T0330288

Innovation and Knowledge Management

NEW HORIZONS IN MANAGEMENT

Series Editor: Cary L. Cooper, *CBE, Professor of Organizational Psychology and Health, Lancaster University Management School, Lancaster University, UK*

This important series makes a significant contribution to the development of management thought. This field has expanded dramatically in recent years and the series provides an invaluable forum for the publication of high quality work in management science, human resource management, organisational behaviour, marketing, management information systems, operations management, business ethics, strategic management and international management.

The main emphasis of the series is on the development and application of new original ideas. International in its approach, it will include some of the best theoretical and empirical work from both well-established researchers and the new generation of scholars.

Titles in the series include:

Human Nature and Organization Theory
On the Economic Approach to Institutional Organization
Sigmund Wagner-Tsukamoto

Organizational Relationships in the Networking Age
The Dynamics of Identity Formation and Bonding
Edited by Willem Koot, Peter Leisink and Paul Verweel

Islamic Perspectives on Management and Organization
Abbas J. Ali

Supporting Women's Career Advancement
Challenges and Opportunities
Edited by Ronald J. Burke and Mary C. Mattis

Research Companion to Organizational Health Psychology
Edited by Alexander-Stamatios G. Antoniou and Cary L. Cooper

Innovation and Knowledge Management
The Cancer Information Service Research Consortium
J. David Johnson

Managing Emotions in Mergers and Acquisitions
Verena Kusstatscher and Cary L. Cooper

Employment of Women in Chinese Cultures
Half the Sky
Cherlyn Granrose

Innovation and Knowledge Management

The Cancer Information Service Research Consortium

J. David Johnson

University of Kentucky

NEW HORIZONS IN MANAGEMENT

Edward Elgar
Cheltenham, UK • Northampton, MA, USA

Published by
Edward Elgar Publishing Limited
Glensanda House
Montpellier Parade
Cheltenham
Glos GL50 1UA
UK

Edward Elgar Publishing, Inc.
136 West Street
Suite 202
Northampton
Massachusetts 01060
USA

A catalogue record for this book
is available from the British Library

Library of Congress Cataloguing in Publication Data

Johnson, J. David.
    Innovation and knowledge management : the Cancer Information Service
Research Consortium / J. David Johnson.
        p. cm. – (New horizons in management)
    Includes bibliographical references and index.
        1. Cancer–Research–United States. 2. National Cancer Institute (U.S.). Cancer
Information Service Research Consortium. 3. Knowledge management. I. Title.
II. Series.

RC267.J64 2005
616.99'4–dc22

                                                                2005044032
ISBN 1 84376 910 7

Printed and bound in Great Britain by MPG Books Ltd, Bodmin, Cornwall

Dedication

To Amanda, our one and only Cinderella, who has come to expect no less.

Contents

List of figures, tables   *viii*
Acronyms   *x*
Preface   *xi*
Acknowledgements   *xiii*

1 Introduction and overview   1
2 Levels of knowledge management innovations   11
3 Organizing for knowledge management: the
   Cancer Information Service   23
4 Organizing for knowledge generation: the
   Cancer Information Service Research Consortium   67
5 Organizing informally for innovation   97
6 Comparing attributes of knowledge delivery and
   information technology innovations   143
7 Innovation in knowledge management
   organizations: lessons learned   197

Bibliography   223
Index   273

List of figures, tables

FIGURES

5.1 Intervention strategies links over time   127
5.2 Models of perceived organizational innovativeness   134

TABLES

2.1 Closer ties factors and goals   17

4.1 Radial communication contacts for regional offices in the CIS   74
4.2 Mean perceptions of the CIS as an innovating organization   79

5.1 Means for interpersonal channel   109
5.2 Means for e-mail channel   110
5.3 Means for written and facsimile channel   111
5.4 Network analysis parallels between knowledge transfer and
    innovation stage   114

6.1 Perceptions of attributes for CISRC Project 1   149
6.2 Perceptions of attributes for CISRC Project 2   152
6.3 Perceptions of attributes for CISRC Project 3   155
6.4 Computerization attributes for telephone service   165
6.5 Computerization attributes for outreach   169
6.6 Computerization attributes for communication   173

6.7   Computerization attributes for office management   177
6.8   Information specialists' perceptions of computerization attributes
      for record keeping   181
6.9   Information specialists' perceptions of computerization attributes
      for information resources   184
6.10 Information specialists' perceptions of computerization
      attributes for mailing   187

Acronyms

ACS	American Cancer Society
CAG	Computerization Advisory Group
CIS	Cancer Information Service
CISRC	Cancer Information Service Research Consortium
CoP	community of practice
CRF	Call Record Form
IS	Information Specialists
KM	knowledge management
NCI	National Cancer Institute
NIH	National Institutes of Health
NLM	National Library of Medicine
OCC	Office of Cancer Communications
OM	Outreach Managers
PDQ	Physician Data Query
PI	Principle Investigator
PD	Project Directors
PP	Program Project
R&D	Research and Development
RO	Regional Offices
RPR	researcher–practitioner relationship
TEAM	Team for Evaluation and Audit Methods
TSM	Telephone Service Managers

Preface

I wrote this book for a combination of personal and professional reasons. Firstly I am a long-term cancer survivor who would not have been able to write this book if it were not for the early detection of a melanoma in 1978. Cancer has many effects, some of them beneficial. I did not get serious about my profession or my writing until it was apparent that what looked like decades that stretched before me to accomplish my goals might be only years or months. So, cancer focused my energies and was by and large responsible for any professional success I have had. I have been fortunate over the last several years to combine my personal interest in cancer with a programme of research related to cancer-related information seeking. I have been doubly fortunate with this project to combine this interest with my long-standing professional work in organizational communication, network analysis, knowledge management and innovation.

Cancer-related knowledge management has taken on enhanced importance in recent years because of the growing emphasis on the consumer or client in the health arena. Individuals increasingly find that they must choose between an array of alternatives in relationship to prevention, detection, and treatment. Thus knowledge, quite literally, is an important survival tool for individuals. This orientation also requires considerable re-evaluation of the traditional approaches to knowledge delivery. It implies a shift away from the development of health campaigns with one unitary message to a recognition that alternatives must be provided and options discussed. Indeed health agencies are adopting the role of information-seeking facilitators through the creation of telephone services and sophisticated databases. Thus the Cancer Information Service can play a critical role in this new information environment by managing knowledge in an innovative manner for the public.

This book is intended for three primary audiences. Firstly it could be used by practitioners and policy–makers in the fields of health, communication, knowledge management, information science and management. Secondly the book is intended for a scholarly audience. Thirdly this book would be most useful as a case study for advanced undergraduate- and graduate-level courses in health, communication, informatics and knowledge management..

As the reader will soon discover, this work is based on an extensive four-year research project that unfortunately cannot be contained within the confines of one book. Throughout I refer to technical reports, journal articles, convention papers and other background material to support my conclusions. Many of these materials are available for the interested reader at my website: http://www.uky.edu/CommInfoStudies/dean/deanpage.html.

Several people have helped me in the writing of this book. I would like to thank the many other people within the Office of Cancer Communications, especially the Cancer Information Service and the Cancer Information Service Research Consortium, who talked about one or another of the topics in this book with me while waiting for airplanes, while on the Metro, while on shuttle buses, while at dinners and lunches, and while at the many meetings of the CIS I have been fortunate to attend.

Acknowledgements

Research supported by: Subcontract No. 737-4241 from the AMC Cancer Research Center for P01 CA57586-01A1 grant from the National Cancer Institute. The conclusions reached in this volume are solely those of the author and do not necessarily reflect the views of the National Cancer Institute or the AMC Cancer Research Center.

Cancer Information Service: I would like to thank the Office of Cancer Communications (the labels used here are those in use during the time period of this study), as well as the following CIS Regional Offices that participated in the data collections: Region 1: (CT, ME, MA, NH, RI, VT) CIS at Yale Cancer Center; Region 2: (NYC, Long Island, Westchester County, NY) Memorial Sloan-Kettering Cancer Center Office of Cancer Communications; Region 3: (NY State, WestPA) CIS at Roswell Park Cancer Institute; Region 4: (DE, NJ, EastPA) CIS at Fox Chase Cancer Center; Region 5: (D.C., MD, NorthVA) CIS at Johns Hopkins University Oncology Center; Region 6: (GA, NC, SC) CIS at Duke Comprehensive Cancer Center; Region 7: (FL, PR) CIS at Sylvester Cancer Center; Region 8: (AL, LA, MS) CIS at University of Alabama at Birmingham; Region 9: (AR, KY, TN) CIS at Markey Cancer Center; Region 10: (OH, WV, SouthVA) CIS at Mary Babb Randolph Cancer Center; Region 11: (WI, IA, MN, ND, SD) CIS at University of Wisconsin Comprehensive Cancer Center; Region 12: (MI, IN) CIS at Barbara Ann Karmanos Cancer Institute; Region 13: (IL, KS, MO, NE) CIS at University of Kansas Medical Center; Region 14: (OK, TX) CIS at M.D. Anderson Cancer Center; Region 15: (AK, NorthID, MT, OR, WA) CIS at Fred Hutchinson

Cancer Research Center; Region 16: (AZ, CO, SouthID, NM, UT, WY) CIS at Penrose St Francis Healthcare System; Region 17: (NorthCA, NV) CIS at Northern California Cancer Center; Region 18: (SouthCA) CIS at Jonsson Comprehensive Cancer Center/UCLA; Region 19: (HI) CIS at Cancer Research Center of Hawaii.

Special thanks: I would like to thank: the staff at Edward Elgar for their unflagging professionalism; Dr Sally Johnson for reviewing an earlier version of this manuscript and for assisting me in the preparation of the manuscript; Julie Berry for her help with the manuscript; Betty Hartman for her help with the index; Nathaniel E Johnson for assisting in the network analyses in Chapter 5; Deb Tigner for her help in preparing and mailing the questionnaires; the other members of the Network Analysis Advisory Board for their help throughout the many phases of the research process: Donna Cox, Jo Beth Speyer, William Stengle, Marsha Woodworth, Maureen McClatchey and Diane Ruesch; and finally, the other members of the Team for Evaluation and Audit Methods: Judy Berkowitz, Hui-Jung Chang, Caroline Ethington, Toru Kiyomiya, Betty LaFrance and Marcy Meyer.

1. Introduction and overview

1.1 INTRODUCTION

This work focuses on three issues critical to the success of modern organizations: knowledge management (KM), innovation and consortial arrangements. I will examine the interplay of these factors in the operation of the Cancer Information Service (CIS) in a critical four–year period in its history. The CIS was essentially a KM organization, charged with delivering up–to–date information to the public related to scientific advances concerning cancer. But although the forerunner of many other knowledge delivery organizations, it also was coming under considerable pressure not only to distribute knowledge, but to generate it. So a consortium which contained many of the elements of a community of practice (CoP), the Cancer Information Service Research Consortium (CISRC), was formed between practitioners within the CIS and researchers outside of it to examine various innovative intervention strategies. The intersection of KM, innovation and consortial arrangements in this case provides a unique opportunity to examine no less than the future of organizations.

Modern organizations must constantly adapt to survive in today's rapidly changing environment (Foray, 2001). A stagnant organization, that cannot innovate to meet evolving environmental conditions, will eventually find itself no longer competitive in an increasingly complex and technologically sophisticated economy (Johnson, 1993). Economic prosperity increasingly depends on the development of new products and services (Hage, 1999). Government organizations, as well as private industry, are experiencing similar pressures to reinvent themselves (for example Osborne and Gaebler, 1993). Innovation processes are crucial to organizational success in terms both of establishing new directions for a company (Wager, 1962) and for organizational effectiveness generally (Rogers and Agarwala–Rogers, 1976). Innovation processes often determine how rapidly private and governmental organizations change to survive in an increasingly competitive world. Perceptions of innovativeness within their organization by organizational members can also have an impact on perceptions of its overall climate, member's satisfaction, and the likelihood of members initiating innovations (Hurt and Teigen, 1977). Innovative organizations are also more likely to expand their resources by creating joint programmes with others in consortia, thereby increasing their resources (Hage and Aiken, 1970).

In many ways KM can be viewed as an innovation that is rapidly diffusing among organizations. It also falls in a class of meta–innovations that enable other innovations to occur in an organization. Indeed the pursuit of KM often is based on the premise that it will lead to better decision–making and a flourishing of creative approaches to organizational problems. So the ultimate outcome of effective KM is the rapid adoption or creation of appropriate innovations that can be successfully implemented within a particular organization's context (Holsapple and Joshi, 2003; Myers, 1996; Swan, 2003). In the case of the CIS there was an even broader mandate, a latent purpose to insure the rapid diffusion of state–of–the–art medical care to patients across the country (NCI, 2003). Greater knowledge intensity leads to greater profitability for commercial firms (Stewart, 2001), higher levels of innovation (Kanter, 1988a) and, ultimately, knowledge has become the source of wealth creation and economic growth (Florida and Cohen, 1999; Leonard, 1995).

Increasingly innovation is the outcome of complex interrelationships between parties involved in consortia that often represent new organizational forms. Both parties have substantial potential common benefits from a successful researcher–practitioner relationship (RPR) including securing physical and material resources and intellectual stimulation (Cullen et al., 1999; March, 2000). In addition, participation of practitioners early on is positively related to utilization and favourable attitudes towards innovations (Beyer and Trice, 1994). It is also obvious that policy–makers see substantial benefits to be had from interactions between the various parties in the research enterprise (De la Mothe, 2001), with increasing calls from the National Institutes of Health (NIH), the National Science Foundation and Fund for the Improvement of Postsecondary Education (2003) among others, for holistic examinations of research problems through the development of synthetic relationships among often fractured disciplines.

While there has been a wealth of literature related to innovation, and encyclopedic treatments of it (Rogers, 1983, 1995, 2003), overview articles have identified a need for new approaches and for new paradigms (partially because of the lack of a coherent existing one in organizational research) (Drazin and Schoonhoven, 1996; Fiol, 1996). In spite of numerous studies, innovation research has resulted in few unequivocal, strong findings, with such descriptors as 'fragmentary', 'inconsistent', 'contradictory' and 'beyond interpretation' applied to the literature (Drazin and Schoonhoven, 1996; Fiol, 1996; Meyer and Goes, 1988). While recent approaches have focused on ever more narrow questions, what is most needed is a look at major overarching themes of this literature and their interconnections. Here I will focus on the interaction of these issues within the CIS, itself an innovative organization, that was the forerunner of many government and non–profit health knowledge delivery organizations.

1.2 THE CANCER INFORMATION SERVICE

Once again, the CIS is in transition. It is in the process of implementing new program concepts. The immediate challenge is the phaseout of the old and adoption of a new, different program structure. With new challenges come new opportunities. The program has never been and will never be static. It moves with the times, evolving to meet changing needs – to be on the front lines of cancer communications, available to all Americans. (Morra, Van Nevel et al., 1993, p. 32)

The CIS is an award–winning national information and education network, which has been the voice of the National Cancer Institute (NCI) for more than 30 years (Marcus, Woodworth, and Strickland, 1993; Marcus, Morra et al., 1998). The CIS also represents a new organizational form, a contractual network, representative of the many new organizational arrangements sweeping the health care industry, since its work is done through nearly a score of regional offices (RO) who work under contract. While the CIS has extensive outreach programmes dedicated to reaching the medically underserved (Thomsen and Maat, 1998), it is probably best known for its telephone service that has a widely available 800 number (1–800–4–CANCER). There is a strong normative thread that runs through the activity of this contractual network; a commitment to providing high–quality information, free to the public, concerning cancer (Morra, Van Nevel et al., 1993). The public has expressed very high levels of satisfaction with this service (Darrow et al., 1998; Maibach et al., 1998; Morra, 1998; Ward et al., 1998).

Over time the CIS has, in addition to its original mandate, become a community–based laboratory for state–of–the–science communication research (Morra, Bettinghaus and Marcus, 1993; Marcus, Morra et al., 1998). For the most part, before 1993, this research was conducted on an ad hoc basis and performed episodically by interested researchers with a variety of partners in RO and national headquarters. The first four–year funding wave of the unique CISRC represented a strategic alliance between researchers from a variety of institutions; and practitioners within the CIS arranged to implement and evaluate three new intervention strategies designed to facilitate the dissemination of cancer information to the public (Marcus, 1998b; Marcus, Morra et al., 1998). The first (Marcus, Heimendinger et al., 1998) and third innovations (Boyd et al., 1998) were connected to the CIS 1–800–4–CANCER telephone service, utilizing the toll–free number as a nexus from which to disseminate cancer information to targeted populations. The second (Crane et al., 1998) and third projects were tailored to the health information needs of traditionally underserved sectors of the American public (Boyd et al., 1998), a particularly important policy issue for the CIS (Morra, Van Nevel and Stengle, 1993; Marcus, Morra et al., 1998).

I will focus on the intersection of KM, innovation and consortial issues in this unique, four–year longitudinal study of the CISRC. During this time period the CIS was also facing the sort of downsizing, reorganization and survival threats that have so characterized the health services administration area in recent years. In part, in response to these trends, the CIS also was adopting a series of information technology innovations during this period. The CISRC was designed to develop the research potential of the CIS, foster collaboration among investigators and the CIS network, and move the service toward high–quality, peer–reviewed research (Fleisher et al., 1998). The CISRC innovations were clearly seen by leaders of the CIS as a way of satisfying key decision–makers within the NCI by demonstrating that the CIS could also contribute to the NCI's research mission, but there was considerable debate within the CIS as to the centrality of research in relation to its traditional vision and mission statements (Fleisher et al., 1998; Marcus, Morra et al., 1998). Ultimately this book is also about how we can more effectively deliver vital health information to those who need it – a central KM issue.

1.3 KNOWLEDGE MANAGEMENT

KM is one of the hottest concepts in the management literature and has been loosely applied to a collection of organizational practices related to generating, capturing, storing, disseminating and applying knowledge (Dierkes, 2001; Nonaka and Takeuchi, 1995; MacMorrow, 2001; Stewart, 2001; Zorn and May, 2002). In this sense, which was certainly the organizing thrust of the CIS that we will return to in Chapter 3, KM can be viewed as a system for processing information. It is strongly related to the areas of information technology, organizational learning, intellectual capital, adaptive change, identification of information needs, development of information products and decision support (Choo, 1998; Fouche, 1999; Schulz, 2001; Stewart, 2001), so intimately that it is often difficult to say where one approach stops and another begins. Knowledge itself runs the gamut from data, to information, to wisdom, with a variety of distinctions made between these terms in the literature (for example Boahene and Ditsa, 2003; Burton–Jones, 1999; Holsapple, 2003; Schulz, 2001; Swan, 2003). Special weight in the context of the CIS is given to a consensus surrounding refereed scientific findings that can be translated to the public to improve cancer prevention, detection and treatment.

Increasingly generating and manipulating knowledge is seen as a core function of our modern economy, the 'only sustainable way for organizations to create value and profitability in the longer term' (MacMorrow, 2001, p. 381). Of course, in commercial settings this is not done for altruistic purposes, but to insure competitive advantage for the firm (Stewart, 2001). In government and non–profit organizations the motives may be slightly different: enhanced prestige and better services for clients, as well as reacting to demands of stakeholders (Eisenberg et al., 1998). So we are often forced to ask the more functional question of KM to what end: be it fostering creativity, enabling innovation or increasing competencies (MacMorrow, 2001). As we will see, the answer to this question is often quite complex, with multiple purposes, often representing different groups, simultaneously at play.

Governments often see a substantial role in stimulating KM. Sometimes this is done quite explicitly, with substantial fanfare touting the dire economic consequences that will ensue if high–tech innovations are not pursued (for example Center for Information Technology Enterprise, 2002; New Economy Regional Plan for the Greater Lexington Area, 2001; Larson and Brakmakulam, 2002). Making sense of innovations within the CIS, often a key component of KM in some approaches (Choo, 1998), was often contentious, with many different goals associated with it at different levels. At other times, and this was a central reason the CIS was founded initially, it was a latent purpose for this organization.

1.3 INNOVATION

Innovation may be the ultimate service provided by KM organizations. Indeed knowledge is often seen as the primary driver of innovation (Amidon and Mahdjoubi, 2003; Nonaka and Takeuchi, 1995; Swan, 2003). It implies bringing something perceived as new into use (Rogers, 1995). I will not focus on invention, a more creative process that implies bringing something new into being. Innovation can be related to: (1) a product or service; (2) a production process; (3) organizational structure; (4) people; and (5) policy (Zaltman et al., 1973). I will primarily focus on the first three types in this book, describing the implementation of three new KM services, the implementation of various information technologies related to KM, and the creation of a new organization, a consortia with many elements of a CoP, designed to conduct research related to KM services. These different types of innovation are also associated with different levels of analysis within organizations, a topic I will expand on in Chapter 2. More indirectly, these innovations also resulted in changes in people and policy within the CISRC.

Several factors can potentially determine the success of innovation processes, including the interdependence of components of the system, their diversity, the nature of the formal management system, external conditions (Galbraith, 1973), the general organizational cultural norms toward innovation (Deal and Kennedy, 1982), and the openness of the organizational system (Rogers, 1983). These factors also play a role in the success of KM, providing a general context for action in an organization.

Innovation is ultimately a social process of information seeking and sharing of ideas perceived as new (Rogers, 2003). Since new ideas are often perceived as risky and uncertain, often there is resistance to them. Communication plays a key role in overcoming resistance to innovation and interpersonal channels play a crucial role in promoting awareness that leads to the adoption of innovations. The nature of the information transmitted concerning an innovation can be grouped into three general categories: (1) information concerning the innovation; (2) information related to influence and power; and (3) information concerning operationalizing the innovation (Fidler and Johnson, 1984). The centrality of communication becomes even more pronounced when innovation occurs in the operation of consortia that have additional informal, coordination pressures not found in more conventional unitary organizations.

Successful implementation of an innovation can be conceived of as the routinization, incorporation and stabilization of the innovation into the ongoing work activity of an organizational unit. For organizations, 'the bottom line is implementation (including its institutionalization), and not just the adoption *decision*' (Rogers and Adhikayra, 1979, p. 79). It has become widely recognized in the literature that most approaches to innovation have a pro–innovation bias (Rogers, 1995), partly because of underlying cultural beliefs in progress through technology. All of us, especially in our personal technological purchases (for example betamax VCRs), increasingly realize that early adoption can be risky and, at the very least, it is sometimes cheaper (for example personal computers) to wait to adopt innovations. There are also real organizational costs to innovations:

wasting resources on inappropriate technology, constant uncertainty resulting from perpetual change, lowered morale from unsuccessful adoption efforts, to name but a few. Implicit in most KM approaches is a return to a more optimistic view of the impacts of innovations on organizations and societies (MacMorrow, 2001).

1.5 CONSORTIA OF RESEARCHERS AND PRACTITIONERS

The knowledge that researchers, teachers, consultants, and practitioners learn by themselves is different and partial. If it could be co–produced and combined in some novel ways the results could produce a dazzling synthesis that could profoundly advance theory, teaching, and practice. (Van de Ven, 2000, p. 5)

In this book I will examine a unique organizational form, the CISRC, which like other new forms has emerged to meet a number of pressing environmental demands. In the health arena pressures concerning health reforms, relating particularly to the growth of information technologies and associated economic pressures, have resulted in a number of different approaches to consortiums. A considerable literature has developed related to new organizational forms (Miles and Snow, 1986; Romanelli, 1991), especially the proliferation of new types of quasi–forms associated with more complex interorganizational relationships (Ring and Van de Ven, 1994; Schopler, 1987). Examples of differing types of interorganizational relationships abound: trade associations, agency federations, joint ventures, social service joint programmes, agency–sponsor linkages (Oliver, 1990), hybrid arrangements (Borys and Jemison, 1989), franchises, strategic alliances, research consortia, network organizations (Ring and Van de Ven, 1994) and quasi–firms (Luke et al., 1989). A major sub–area of this literature relates to health organizations (Arnold and Hink, 1968; Farace et al., 1982; Luke et al., 1989).

A host of environmental factors are contributing to the development of new organizational forms; concerns about personnel costs (for example pensions, health costs); external pressures to keep the number of members on their permanent staff low; uncertainty reduction; needs to pool knowledge and information or to create it in the case of research and development (R&D) firms; and affiliation (for example with a more credible national organization). While the need for new organizational forms and the pressures to create them are great, success is difficult to achieve, particularly in the health area (Arnold and Hink, 1968; Farace et al., 1982). Many barriers have been identified: the specific missions of cooperating agencies are often different (for example providing social support vs. treatment for cancer patients); relatedly, outcome and effectiveness measures differ between agencies; and the coordination costs are heavy to integrate truly the efforts of diverse organizations (Arnold and Hink, 1968). In addition, members of coalitions may have multiple goals (Stevenson et al., 1985), they may also resent the loss of decision–making latitude, and the cost of managing their linkages increases (Oliver, 1990).

The CIS is unique in many ways. It is not a formal organization in the conventional sense, nor is it an interorganizational network. It is a new organizational form which, while incorporating many of the features of organizational forms previously identified in the literature, has its own idiosyncratic combination of characteristics. This unique combination of organizational characteristics makes it even more critical that intensive efforts be spent on integrative communication activities (for example national conferences).

There is an increasing need to develop new theories and fresh perspectives based on empirical data of the operation of these new organizational forms (Luke et al., 1989; Child and McGrath, 2001). The ability of a society to create them directly affects its ability to adapt to new environmental circumstances (Romanelli, 1991). Perhaps the best label for the new organizational form represented by the CIS is that of a contractual network. The most unique characteristic of the CIS is its geographic dispersion in 19 ROs serving the entire US (Marcus, Woodworth and Strickland, 1993). What brings all of the ROs together is a classic fee–for–services contract, which in effect hires existing organizations for a specified time, to provide services toward the accomplishment of a common goal. Although the ROs are technically temporary, many of the offices have been in service to the CIS for over 20 years and have successfully competed for contract renewals (Morra, Van Nevel et al., 1993). These offices however still retain their membership in their local sponsor or parent organizations (for example cancer centres) and identify with and address their regional concerns. Yet there is also a strong normative thread that runs through the activity of this network, a commitment to providing high–quality information, free to the public, concerning cancer (Marcus et al., 1993).

Throughout this book I will focus on the factors that lead to the successful development of KM innovations in consortia. A consortium can be defined simply as a collection of entities (for example companies, public sector organizations) brought together by their interest in working collaboratively to accomplish something of mutual value which is beyond the resources of any one member (Cullen et al., 1999; Fleisher et al., 1998).

Here I will use the CISRC, a consortium of cancer–control researchers and practitioners who formed a coalition to implement trials related to three major cancer control projects, to illustrate my major substantive points. Innovation often occurs within such CoPs whose members share a common set of goals and a core of shared knowledge (Fouche, 1999). The creation of a consortia of researchers and practitioners represented by the CISRC added yet another level of complexity to the CIS. In general for researchers there are considerable benefits that can ensue from interacting with practitioners: in fact they may have more to gain from RPRs than do practitioners. While both parties have things to gain from RPRs, they often have even more to lose, and this is seldom explicitly discussed. The operation of consortia has been increasingly central to theoretical work on organizations and, not so coincidentally, it is of increasing pragmatic concern to organizations, particularly related to the development and implementation of KM and innovations.

1.6 PLAN OF THE BOOK

One fundamental question related to KM that is often avoided in the literature is what is its ultimate purpose. Here I will systematically relate KM to innovations. As we will see in more detail in the next chapter, innovations within the CISRC occurred in three areas. One set of innovations dealt with testing new interventions related to knowledge delivery within the CIS. In addition, internally, the CIS, recognizing the importance of information technologies, had also been innovating with production processes relating to computerization of their services to facilitate the manipulation and storage of information. The CISRC itself was a meta–innovation designed to develop the research potential of the CIS, foster collaboration among investigators and the CIS network, and move the service toward high–quality, peer–reviewed research (Fleisher et al., 1998).

Chapters 3, 4 and 5 focus in one way or another on organizing for KM and innovation within this consortia and its constituent parts. Chapter 3 develops a more complete picture of the history and formal structure of the CIS, focusing on both broader societal level trends in knowledge dissemination and the CIS's prototypical role in the development of KM in health services. In Chapter 4 we provide a more complete description of the CISRC Program Project (PP) grant and the role of consortia in knowledge generation and the implementation of knowledge delivery innovations. Chapter 5 focuses on the rich array of informal communication channels used by CISRC members to communicate about innovation. Informal communication, represented by network analysis, has been centrally associated with innovation processes in the literature.

Chapter 6 reports the results of our research on the innovations that are the heart of this work, describing their ultimate success at the different levels. Finally, in Chapter 7 I focus on the lessons learned from this four–year project discussing their implications for KM, innovations and consortia. I also explore in this chapter the notion of success in innovation implementation and provide a postscript on the current and future state of the CIS and CISRC.

2. Levels of knowledge management innovations

2.1 INTRODUCTION

> The role of top management is to give employees a sense of crises as well as a lofty ideal. (Nonaka, 1985, p. 142 cited in Nonaka and Takeuchi, 1995, p. 79)

The successful implementation of innovations within organizations is often problematic. Indeed improved innovation processes are often seen as the major benefit of improved KM systems within organizations. In Chapter 6, after the appropriate groundwork has been laid, I will more formally assess the relative success of the various innovations associated with the CISRC. Here I introduce the notion of levels of innovation and the associated factors that contribute to successful implementation. These issues are critical for how organizations go about making sense of what they are doing vis–a–vis their environment, a major underlying theme of the KM literature (Choo, 1998; MacMorrow, 2001). In the history of the CISRC project, people came to understand these distinctions slowly, in part because of the different views of different groups, which needed to be confronted in dialogue surrounding key historical events in the project, primarily related to what the project's ultimate goals were.

2.2 LEVELS

Innovation proceeded in three areas within the CISRC: creating a consortium to generate knowledge, innovations in information technology and structure, and testing innovations related to knowledge service delivery.

The first two of these areas are examples of meta–innovations, establishing structures and processes that promote the possibility of further innovations. The latter is more commonly associated with the creative processes of introducing products and services related to new knowledge. Within the CISRC these different areas became closely associated with different views of the consortium and different goals of the various parties. At times innovations became hotly contested symbols of what the consortium was all about.

More generally, I have argued that successful implementation of innovations depends on positive weightings of three distinct factors: framing, innovation environment and innovation attributes. Framing refers to the couching of an innovation in terms of the political and strategic imperatives of the organization. The innovation environment refers to the internal tactical environment (for example the presence of enabling information technologies) for innovation implementation. Innovation attributes refers to the characteristics of an innovation such as trialability. Neither framing, environment nor attributes are sufficient by themselves to ensure unequivocal success, although they may lead to partial success (Johnson, 2000, 2001).

Each of these factors is associated with a voluminous literature, but partially because of their differing epistemological and methodological approaches, the interactions between these literatures are seldom specifically addressed. The interplay of differing innovation levels, as others have suggested (Kanter, 1988a; Klein and Sorra, 1996), offers interesting new lines of inquiry for an area of research that sorely needs them (Drazin and Schoonhoven, 1996; Fiol, 1996; Klein et al., 1999). Understanding the interplay of these major competing levels can result in more effective individual and institutional change strategies (Bolman and Deal, 1991; Fairhurst and Sarr, 1996; Schon and Rein, 1994).

Not only are these factors at different levels of abstraction (Rousseau, 1985), they are also related to different hierarchical management levels, with attendant differential access to power and resources that can play critical roles in innovation implementation. Framing is essentially a tool used by top–level managers (although others can evoke it too in their persuasive appeals and issue selling to top management: Dutton et al., 2001), to influence external stakeholders. The internal innovation environment is normally the province of middle managers, while innovation attributes are primarily an operational concern of those actually implementing an innovation. This creates substantial problems for internal dialogue within an organization since key groups are using a different vocabulary and set of assumptions (Drazin et al., 1999; Johnson, 2000). For example, lower–level organizational personnel have a tendency to view innovations in terms of their operational attributes, value effectiveness gains in their routine work, and resulting enhancements in their self–efficacy and sense of self–actualization. On the other hand, top–level managers may value an innovation for its ability to immediately and directly address the needs of major external stakeholders. They seek innovations that provide an image that their organization is on the cutting edge and prestigious.

Framing

> We see policy positions as resting on underlying structures of belief, perception, and appreciation, which we call 'frames.' ... the frames that shape policy positions and underlie controversy are usually tacit, which means they are exempt from conscious attention and reasoning. (Schon and Rein, 1994, p. 23)

This distinction between tacit and explicit knowledge is a fundamental one in the KM literature (Choo, 1998; MacMorrow, 2001; Nonaka and Takeuchi, 1995) and, as in other situations, it took a while for explicit understanding to come to the fore within the CISRC. This distinction also affects the ways issues are framed within organizations. Frames have recently received renewed interest in organizational communication theory (Johnson, 1997b, c). The framing concept has a long history in the social sciences, especially in relation to more micro discourse processes. Frames perform many critical functions for interactants: they are shared conversational resources, they provide a common emotional tone, they insure quicker responses, and they also provide a basis for temporal stability by insuring more continuous responses. In short, frames are a basis for coordinated action in collectivities, since cooperation requires a 'reading' of the other's actions and intentions (Johnson, 1997b, c). The concept of frames is most commonly used to indicate a way of viewing the world and interpreting it, acting as a sense–making device that establishes the parameters of a problem (Johnson, 1997b).

Organizational innovation orchestrators manipulate information, control resources, set agenda, acquire power bases, and frame decision premises to promote the political capital that they have invested in a given innovation (Frost and Egri, 1991). Here the focus is on how innovations are framed in terms of the expectations of key external stakeholders (Mitchell et al., 1997). Satisfying these external stakeholders is critical to the flow of resources in large public sector organizations, where new investments often depend on the matching of agency efforts with new political initiatives.

Fairhurst and Sarr (1996) have suggested that managerial effectiveness rests on the management of meaning that is largely accomplished through framing. They concentrate on framing 'skills' including context sensitivity, tools (for example metaphor, stories and spin), avoiding mixed messages, framing preparation and establishing credibility. Similarly, Bolman and Deal (1991) also see frames as tools for leaders: 'The truly effective manager and leader will need multiple tools, the skills to use each of them, and the wisdom to match frames to situations' (p. 12).

Many of the decisions relating to major national initiatives (for example prostate cancer, breast cancer, affiliations with other organizations) are made outside the context of the CIS (for example Health and Human Services, the NIH) with the CIS left to implement them. In turn, formally generated innovations originate in upper management, using the traditional authority structure as the primary impetus underlying adoption. This is a unique feature of innovation within organizations; an entity of higher status and authority can decide to adopt an innovation that another segment of the organization must implement (Rogers, 2003). In organizations the former unit has been termed the adoption unit and the process as a whole has been called authority innovation decision (Rogers and Shoemaker, 1971). This has been the typical pattern of innovation within the CIS programme in that innovations implemented are consistent with the broad policy objectives as set forth through the Office of Cancer Communications (OCC).

The CISRC was conducted within the larger political context of an evaluation of a federal government health information programme: one implicit understanding related to the research was that the results would be utilized to demonstrate that the CIS could be used as a research arm of NCI. Thus the CISRC was designed to develop the research potential of the CIS, to foster collaboration among investigators and the CIS network, and to move the service toward high–quality, peer–reviewed research (Fleisher et al., 1998). The CISRC innovations were clearly seen by leaders of the CIS as a way of satisfying key decision–makers within the NCI by demonstrating that the CIS could also contribute to the NCI's research mission, but there was considerable debate within the CIS as to the centrality of research in relation to its traditional vision and mission statements (Fleisher et al., 1998; Marcus et al., 1998). Often environmental 'jolts' associated with organizational stakeholders are necessary to stimulate innovations (Marcus and Weber, 1989).

Innovation Environment

Several innovation environment factors can potentially determine the success of innovation processes, including the interdependence of components of the system, their diversity, the nature of the formal management system, external conditions (Galbraith, 1973), types of power and influence used to secure involvement (Fidler and Johnson, 1984), the climate of an organization (Johnson et al., 1997), the general organizational cultural norms toward innovation (Deal and Kennedy, 1982) and the openness of the organizational system (Rogers, 1983). We discuss these issues in more detail in Chapters 3 and 4.

The initiation of innovations in organizations is more likely to occur in an internal environment where: people have easy access to information; there are permeable boundaries between organizational units; there are rewards for sharing, seeking and utilizing new information; there are rewards for risk taking, accepting and adapting to change; and the organization encourages its members to be mobile and to develop interpersonal contacts (Goldhar et al., 1976).

Attitudes towards innovativeness within their organization held by organizational members can also have an impact on the overall climate of an organization, members' satisfaction and the likelihood of members initiating innovations (Hurt and Teigen, 1977). For innovation to flourish, the organization's climate must be supportive of it (Kanter, 1983; Klein and Sorra, 1996) and conducive to a willingness to change (Hurt et al., 1977). These climate, cultural and structural factors combine to determine the tactical internal innovation environment of an organization which, as I cover in more detail in Chapters 3 and 4, was different for innovations within the CIS and the CISRC.

Innovation Attributes

Historically, researchers have described innovations in terms of their attributes, or perceived characteristics, based on respondents' subjective judgements, which play a significant role in the diffusion of innovations (see Chapter 6 for more detail). Rogers (1983, 1995, 2003) has developed the most commonly recognized scheme for examining differing properties of innovations focusing on five perceived attributes of an innovation: relative advantage, compatibility, complexity, trialability and observability. Ultimately, attributes relate best to the inherent properties of concrete, explicit services and products. More broadly, recent approaches have indicated that the innovation attributes of relative advantage, observability, adaptability and acceptance tap an overarching trait, pros, while complexity and risk comprise cons (Johnson, 2000, 2001).

2.3 THE GOALS OF THE VARIOUS CISRC PARTIES

Maximizing the full research potential of the CIS was viewed by many as helping the CIS become even more closely aligned with the primary mission of NCI which, like all of the National Institutes of Health, is primarily dedicated to research. (Marcus, Morra, et al., 1998, p. S13)

Although the CIS contract encourages support of and participation in research, it is not a primary function of the program. (Fleisher et al., 1998, p. S88)

However, what remains unclear are the criteria that might be used to make these policy decisions and, ultimately, the extent to which these findings will actually impact the day–to–day operations of the CIS. (Marcus, 1998a, p. S95)

Often the tensions between RO practitioners and CISRC researchers resulted from how they saw each other in terms of their ultimate individual goals. While there has been considerable debate concerning how much of organizational behaviour is truly rational or goal oriented and, somewhat relatedly, how conscious members are of their goals before they act (see Weick, 1969), it is useful to examine goals as a reference point for the different orientations and frames of the various parties involved in the CISRC. While Goes and Park (1997) have suggested complementarity of goals is a key factor in the continuation of joint ventures, it may be unrealistic to expect, in the often political internal environment even of unitary organizations, that there will be consistency across groups in goals (Augier, 2004).

Ironically, often the goals of different parties only became explicit through interactions with other parties which have clearly different ones (Sennett, 1998). The fundamental goal issue within the CISRC was 'what is the innovation we are focusing our efforts on?', in other words what was the ultimate desired outcome expected of the CISRC project. This issue came to the fore in one memorable circular call, a party call containing both practitioners and researchers, of the Publication Subcommittee (Fleisher et al., 1998; Marcus et al., 1998). The call focused on the publication of Time 2 of the innovation attributes data of the three CISRC projects (see Meyer, Johnson, Cox and Speyer, 1997; Meyer, Johnson and Ethington, 1997). So the explicit recognition of these issues came well into the project and echoes issues around tacit and explicit knowledge (Nonaka and Takeuchi, 1995).

As the call unfolded, it was clear that the groups even within the CISRC had fundamental differences on this basic issue. The principal investigator (PI) of the Survey Methods Core (SMC) insisted that the innovation was really the CISRC itself, a communications laboratory for NCI, the implementation of a consortium of researchers operating within the CIS (Innovation Theme 1 in Table 2.1). Thus innovation really proceeded at two levels: the specific research interventions, and building the infrastructure to support future innovations and related knowledge generation, a not uncommon approach in cancer–control research (McKinney et al., 1992), including research that the SMC PI had been involved in (Kaluzny et al., 1993; Kaluzny and Warnecke, 1996). Within the CISRC, the SMC PI had a more limited form of internal brokerage focusing on individual research projects because he conducted the surveys associated with them. In addition, he had independent links to the research establishment within the NCI because of his long–standing research programme, which perhaps gave him the broadest vision of the CISRC as an innovation in and of itself.

Table 2.1 *Closer ties factors and goals*

Closer ties factor	Groups		
	Researchers	Regional Offices	OCC
Homophily	Long time frame	Short time frame	Mid–range time frame
	Social science	Helping prof–essions	Contract officer
Shared Interests	CIS as research laboratory	CIS as research laboratory	CIS as research laboratory
	Innovation theme 1, 2	Innovation theme 3	Innovation theme 1
	Practice/ policy	Practice/ management tool	Practice/ account–ability
Threats	Identification with research community	Identification with regional office	Identification with NCI
	Interference with research	Interference with service	Interference with contract

The CISRC PI, who had the longest–standing and broadest contacts within the consortium, and was the person who brought everyone together initially, curiously had the narrowest substantive vision for it. He maintained that what the CISRC was doing was neither implementing nor testing innovations, but instead conducting 'little, tiny research trials' (Innovation Theme 2). In a later face–to–face meeting, he went on to suggest that the goal was not even to demonstrate an intervention effect, but rather to provide a fair test. The CISRC PI and other researchers at this meeting suggested that their obligation was to provide clear results. It was up to others to apply them; this view clearly represented the classic views of researchers.

The Team for Evaluation and Audit Methods (TEAM) PI, in the conference call, argued that the CISRC was conducting pilot studies to test the efficacy of full–scale implementation of innovations throughout the CIS of improved knowledge dissemination practices (Innovation Theme 3). This view was shared by the practitioner members of the CIS, who were the primary focus of TEAM research detailing their reactions to the innovations (see Meyer, Johnson, Cox and Speyer, 1997; Meyer, Johnson and Ethington, 1997), as later revealed in the face–to–face CISRC meeting and in a subsequent summary of their experience with the CISRC written by project directors (PD) (Fleisher et al., 1998). The PDs saw this as a critical shortcoming of the CISRC: there were not adequate mechanisms for translating research findings into actual programmes, nor were there mechanisms to create future CIS staff–initiated projects (Fleisher et al., 1998). In addition the Acting Chief of the CIS pointed out in the face–to–face meeting that there were enormous hidden costs (conference calls, paper or protocol reviews, and so on). This point was also emphasized in the CISRC PI's summary of the overall project and its impact on PDs (Marcus, 1998b). These fundamental disagreements about goals, directions and concomitant action shaped many of the tensions between researchers and practitioners and often dictated their patterns of relations.

For PDs participation in research was part of the new contract, as well as part of the institutional expectations of RO, especially those in academic settings. OCC had a similar interest in convincing other elements of the NCI that the CIS could also serve as a research arm (Innovation Theme 1). So involvement in the project ran the gamut of classic types, calculative to normative, identified in the literature (Etzioni, 1964). 'One of the major management challenges at the regional level was to transmit to staff the excitement and value of conducting research in a mainly service program. For the regional staff, the research projects represented a major change in the way they performed their daily work' (Fleisher et al., 1998, p. S88).

Yet another group who, while not involved in adoption decision–making, played a critical role in implementation was the information specialists (IS). They represented a significant management challenge for PDs who often acted as boundary spanners between them and the CISRC Program Project (PP) staff (see Chang et al., 1997). IS training and socialization emphasized many factors that were antithetical to the research projects as they came to be implemented. In the Denver meeting in the third year of the project a discussion concerning the projects highlighted the ways in which the research projects did not match stated CIS priorities: they focused on counselling more than information provision; they focused on prevention, more than dealing with patients and their families, the predominant mode of operation within the CIS; and the strict adherence to research protocols deprived IS of autonomy and flexibility in responding to callers that threatened their professionalism.

In fact the strong normative commitment of ISs to the traditional role of the CIS in providing information to callers, who had compelling needs (for example, how should my mother be treated for cervical cancer? How do I deal with chemotherapy?) may have been the biggest barrier to their involvement in the CISRC projects. Most CIS offices had substantial call volumes during this period, with attendant busy signals during peak periods (Morra, Van Nevel et al., 1993), with representative monthly reports of 26 per cent busy rates (Steverson, 1995). ISs in implementing CISRC protocols would take substantial additional time implementing the interventions, ranging from 4 minutes to 50 minutes (including preparation time) across the various projects per call (Boyd et al., 1998; Crane et al., 1998; Marcus, Hiemendinger et al., 1998). This directly impinged on their ability to provide normal service. In most offices, while implementing protocol scripts, they could literally see the blinking lights on their telephone signifying waiting calls. The abstract value of eventual return of research results to policy issues affecting the CIS thus directly clashed with the immediate compelling needs of callers. Perhaps reflecting the persuasive abilities of PDs, one–half of ISs responded affirmatively that research should be part of the CIS programme (Fleisher et al., 1998).

Interestingly, superordinate threats from third parties may be a major inducement for cooperative relationships (Gibson and Rogers, 1994; Browning et al., 1995). Indeed Lawrence and Lorsch (1967c) define integration in terms of the collaboration needed to respond to environmental demands. During this time period, the very existence of the CIS was threatened (Chang et al., 1997; Pobocik et al., 1997; Johnson, 2000, 2001, 2002), drawing both researchers and practitioners closer together than they might have been in other circumstances, since all of the parties clearly had a shared goal of the continued existence of the CIS.

Framing ideas in terms of overcoming resistance to change, probably the most popular approach in the literature traditionally, may be exactly the wrong approach for proactive organizations (Armenikas et al., 1993) like the CIS. Rather, a more promising approach seems to be to identify sustaining mechanisms, for example broad–based support of organizational members, that will pull people toward an attractive future (Drucker, 1995; Klein and Sorra, 1996; Ross, 1974). Indeed Mohr (1969) suggested the primary motivation for public health organizations to innovate was the quest for prestige (see also Becker, 1970) rather than issues of internal effectiveness and efficiency. Similarly, Brenner and Logan (1980) argued, based on their analysis of the diffusion of medical information systems, that outside innovation factors were much more important in the diffusion of innovation process than is represented in the prevailing view in the literature. While the classic Rogers (1983, 1995, 2003) attributes of innovation may be important in persuading individuals to implement innovations adopted by others, in the larger organizational context these are clearly secondary factors, more associated with 'fine–tuning' an innovation. As the CIS case makes clear, framing and the innovation environment may play more critical roles.

In part, readiness to change also reflects an individual's believed potential to gain (or lose) from particular innovations (Frost and Egri, 1991). Bach (1989) has argued that the greater an organization's emphasis on efficiency, the slower its rate of change; partially because the innovation process will make the organization less efficient, at least for a time, which suggests top management can play a critical role in pushing organizations in different directions by overcoming the inertia of lower–level organizational members.

Not only can managers utilize information about stakeholders' perceptions of innovation to facilitate the adoption and implementation of innovations in the interest of meeting specific strategic objectives; the ways in which managers respond to stakeholders' attitudes towards innovation may influence the organization's ability to generate future innovations. Managers who validate organizational members' attitudes toward innovation, perhaps by incorporating feedback to modify innovations mid– stream, are also cultivating the climate of innovativeness within their organization (Damanpour, 1991; Hurt and Teigen, 1977). If organizational members feel that their voices are heard, then they will believe that they have a higher level of participation in innovation processes, which in turn will produce more involvement on their part (Albrecht and Ropp, 1984; Fidler and Johnson, 1984; Johnson, 1990; Johnson, Donohue et al., 1995b; Johnson, Meyer et al., 1997). Managers who are sensitive to the needs of all parties in an innovation process, in the pluralistic modern organization, have the potential to sustain and to build an organization's innovation environment. Thus they also need to pay attention to middle management's organic bridging role and their concerns with costs and benefits, as well as efficiency.

2.4 CONCLUSION

Traditional approaches to innovation research in organizations, such as a focus on such factors as attitudes, have little or no relation to the innovation environment (Hoffman and Roman, 1984) and the structural and environmental factors that are often the critical determinants of innovation implementation (Baldridge and Burnham, 1975; Dougherty and Hardy, 1996). Innovation is a dynamic process, with often subtle and unexpected relationships between levels. As organizations become more concerned with the strategic implications of innovations and the associated need to create more innovative environments, it is time for a new approach, one with a more critical edge (for example incorporating political processes essential to managing innovations), for innovation research.

The most important issue may be the interaction of multiple levels, each with different interpretations and different cost–benefit equations (Meyer and Goes, 1988), which also offer some hope of bridging micro and macro levels of organizational behaviour related to innovations (Lewis and Seibold, 1996). Unfortunately different epistemological, methodological and theoretic frames for academic research must be negotiated in this process. In fact it was not until the anomalous results of more narrow, separate empirical research projects on two of the three levels suggested a clear need, which we will soon turn to, that the broader perspective on these processes articulated in this chapter was developed.

3. Organizing for knowledge management: the Cancer Information Service

3.1 INTRODUCTION

Fundamentally, the CIS is charged with providing high–quality information to its clients, primarily callers to its 800 telephone number. It represents an integrated KM system designed for effective use of information. It obtains the consensus–based scientific information it transfers from its parent organization, the NCI. Unfortunately a number of scientific controversies in well–established areas have emerged in recent years that even conventional scientific peer review may not successfully address. For example while there had been over 14 000 citations in the mid–1990s on screening for breast cancer (Hoke, 1995), the NCI and the American Cancer Society (ACS) interpreted this evidence differently for women between 40 and 50 (for example Mettlin and Smart, 1994). What is knowledge, is often a matter of intense negotiation between various stakeholders as evidenced by this controversy related to mammography (HHS, 2002).

The KM structure of the CIS is fundamentally a responsive one, very dependent on changes in the larger biomedical environment. It does not have the luxury of operating in a command environment; it must respond to the diversity, complexity and sense–making abilities (health literacy) of its audience, placing it clearly in more postmodern conceptions of KM (Dervin, 1998). It has to be organized in such a way that it provides consistent, quality information, in a manner that is often not immediately apparent to any one caller. The information it provides also must be translated in a manner that can result in meaningful responses on the part of callers (for example, course of treatment) that transforms basic information into knowledge (and perhaps in some cases even into wisdom and ultimately action). Thus the service the CIS provides is ultimately to make information purposeful and relevant to individuals that need it, who are often in dire circumstances.

In a broader sweep, the role of health professionals in our modern consumer–driven health environment comes in facilitating the flow of health information, ensuring that there is support for the nation's information infrastructure. Many health organizations have realized that there are real strategic advantages, especially in enhancing quality, maintaining market share and developing innovations in promoting information technologies. As Porter and Millar (1985) point out, competitive advantages come not just from enhancing performance, but also from giving organizations new ways to outperform competitors and in developing new information businesses. Improving information management (White, 1985), associated analytic skills (Cronin and Davenport, 1993) and knowledge utilization (Menon and Varadarajan, 1992) should be a top priority then of health care management (McGee and Prusak, 1993). Indeed it has become commonplace for almost all hospitals and managed care providers to have very active information programmes for their clients (McKinnon, 1995). Because of the critical role of these broader societal trends we will turn to a discussion of them before describing the basic organizational structure of the CIS.

3.2 WHY IS CANCER–RELATED INFORMATION SEEKING IMPORTANT?

Effective adherence requires accurate information for making informed decisions about health behavior changes. Several studies show, however, that Americans' knowledge of cancer risks, symptoms, and preventive actions is far from optimal. (Lerman et al., 1989, p. 4956)

Although knowledge is not a sufficient condition for appropriate care–seeking, it is certainly a necessary one. (Loehrer et al., 1991, p. 1669)

The aim should be to aid and foster a self–reliant, self–actualizing consumer who can make the most of decisions and play an equal role with the sellers in the marketplace. The key to such consumer emancipation is better information. (Thorelli and Engledow, 1980, p. 9)

Information is an important first step in health behaviour change (Freimuth et al., 1989; Seibold et al., 1984). The consequents of information–carrier exposure and seeking are many,   including   information   gain, effective support, emotional adjustment, social adjustment (Zemore and Shepel, 1987), attitude change, knowledge change, behaviour maintenance (Anderson et al., 1989), a feeling of greater control over events, reduction of uncertainty (Freimuth, 1987) and compliance with medical advice (Street, 1990). Much health behaviour (for example breast cancer screening) involves acting on the basis of personal (Lenz, 1984) and informed judgement (Atkin, 1973). The scope and nature of the information on which to base these judgements, the repertoire of alternative courses of action known to the searcher, and ultimately the action taken are affected by individuals' information–seeking behaviours, one of which may be a call to the CIS.

Active information seeking is associated with favourable responses to a variety of health practices (for example having regular medical check–ups and exercise) (Rakowski et al., 1990). Higher levels of cancer knowledge lead to more prompt action when respondents exhibit cancer danger signals. Knowledge also generally increases the likelihood that someone can be persuaded (McGuire, 1989). The amount of information patients have about cancer is positively related to patient satisfaction (Gotcher and Edwards, 1990), partly because a more informed and questioning consumer gets better care (Hibbard and Weeks, 1987). In short, aggressive responses, of which active information seeking by individuals is one, are most likely to lead to positive cancer–related outcomes – prevention, early detection and treatment, and more efficacious treatment. Information seeking also leads to earlier prognosis, which at the very least allows the terminal patient and his/her family more time to adjust to difficult circumstances (Steen, 1993).

There is information available that could prevent one–third of cancers if appropriate behaviours were adopted (for example smoking cessation, better nutrition), but this information is not being effectively disseminated to target audiences (Hibbard and Peters, 2003; Johnson, 1997a). Unfortunately communication campaigns historically have met with limited success in diffusing cancer–related information. One understudied means of ensuring that information gets into the hands of those who need it is an enhanced understanding of information seeking.

Information seeking can be defined simply as the purposive acquisition of information from selected information carriers. Cancer–related information seeking has become increasingly important. Not too long ago, information related to cancer was the exclusive preserve of doctors and other health professionals. In the US, not only is the diagnosis shared, but individuals have free access to an often bewildering wealth of information. With this access has come an increasing shift of responsibility (some might say burden) to the individual to make decisions concerning his or her treatment and adjustment to cancer. Thus processes related to information seeking are becoming increasingly central to how individuals are coping with cancer.

Previous research has documented several misconceptions among the public about the causes of cancer, the chances of cancer survival, and what can be done to prevent the disease. Much of the public's knowledge of cancer is fragmented and some myths about cancer (for example that bruises cause cancer) continue to persist among the public, often over decades (Case et al., in press). These misconceptions may result in a failure to adopt preventive health measures, delay of medical treatment, or use of non–medically sanctioned treatments when cancer is diagnosed. Interestingly, fully half of disadvantaged cancer patients believed that non–traditional treatments (for example faith healing, vitamin therapy) were viable alternative approaches (Loehrer et al., 1991).

Individual Responsibility/Client/Consumer Movement

By now, consumers' freedom to choose, to be informed, to be heard, and to be safe seem to be accepted as classic rights. The right to choose assumes an open market and a true open market assumes informed consumers. (Thorelli and Engledow, 1980, p. 10)

Increasingly the responsibility for health–related matters is passing to the individual (Hibbard and Peters, 2003). Ever since the 1970s patients have been more and more active participants in decisions effecting health care (Robinson and Whittington, 1979; Pettigrew, 1989), with concomitant improvements in the attitude and mental state of patients (Steen, 1993), as part of the growth of health consumerism (Freimuth et al., 1989). The rise of the consumer movement generally can be traced to a speech by John F. Kennedy in 1962 in which he articulated four basic consumer rights: to be informed, to choice, to safety and to be heard (redress) (Jacoby and Hoyer, 1987).

The consumer movement in health is in part actively encouraged by hospitals, insurance providers, and employing organizations who want to encourage health consumers to 'shop' for the best product at the most affordable price (Hibbard and Peters, 2003). It is generally recognized that consumers can be a positive force for change in the health care sector (Hibbard, 2003). It is commonplace for hospitals to provide patients with a statement of their rights. Among these rights, typically is the right to seek information; for example, 'You have the right to seek and receive all the information necessary for you to understand your medical situation' (Beth Israel Hospital, 1992, p. 3).

With each passing year more information is available to interested parties, and there is also more demand for detailed information relating to cancer. This is especially so for such basic issues as choosing health care providers and hospitals. Facilitating and enhancing this consumer movement have been explosive developments in information technologies, which make more specialized media sources available, permitting increased choice in information carriers, and increased connectivity with other interested parties (Case et al., 2004).

Still, the consumer movement assumes increasingly sophisticated individuals who can understand issues ranging from advanced cell biology to psychosocial adjustment to pain management. While 'Man's very survival depends on paying attention to aspects of the environment that change' (Darnell, 1972, p. 61), individuals have free access to an often bewildering wealth of information. Increasingly the focus of health communication campaigns is on getting people to seek more information on health topics (Parrott, 2003; Salmon and Atkin, 2003). There are literally millions of articles published every year in the biomedical and technical literature, making it nearly impossible for even the most dedicated individual, or even the health professional, to keep abreast of recent advances, with estimates of the raw amount of stored information doubling in three years (Lyman and Varian, 2003).

Large numbers of patients do not receive state–of–the–art treatments, partly because physicians cannot keep up with the information explosion (NCI, 2003). The overload of information on health professionals today forces decentralization of responsibilities, with increasing responsibility passing to individuals if they are going to receive up–to–date treatment. The physician is no longer the exclusive source of medical knowledge (Parrott, 2003). Health professionals must be cognizant of the welter of information available and their role in this complex system (Parrott, 2003). Interestingly, results of a national education programme related to skin cancer in Australia found that during the period of the campaign 90 per cent of the total skin examinations were initiated by the patient, not the physician (American Cancer Society, 1995).

In effect, patients must often do the traditional work of doctors, who cannot possibly keep up with the in–depth information related to specific cancer treatments, especially for more exotic cancers. Recognition of the limits of health professionals also requires individuals to be able to confirm and corroborate information by using multiple sources. In fact patients often call the CIS to verify information they receive elsewhere (Freimuth et al., 1989). Paradoxically however there may never be enough information to answer the specific questions posed by patients (Sechrest et al., 1994). Some of the most important questions patients have may never be answerable: for example, how long will I live if I start this new, experimental course of treatment.

Individuals confronted with cancer often find that they must make judgements with an inadequate knowledge base for even understanding basic terminology. Cancer represents a variety of diseases, each with its own etiology, staging and treatment, which makes cancer–related decision–

making very complex. With their increasing responsibility for information seeking, there is also an increasing burden on individuals, who are expected to keep abreast of rapidly changing health and scientific information. It may be unfair to make the client responsible for every aspect of his or her treatment, especially in these highly uncertain times. In this new world, individuals must confront health problems very much as a scientist, constructing practical theories upon which they must act. This may be establishing a set of expectations that only the best educated can achieve. Will people make the right choices? Do they know enough to weigh and decide between the often conflicting pieces of information they will receive? Human beings are far from optimal information seekers, and while information is a multiplying resource, attention by implication is a zero–sum resource (Johnson, 1997a). Attempting to keep track of just prevention information could consume all one's spare time, raising serious questions about the nature of someone's life driven by such obsessions (Zook, 1994). This issue will soon take on even more importance with the advent of genetic testing among the 'presymptomatic ill' for such genes as BRCA–1 which plays a significant role in the development of breast cancer (Johnson et al., in press).

Adding to this mix is the fact that for many people the first time they will think about cancer in a meaningful way is when they are initially diagnosed, so they may not possess the background information and training to make effective choices. For most individuals, information seeking related to health issues is a novel task fraught with many barriers. While they are dealing with an emotionally charged situation, they will be asked to weigh and evaluate often conflicting medical claims, placing a tremendous burden on them (Johnson and Meischke, 1993a).

All this also raises the question of whose information it is anyway. The social norms that cast doctors and public health officials as the brokers of medical information are yielding to an era in which individuals actively seek information (Johnson and Meischke, 1993b), where a balance of power is sought in the patient–provider relationship (Wertz et al., 1988). Cancer patients tend to want much more information than health care providers can give to them, even if willing (McIntosh, 1974). Information that to a client is necessary for coping with cancer, may be seen by doctors as an intrusion into their prerogatives. Exacerbating this problem is the fact that doctors and patients may not share similar outcome goals. Traditionally doctors have viewed the ideal patient as one who came to them recognizing their authority and was willing to comply totally (with enthusiasm) with recommended therapies (Hibbard and Weeks, 1987; Zook, 1994). Yet many, if not most, patients do not comply with treatment regimens (Evans and Clarke, 1983).

Most doctors believe in treating cancers aggressively, even those with low cure rates; however increasingly some more harmful aspects of chemotherapy and other treatments are weighed against the likelihood of success and the quality of life (Steen, 1993). So while doctors typically engage in narrow problem–solving relating to the disease, patients often view cancer as but one component of a complex social system of which they are a part. What good does it do to save me, if I will be but a shell of my former self and my family is bankrupted in the process? (Brink, 1995a).

Perhaps the most threatening aspect of enhanced information seeking for health professionals is their loss of control. Yet no market can operate effectively if information is not freely available; if one group of professionals is granted a monopoly on information (Wennberg et al., 1982). Still, the more control that health professionals have, the less effective they may ultimately be, especially in terms of ensuring that clients act according to consensus views of treatment. While the hoarding and withholding of information often benefits the interests of individuals in privileged or specialist positions (Moore and Tumin, 1949), in many respects doctors have benefited by this shift of responsibility, since their failures are a result of major choices patients have made (for example, should I have just surgery alone, rather than chemotherapy and surgery?). Thus there is less of a feeling among clients that their doctor has betrayed them when things go wrong (Steen, 1993). Increasingly the blame is likely to be placed on the individual for not only choosing the wrong treatment regimen, but also for not engaging in the primary prevention activities that would have allowed them to avoid cancer in the first place (Becker and Rosenstock, 1989).

Most discussions of information seeking tend to focus on the benefits of information seeking. Yet information seeking can be viewed as having many negative consequences: people in authority lose control and the burden on individuals increases tremendously. Many doctors have legitimate concerns about self–diagnosis and patients possessing just enough information to be dangerous (Broadway and Christensen, 1993) and the general preferences of consumers may cause them to avoid unpopular, albeit effective, invasive procedures (Greer, 1994). In spite of (or maybe because of) the abundance of available information, lack of knowledge about important issues is a significant problem. As more and more of us become responsible for our own care, in part because of the rise of outpatient treatments, home care and hospices, these issues will only take on greater importance.

Information Gap/Inequities/Digital Divide

... cutting–edge technology, especially in communication and information transfer, will enable the greatest advances yet in public health. Real health care reform will come only from demand reduction, as individuals learn to take charge of their health. ... Communication technology can work wonders for us in this vital endeavor. ... encouraging personal wellness and prevention and leading to better informed decisions about health care. (Koop, 1995, p. 760)

In the final analysis, it will be the human touch of the system – not the technology – that will determine whether it is successful or not. (Office of Rural Health Policy, 1994, p. 13)

The aim should be to aid and foster a self–reliant, self–actualizing consumer who can make the most of decisions and play an equal role with sellers in the marketplace. The key to such consumer emancipation is better information. (Thorelli and Engledow, 1980, p. 9)

Certainly the disadvantaged are not as likely as the rest of society to change the undesirable conditions of their lives, or to see information as an instrument of their salvation. (Freimuth, 1990, p. 177)

The concepts of an 'information gap' and the 'information poor' have been advanced as important policy issues, generally in terms of their broad societal ramifications. It has been argued that there is a growing difference in access to information between different segments of our society and that increasingly this gap also reflects other demographic classifications, such as socioeconomic status. Perhaps even more importantly, 'informational have–nots' in many respects represent the average US citizen, not a small minority of the population (Dervin, 1989), and these individuals risk becoming members of a permanent underclass.

The Internet creates an increasingly fragmented and privatized information environment, as opposed to the more mass, public access technologies represented by television and radio (Case et al., 2004). In response to these trends, governmental agencies are adopting policies to promote information equity among various segments of our society (Doctor, 1992). Often universal telephone service is used as an exemplar for the emerging uses of the Internet, as one example, but some question whether access to information resources can ever truly be universal, in spite of the best intentions of our policy–makers (Fortner, 1995).

This is partly because of the unwillingness of potential users to avail themselves of information resources. At a societal level surprisingly few people use our existing information infrastructure (Johnson, 1997a).

Clearly, if not a knowledge gap, a utilization gap exists, in the use of CIS by demographic groups that would typically be classified among the information poor (Freimuth et al., 1989). This problem drove the initial round of CISRC research projects that I will discuss in more detail in Chapter 4.

Another major impediment in information seeking for some groups is a lack of necessary information processing skills, some as fundamental as a lack of literacy and lack of knowledge of the primary language in which most health matters are expressed (Friemuth et al., 1989). The information fields in which the poor are embedded typically involve one–way communication from mass entertainment–oriented media, such as television (Freimuth et al., 1989). Added to this mix of impediments is a possibility of mistrust and deliberate rejection of what is seen as 'establishment' positions (Freimuth et al., 1989).

Unfortunately this information gap is also directly related to such critical cancer–related factors as the early detection of the disease and the pursuit of efficacious treatment once the disease is diagnosed. The information gap also directly corresponds to the individuals who are least likely to have access to health care for economic reasons; so these individuals are doubly disadvantaged. In addition, members of these groups are also often at higher risk for many health problems, including cancer (Freimuth et al., 1989).

Beyond the issue of use is the general concern for need, with several user studies of the general populace finding they have few information needs, at least ones they cannot satisfy informally. All this raises the policy question of what level of support should be given to an information infrastructure which receives little general use (Johnson, 1997a).

The knowledge gap hypothesis (Tichenor et al., 1970) argues that over time gaps will increase, since more highly educated individuals assimilate new information faster from traditional mass media than more poorly educated ones; they also have more relevant social contacts who are likely to discuss issues with them. In one form, this hypothesis suggests that these gaps are perpetual, and that, ironically, agency efforts to disseminate information only increase the gaps existing in society, since the educated will assimilate the information more quickly and completely (Viswanath et al., 1993). In addition technology and software access are likely to be greater for privileged groups within our society.

While the knowledge gap has generally been supported in static studies, its exact dynamics over time are still subject to some debate (Freimuth, 1990; Viswanath et al., 1993). Gaps are smaller for topics that are of local interest, that differentially interest certain groups (for example the performance capabilities of a BMW versus a GMC Envoy), and when they are couched in non–textbook terms (Freimuth, 1990).

Several underlying dynamics have been suggested for the existence and persistence of gaps. The deficit or individual blame bias suggests that information 'haves' possess superior communication skills (for example reading, listening), a framework for understanding new information, and a greater range of social contacts. The difference position notes that many barriers exist to knowledge acquisition among groups in our society, including: literacy (non–native language speakers); 'information ghettos', where there is primarily a one–way flow of information; exclusive within–group communication that further reinforces ignorance; and the often fatalistic cultures of disadvantaged groups. While the set of conditions described in the deficit position are fairly intractable, and often lead to blaming the victim, the second set focus on key information–seeking differences between groups that might be overcome more easily (for example messages could address fatalism, as well as the substantive issue at hand) (Freimuth, 1990).

It has been argued that the use of mass media can act to reduce gaps relating to issues that are of interest to normally disadvantaged groups (Freimuth et al., 1989; Freimuth, 1990) and, further, at some point the 'haves' become satiated and the poor can catch up (Dervin, 1980). Another way of stating this is to suggest that there are ceiling effects for some knowledge. So simple messages (for example, wear your seat–belt) and finite knowledge of a particular event (for example, Betty Ford has breast cancer) increase the possibility for reduced gaps between audience members (Freimuth, 1990).

It has also been suggested that motivation can make the critical difference, overcoming problems represented by lack of education and social position. These issues were examined in an interesting study done by Viswanath et al. (1993) examining education, motivation, group membership, information functionality and knowledge gain over time in a community–based training programme on diet, nutrition and cancer–risk. Community members volunteered for a home–based course (a prime indicant of motivation; the others being perceived risk and efficacy), while the public was incidentally exposed to information in the mass media and grocery stores. In essence the study found that there was a complex interaction among these variables and that motivation alone could not overcome lack of education. For dietary fat knowledge, the study found that for the home–based course group the knowledge gap persisted over a one–year period for the subgroups with differing levels of education, although the gap was less than for the general population, and the motivated but less educated surpassed the level of knowledge of the less–motivated general population groups. For the dietary fibre study, for the motivated group, the gap widened slightly between the more and less educated, although for the general population group it decreased slightly. This may have been attributable to the higher general interest in dietary fibre and the greater general flow of knowledge related to it in the mass media, which resulted in a higher general level of knowledge among all groups related to this issue. In sum, this study found that while motivation increased knowledge levels, it did not overcome initial differences between groups in level of education.

Inevitably, differential access to information produces differential participation rates in our society (Lievrouw, 1994). Classically our mass media infrastructure has produced information fields that are informative. They are geared to providing information they select that is then consumed by their audiences. Increasingly information technologies offer the possibility of involving audience members through their interactive capabilities and enhanced possibilities for information seeking (Lievrouw, 1994). It has been suggested that policy–makers should strive to create information equity among different segments of our society, as well as more globally (Siefert et al., 1989). One underlying reason for creating equity is that the wider the range of ideas available to individuals, the more likely it is that a plurality will gravitate toward the correct one.

Disconcertingly, it is also possible that people will become so overloaded with information that they will 'escape,' turning to demagogues who offer simple solutions to increasingly complex problems. The dark side of the quest for uncertainty reduction is that once an answer is arrived at, a decision made, blockage from future information seeking may occur (Smithson, 1989).

One step in reducing information gaps is greater knowledge of the factors affecting information seeking. Information seeking clearly differs by the educational levels of individuals (Chen and Hernon, 1982; Doctor, 1992). So it is important not only to provide access to the information superhighway; people must also receive the training necessary to use it (Doctor, 1992). Rather than stressing simple access to ideas, it may be better to stress access to playful intellectual tools that allow individuals to make sense of an overwhelming information environment (Entman and Wildman, 1992).

Even if there is not a knowledge gap, there is a utilization gap. This utilization gap arises in part because some individuals are consciously deciding to decline membership in the information society (Fortner, 1995). Some people have just reached a saturation point; they cannot spend any more time communicating (Fortner, 1995). Some groups, such as unions, have historically mistrusted the application of new technologies (Palmquist, 1992) and deliberately rejected 'establishment' positions. Others decide, for aesthetic or lifestyle reasons, not to adopt new information technologies. So instead of surfing the Internet, they prefer more civil discourse with their friends (Fortner, 1995).

We have always had among us Luddites who reject new technologies because they are socially and economically disadvantaged by them. We also have many individuals who we typically do not like to talk about, who really do not want to know things, who are more interested in 'vegging out' and being entertained (Fortner, 1995). While over and over again on a societal level we emphasize the need for individuals who will constantly grow and develop into perpetual learners, it must be acknowledged that some individuals would prefer a comfortable world where they do not need to change nor expend the necessary effort to become full–fledged participants in the information society. Even more disturbing is the process of information alienation arising from the frustrations of a failed search, where people come to believe that the information they seek will never be available to them (Dervin, 1980).

Indeed it has been estimated that as little as 10 per cent of top executives use the information technologies they have (Fortner, 1995). Some more cynical observers of information seeking in the professions suggest that perhaps the most powerful motivation for doctors to keep up to date is the ever–present threat of a malpractice suit (Paisley, 1993). Most other professions do not have similarly compelling external motivations to keep current; they do not have sanctions for 'remediable ignorance', for actions which duplicate or overlook existing knowledge (Paisley, 1980). These professions can in effect conspire to say it is pointless to try to keep up.

Even more disturbing than the information gap is the understanding gap that is developing between individuals who have access to a rich array of diverse information sources and the resources necessary to synthesize information (Viswanath et al., 1991); 'bad ideas spread more rapidly among the ignorant than among the informed, and good ideas spread more rapidly among the informed than the ignorant' (March, 1994, p. 246). Our elites, both institutions and individuals, are developing a considerably different view of the world than other members of our society, in part because of their differential levels of information–seeking capacities and skills. Even between elites, constant self–selection of differing information sources is producing different views of the world. The information revolution is contributing to the accelerating fragmentation of our culture (Fortner, 1995).

This has led to considerable concern that individuals and organizations with resources and access will perpetuate (or even widen) gaps in information to preserve or enhance their power and economic advantages (Doctor, 1992). Increasing information levels among the public, especially of prevention information, offer the greatest possibilities of both improving health and reducing costs (Koop, 1995; NCI, 2003). It has been estimated that 70 per cent of premature deaths could be postponed by a focus on disease prevention and health promotion; this is especially true for factors related to tobacco, diet and activity patterns, and alcohol that are implicated in one–third of deaths in the US (Koop, 1995). It has also been estimated that company wellness programmes that encourage prevention–oriented programmes cut company medical bills an average of 20 per cent (Leutwyler, 1995). Yet an increased focus on secondary prevention, involving screening and early detection, is not without substantial costs. Disconcertingly, it has been estimated that the costs of most screening programmes exceed the costs of therapy if the cancer were undetected at early stage (Leutwyler, 1995).

Many have suggested that we need to change our focus to more modern conceptions of health, which include wellness and primary prevention, rather than our traditional narrow preoccupation with the treatment of specific medical disorders (Freimuth et al., 1993; Koop, 1995). A key element of the change to broader conceptions of information is increased access to a national information infrastructure (Clark, 1992). There is broad public support for providing additional information related to health (Research!America, 1995).

3.3. CREATING RICH INFORMATION FIELDS

Creating rich information fields through such practices as 'self–serving' to information from databases, should make for a more informed consumer, who is likely to consume less time of health professionals being 'brought up to speed' on the basics of his or her disease and its treatment. Health professionals must make it easy for people to use information technologies, since most individuals will resist change, especially change related to information technology (Hoffman, 1994). Unfortunately this has been historically true of doctors, and because of their role as the key decision–makers in hospitals, the benefits of advances in information technology have been slower to come in the health arena than in more commercial sectors of our society (Brenner and Logan, 1980), lagging from seven to ten years behind other industries (Clark, 1992). Doctors find information technology threatening on several levels: it removes their exclusive control over information; it increases the possibility that their behaviour will be monitored (for example through assessment of medical records of their patients); and many doctors are loathe to admit ignorance in any area, a key problem when they need to learn new technologies (Schuman, 1988). Countervailing pressures to drive down costs from insurers and government agencies are overcoming the traditional resistance of health professionals to information technologies (Johnson, in press).

Information Processing Technologies

The information–seeking possibilities created by new technologies are facilitated by an information architecture that has three primary components: data storage, data transport and data transformation. While I will discuss these components separately, increasingly it is their blending and integration that is creating exciting new opportunities for information seeking, primarily through the ubiquity of the Internet (Case et al., 2004).

In the health arena these benefits and possibilities are often captured under the heading of telemedicine or health informatics. Consumer health information is perhaps the fastest–growing area of this specialty (MacDougall and Brittain, 1994). The purported benefits of telemedicine are many: increased access to information, increased consistency in medical decision–making, matching diagnostic and management options to patient needs, increased quality of care, more interpretable outcomes, increased efficiency, increased efficacy, decreased costs and a more uniform structure for health care (Turner, 2003).

Traditionally data storage has meant physical storage of information in filing systems, but with the volume of information related to health, paper–based systems are increasingly unwieldy (Tilley, 1990). Information systems retain organizational memory through records held in electronic databases, such as the Cancer Information Service's Call Record Form (CRF). These databases can result in later secondary analysis that advance knowledge (for example Freimuth et al., 1989).

Databases are repositories of information that become key elements of a profession's memory. There has been explosive growth of databases. Essentially databases provide a means for storing, organizing and retrieving information. Shared databases are at the core of developing information systems, since they provide a common core of information. Databases must be combined with sophisticated electronic access, such as the Internet, to achieve their full potential for information seeking.

Databases, when coupled with powerful search engines and the linking capabilities of modern relational databases, also encourage ever more complex questions. Associative databases, with data–mining or knowledge discovery programmes, can automatically search for information on increasingly remote or tenuous relationships to provide answers we never expected (or at least would have been unable to uncover) (Benoit, 2002).

Modern conceptions of storage have broadened this function considerably to include verification and quality control of information entering a storage system. Security systems, which directly relate to information seeking for the stored information, are also increasingly important. For example who should have access to personal information? Security issues also involve means to insure that no one can tamper or change information residing in a database (Hoffman, 1994).

Information pollution has become an increasing concern of even the popular press because of the wealth of information found in resources like the Internet and the difficulty in determining its accuracy. There is also reason to be concerned about the commercial motivations of many providers of information. One unresolved area is who is liable for erroneous information in a database: its provider, the author of a message or the person providing the information? Doctors are reluctant to lodge too much authority in these systems because they are ultimately responsible for any advice they give patients, even if they are just relaying information from a database (Schuman, 1988). However, since most malpractice suits are based on a standard of reasonable care, as more physicians use information technologies, it may also be the case, that not using them could be a basis for a malpractice claim (Diamond et al., 1994). Doctors have historically mistrusted medical information systems because they may not capture the subtlety and nuance that only their long experience and training can bring to a situation (Shuman, 1988). They also do not provide much assistance to health professionals in areas where there is low consensus knowledge (Brittain, 1985).

On the other side are consumer activists and former cancer patients or family members who suggest, especially in areas where there is not effective treatment, that all information, regardless of source, should be made available. Users should be the only ones who determine the utility of information and peer review often serves to preserve the status quo. It may even be the case that knowledgeable lay people may have more knowledge than general practitioners and even oncologists in limited areas (Hoke, 1995).

The previously mundane world of data transport is increasingly the stuff of lead stories in the evening news, such as providing easier access to information on the Internet, or providing new business opportunities through revised telecommunication laws. Essentially data transport involves the acquisition and exchange of information.

Telecommunication systems such as fibre–optic cables and satellite systems provide the hardware that links individuals and provides enhanced access to systems. Telecommunication systems maintain communication channels (for example e–mail) through which information is accessed and reported. They can specifically enhance the information seeking of patients by creating new channels for sending and receiving information, helping them in filtering information, reducing their dependence on others, leveraging their time to concentrate on the most important tasks, and enhancing their ability for dealing with complexity.

New communication technologies, like bulletin boards, permit the sending of messages to a communication space that is characterized by potential similarities of messages and communicators, rather than to specific individuals. This enhances participation and access by saying that all individuals who share a similar interest can come to the same electronic space to communicate (Culnan and Markus, 1987). Increasingly cancer support groups are meeting in cyberspace on locally supported electronic bulletin boards.

For information seeking, the critical issues revolve around the carrying capacity of a particular system and the ease, range and timeliness of access. Fibre–optic broadband systems are vastly superior to traditional metal wire systems because of their carrying capacities that now permit the transmission of moving visual images. Without this increase in carrying capacity, represented by broadband applications, the current movement toward telemedicine, especially such applications as distant surgery, would be impractical. Some cancers, such as melanoma, are much more easily understood when the rich visual imagery and interactivity of computerized telemedicine systems are brought into play (Sneiderman et al., 1994).

Networks, like the Internet, usually combine enhanced telecommunication capabilities with software that allows linkage and exchange of information between users (one of which is often a database). One reason for the excitement behind the Internet is its easy access (in terms of both costs and lack of other barriers) and the increasing user–friendliness of software that permit access to websites. In addition, commercial on–line services offer unique resources (for example chat–groups, bulletin boards and access to in–house experts) as well as access to the Internet. The proliferation of home pages and websites where users can exchange information related to specific topics is proceeding at an incredible pace. Combining databases and telecommunications with software creates telematics that allows for the possibility of increasingly sophisticated searches for information and analysis or interpretation of it once it is compiled.

The integration of data storage and transport with sophisticated software offers unique opportunities for software solutions that transcend the limits of individual information processing, especially that of novices. For example, data–mining programmes are a form of artificial intelligence expert system that are continually looking for new statistical and visual representations of data linked in ways that it would be very difficult for even the most diligent human researcher to have the patience for. These systems embody many of characteristics of artificial intelligence systems. They can result in more thorough and consistent decision–making.

The Internet has spawned many flexible information search and retrieval services that determine its substantial benefit. Expert search engines try to accommodate different learning and search styles of different users adopting their approach to specific individuals. Intelligent information–sharing systems address the problem of filtering information on several levels that is sent to a respondent on electronic data systems. Messages might be screened, sorted and prioritized based on several categories: the urgency with which a response is needed, cognitive domains (for example key words), social dimensions (for example more attention given to friends, those higher in the hierarchy), future communication events (for example the agenda for an upcoming meeting) and so on (Johnson, 1997a).

These systems, and their associated tools of simulation and of modelling, in effect can overcome the limits of individual cognition and bounded rationality by providing humans with answers without concerning them with an enormous range of variables and potential scenarios and options that these systems automatically consider. These computer programmes increasingly rely on powerful graphic images of data, assuming that for interpretation of information a picture is literally worth a thousand words. In some ways they are similar to shared decision–making programmes that allow patients to explore on their own information related to their problems, which is then used to facilitate joint decisions with their physicians about treatment options. These programmes have been met with enthusiasm when implemented by both patients and clinicians; however, they are very expensive to maintain and develop (Johnson, 1997a).

Summary

All this suggests the increasing importance of information as a strategic asset that should be systematically incorporated in the planning of health professionals, especially those in clinical practices. Health institutions need to recognize the potential benefit of marketing unique corporate knowledge and expertise to other information seekers (Johnson, in press). For example cancer centres may have developed unique ancillary knowledge related to genetic markers that could lead to new spin–off industries that others would like to acquire. Health professionals also need to lobby the government to maintain critical information infrastructures.

These trends also suggest a need to reintroduce simplicity, partially by establishing more direct communication linkages with the primary source of information (Keen, 1990), and to think carefully about what information should be excluded from an individual's information processing. While more and more information can be produced more efficiently, there is a concomitant increase in the costs of consuming (for example interpreting, analysing) this information (More, 1990).

Somewhat relatedly, to coordinate most effectively there must be compatibility among various information systems and some form of standards for information processing. Coordination costs increase with distributed work and more extensive lines of communication and the problem of information asymmetries (for example quality) may be insurmountable in terms of creating totally open health information infrastructures (Johnson, 1997a). For example in hospital settings CEOs received twice as much decision–making information as their boards and three times as much as their medical staff (Thomas et al., 1993). This suggests there are considerably different knowledge bases and interpretive frameworks for individuals in different information–processing roles. In addition the nature of information processed by differing functional specialties also differs, with production–based information more certain and quantifiable than the typical mix of marketing and sales information for example (McKinnon and Bruns, 1992). This specialization, which can be augmented and enhanced by information technology, makes it much harder for differing groups to communicate across their boundaries (Hoffman, 1994).

Increasingly, seeking and interpretation will be delegated to intelligent software (Maes, 1995). These systems will not however be able to make the value (for example is the personal cost of chemotherapy worth it?) and ethical decisions often associated with cancer. It has become a truism that computer–based information and decision systems excel at programmed explicit tasks; they do not perform well, and may even be dangerous, for tacit tasks that are ambiguous and/or that need creativity and judgement (Johnson, 1997a).

There are a number of indications that programmematically the best channels for providing cancer–related information are those channels that constitute a hybrid of the positive properties of both mediated and interpersonal channels, something that the Web is also moving to, supplanting traditional processes of interpersonal communication influence, such as the two–step flow of opinion leadership (Case et al., 2004).

Telephone information and referral services

Information and referral centres can take many forms, such as call centres, customer support, hotlines, switchboards and units within organizations (for example nurses' medical helplines) where individuals can go to get answers to pressing concerns. They are an ubiquitous feature of our economy with estimates that they employ 3 per cent of all workers in roughly 100 000 call centres (Downing, 2004). These various types of centres serve three primary functions: educating and assisting people in making wise choices in sources and topics for searches; making information acquisition less costly; and being adaptable to a range of users (Doctor, 1992). These services have been found to offer considerable help and assistance to callers (Gingerich et al., 1988; Marcus, Woodworth and Strickland, 1993; Ossip–Klein et al.,

1991; Marcus et al., 2002). They are also increasingly integrated with information technology systems, with these services operating as personal guides to clients (for example Mooney et al., 2002).

One example of a hybrid channel is the CIS telephone service that has a widely available 800 number (1–800–4–CANCER). Telephone information and referral services like the CIS represent a unique hybrid of mediated and interpersonal channels, since they disseminate authoritative written information, as well as verbal responses to personal queries (Anderson et al., 1992; Freimuth et al., 1989; Walsh and Phelan, 1974). The hybrid nature of telephone services and referral services is important, since it can overcome some of the weaknesses of other channels. They have the additional advantage of homophily of source, a crucial factor in effective communication (see Rogers, 1983), since the calls are handled by individuals of closer status and background to potential callers than are physicians. It has been suggested that the CIS provides an important link between symptomatic people and health services, since a substantial proportion of callers follow up with more information seeking, passing on information to others, or consultations with health professionals (Altman, 1985). Generally cancer telephone services have also been used effectively with media campaigns, combining the best features of interpersonal and mass communication (Arkin et al., 1993; Sherer and Juanillo, 1992).

The advantages of telephone services as a channel include: they are free, available without appointment and forms and offer a high level of empathic understanding (Carothers and Inslee, 1974); they offer greater client control, permit anonymity for both parties, bridge geographic barriers (Rosenbaum and Calhoun, 1977), provide immediate responses, allow the client to take greater risks in expressing feelings (Adelman et al., 1987), and offer convenience, cost effectiveness and personalized attention (Altman, 1985). All these factors are reflected in respondents rating CIS as the highest–quality source of cancer information (Mettlin et al., 1980) and the extremely high rate of user satisfaction in subsequent surveys (Morra et al., 1993; Ward et al., 1988). These evaluations reflect key sources of CIS strategic advantage, especially in relation to other 'hotlines': NCI research infrastructure, development of authoritative guidelines, a quality monitoring system, and translating this information to the public.

3.4 THE CANCER INFORMATION SERVICE

We need every weapon against cancer, and information can be a powerful, lifesaving tool. ... A call is made, a question is answered. NCI reaches out through the CIS, and the CIS is the voice of the NCI. (Broder, 1993, p. vii)

... one phone call, one conversation, can save a life. This is the true essence of the service and the most rewarding aspect of the program. (Morra, Van Nevel et al., 1993, p. 7)

In broad sweep the CIS has traditionally been the disseminator and translator of consensus–based scientific information from the NCI to broader segments of the public. In some ways the NCI acted to codify knowledge, the CIS then exploited it, while the CISRC eventually explored the creation of knowledge (Schulz, 2001). The CIS's focus has been on actionable knowledge, providing guidance to callers on how they should best respond to often difficult life situations. We can easily organize a description of the CIS around the major functions of KM organizations: transforming information into knowledge; identifying and verifying knowledge; capturing and securing knowledge; organizing knowledge; retrieving and applying knowledge; combining it; creating it; and finally distributing and selling it (Liebowtiz, 2000). Different KM functions imply different communication structures and information flows in organization (Schulz, 2001), as well as different relations to innovation activities. As we have seen in Chapters 1 and 2 and I will describe in more detail in Chapter 4, members of the CIS saw a major strategic advantage in moving to higher–end KM functions, such as generating knowledge.

The Role of the OCC and the NCI

Here I will describe the information services provided to the CIS by the OCC, the National Cancer Institute (NCI) and the National Institutes of Health (NIH) that relate to the classic KM functions of transforming information into knowledge; identifying and verifying knowledge, and capturing and securing it. Needless to say these organizations have continued to refine and develop their KM activities, and here we will focus on what was in existence during the time period of this study. We will conclude the book with a postscript describing the CIS's current structure.

NIH

The NIH, primarily through the National Library of Medicine (NLM), devoted considerable resources and thought to building a national information infrastructure in the US that integrates many of the issues we have been discussing in this section. This was done partially to respond to the concerns of advocacy groups for more rapid dissemination of knowledge, particularly related to AIDS and to breast cancer. Where possible the NIH attempted to work through intermediaries (both the media and various groups) to achieve a multiplier effect in their information dissemination efforts, a point we will return to in the next chapter.

NLM

The NLM, which dates to 1836, is the largest research library focusing on a single professional field in the world (NLM, 1994). While the NLM was primarily in existence to service the needs of health professionals, its databases, such as MEDLINE, provide the critical national information infrastructure for enhancing patient care (Lindberg et al., 1993; Wood, 1994). MEDLINE on–line searches totalled over 6 million in 1994. GRATEFUL MED software allows users to access NLM databases such as CANCERLIT and PDQ from their personal computers, for a nominal fee. Many NLM databases, such as MEDLINE, were available on CD–ROM from various commercial organizations. PDQ was a major resource for the CIS in providing detailed responses to public inquiries.

NCI

The NCI's Information Services programme was composed of the CIS, the PDQ Search Service and the Information Associates Program. The PDQ Search Service was specifically designed to make information available to health professionals who do not have the time or resources to access the PDQ database directly. Ease of access was promoted by a toll–free telephone, toll–free fax and Internet e–mail. Searches were conducted by Certified Search Specialists who acted as information brokers.

The Information Associates Programme was run by the International Cancer Information Centre of the NCI. It represented a very interesting approach to providing comprehensive information services for a modest annual fee. It provided toll–free access to CancerFax, the Electronic Bulletin Board Service and PDQ. It also provided subscriptions to the *Journal of the National Cancer Institute, Journal Monographs*, as well as patient education materials from OCC and NCI bulletins. It also maintained a bulletin board that provided timely updates, e–mail capability and electronic conferencing.

To their credit, the authoritativeness of information has always been a paramount concern for government databases. The NLM's MEDLINE systems cross–referenced corrections to articles (Tilley, 1990). In the cancer area the NCI's PDQ had been paying systematic attention to these issues for over a decade (Hibbard et al., 1995). PDQ was originally designed to address the knowledge gap between primary care physicians and specialists. In a 1989 survey of primary care practitioners, two–thirds felt that the volume of the medical literature was unmanageable and 78 per cent reported that they had difficulty screening out irrelevant information (Hibbard et al., 1995), but doctors in another survey also reported that computerized databases could help in dealing with these problems (Diamond et al., 1994). 'This knowledge gap is responsible for the prolonged use of outmoded forms of cancer treatment resulting in unnecessarily high rates of cancer morbidity and mortality' (Kreps et al., 1988, p. 362). Indeed a major latent function of the CIS historically has been to speed the diffusion of state–of–the–art cancer treatment.

Fundamental to PDQ was the recognition that the rapid dissemination of health information was critical to successful treatment, since at the time it was created in the early 1980s approximately 85 per cent of cancer patients were treated by primary care doctors (Kreps et al., 1988). In its early days one–third of the usage of the PDQ came from the CIS (Kreps et al., 1988), reflecting a high level of usage by the lay public.

PDQ sought to provide a current peer–reviewed synthesis of the state–of–the–art of clinical information related to cancer (Hibbard et al., 1995). PDQ contained three primary components: (1) a full–text file with treatment, supportive, care, prevention and screening information as well as information on newly approved anti–cancer drugs; (2) a file of active treatment protocols; and (3) a directory of physicians (over 21 000) and organizations (over 8000) that provided cancer care. A critical issue facing all databases is how old, irrelevant information is culled from any storage system. A not–so–apparent problem of public databases, like many of those available on the Internet, is the potential lack of timeliness of the information.

The cancer information file of PDQ was reviewed monthly by five editorial boards of cancer experts in different areas (for example adult treatment, screening and prevention). These boards have clear guidelines on levels of evidence for information to be considered for the database (for example level 1 is evidence obtained from at least one randomized control trial). About 14 per cent of the statements in the files were changed each month, often substantially (Hibbard et al., 1995). These procedures clearly set PDQ apart from other data bases in terms of the timeliness and authoritativeness of information it contained. In addition, MEDLINE database searchers could add additional quality criteria within their searches by for example only requesting information from clinical trials (Haynes et al., 1994).

The viability of information, which included issues like shelf life of data, was also an important issue; NCI–based systems were constantly updated and outdated references deleted. The long–term ability of media like computer disks to store and to retrieve information physically was yet another aspect of this problem. Since even hard floppy disks cannot store data indefinitely, increasingly salient is the related issue of the meaningfulness of the keywords and software assumptions that categorized the original information. This area of concern was being addressed in part by the NLM's Unified Medical Language System (UMLS) initiative to try to establish some standards for on–line information resources (MacDougall and Brittain, 1994).

Office of Cancer Communications

The CIS was one section of the larger division of the OCC during this time period. The OCC was organized around several classic KM functions, providing comprehensive services for the NCI. The Patient Education Office was charged with developing education programmes for key initiatives and resources for patients and health professionals, especially related to the persistent NCI strategic problem of recruiting individuals for clinical trials. The CIS was one of three sections within the Reports and Inquiries Branch which was generally charged with responding to requests from stakeholders outside of the NCI for information. The Public Inquiries Section responded to direct requests from the public, monitored NCI–controlled correspondence, made clinical trial referrals, and provided technical content review of information products. The Reports Section responded to press inquiries, conducted NCI press conferences, prepared press releases and, as part of the *Journal of the National Cancer Institute* news section, covered scientific meetings. The Information Projects Branch consisted solely of the Health Promotion Section. This branch focused on public education (for example tobacco, nutrition, early cancer detection) and outreach, special populations education, and communications research. The Information Resources Branch focused on printing (for example brochures) production, editorial clearances and Freedom of Information and Privacy Act issues. The Graphics and Audiovisual Section focused on design and graphics of NCI information materials. The Library and Information Section developed and maintained databases, conducted database searches, provided reference services and maintained the library collection. Thus the CIS had a well–defined role within a comprehensive KM operation.

KM Services of CIS

The National Cancer Institute's Cancer Information Service (CIS), the foremost public resource for cancer information, was founded based on the conviction that constant advances in scientific research combined with the public's knowledge, understanding, and use of these medical findings saves lives. Believing in the importance of person–to–person interaction as well as the application of advanced technologies, the CIS is committed to using a range of communications approaches to ensure that as many people as possible have access to our service. By providing the latest, science–based information about cancer in understandable language, the CIS helps people become active participants in their health care.(CIS Vision statement from *Cancer Facts*, NCI, December, 1996)

As we have seen, the CIS focused on the classic KM functions of retrieving and applying knowledge, combining it, and finally distributing and selling it. The CIS was implemented in 1975 by the NCI to disseminate accurate, up–to–date information about cancer to the American public, primarily by telephone (Ward et al., 1988; Morra, Van Nevel et al., 1993). Information was available free of charge from the CIS to anyone who called 1–800–4–CANCER. (All descriptions here are based on the time period of this study; the CIS is constantly being reorganized both for its location within the NCI and often more radically during its periodic – roughly every four to five years – contract renewals for the geographic coverage of its ROs. See Morra, Van Nevel et al., 1993.) By any measure the CIS distributes vast amounts of information to the public. At the start of our study period there were 550 000 inquiries by the public, 127 641 calls ordering publications, a total of 18 million pieces of literature sent (for example brochures), and 30 000 PDQ computer data base searches (NCI, 1993). The impetus underlying the creation of the CIS was the assumption that all cancer patients should receive the best care with a latent purpose of diffusing up–to–date information to clinical settings (NCI, 2003). To accomplish that end it was felt that free and easy access to credible information was critical (Morra, Van Nevel et al., 1993).

The CIS as a Contractual Network

The CIS's primary activities focus on providing information about cancer and cancer–related resources to the public primarily through a telephone service and various outreach activities (Morra, Van Nevel et al., 1993). Established in 1975, it was one of the first federally–funded health–related telephone information systems in the nation (Marcus, Morra et al., 1993). The CIS is not a formal organization in the conventional sense, nor is it an interorganizational network. It is a new organizational form which, while incorporating many of the features of organizational forms previously identified in the literature, has its own idiosyncratic combination of characteristics.

The relationships between the OCC staff charged with oversight of the CIS and the 19 ROs can be couched in terms of the classic relationship between headquarters and subsidiary units in multinational corporations (Pahl and Roth, 1993). Luke et al. (1989) have described the pressures for increased integration and formalization as 'implosive' within new organizational forms and the countervailing pressures for them to disintegrate as 'explosive'. Throughout the history of the CIS there has been a tension between centralization and formalization of its operations and the decentralizing forces characteristic of its RO structure (Morra, Van Nevel et al., 1993).

Formalization was evidenced in an elaborate set of rules and procedures governing behaviour of contractors in ROs. Quality was also ensured by an innovative programme of quality assurance, which set it apart from competing services, involving CISTERS (Cancer Information Service Telephone Evaluation and Reporting System) (Kessler et al., 1993). This test–call system involved computerized protocols of scenarios involving 'typical calls' that were compared to responses of actual calls with randomly selected TSMs these evaluations were used to trigger training and other responses to deviations from national standards. Test–call scenarios evaluation criteria fell into three categories: objective measures relating to the mechanics (for example number of rings before an answer) of calling a CIS RO; completeness measures relating to the technical information provided to a caller; and quality measures reflecting the manner (for example communication skills of the IS) in which information was conveyed.

There is an increasing need to develop new theories and fresh perspectives based on empirical data of the operation of these new organizational forms (Luke et al., 1989); particularly concerning the nature of the communication channels needed to maintain them. Because of geographic dispersion, day–to–day communication is mediated, although some of it is more interpersonal (for example by telephone) than others, reflecting the powerful role of distance in determining choices of communication channels (Johnson, 1993). Indeed, when taken *in toto*, the CIS is in many ways a precursor of the emerging contemporary organization.

KM Roles in the CIS

To accomplish its KM work the CIS has developed several specialized, functional roles in its ROs. These roles – PD, telephone service managers (TSM) and outreach managers (OM) – differ both in their position requirements and in their organizational status level, with PDs having higher status than the TSMs and the OMs (Morra, Van Nevel et al., 1993). PDs are the day–to–day managers for the regional CIS offices. Most of them possess a masters degree in public health, social work, education or the arts. A portion of their time is spent coordinating work with the OCC, other ROs, or their local cancer centres (Johnson, Berkowitz et al., 1994b).

TSMs are in charge of managing the telephone service and the referral resources (some offices also have separate resource specialists who perform this more specialized KM role). They supervise ISs who directly serve callers. All of them possess a nursing degree or a bachelor's degree (Morra, Van Nevel et al., 1993). They are responsible for the day–to–day management of the telephone service, including quality assurance. They utilize more formal channels of communication such as memos, letters and e–mail (Johnson, Berkowitz et al., 1994b). TSMs because of their control functions in the implementation of formal procedures rely primarily on written channels, but for breaking advances in cancer control research they also utilize e–mail and interpersonal contacts. TSMs enforce very specific rules and procedures. Written channels allow them to overcome ambiguity and provide them with the authoritative information from the OCC that they pass on to the public.

The ISs within the CIS, who in many ways serve as knowledge brokers, have a unique cluster of skills: though the CIS is not a help or counselling 'hotline', callers are often very anxious; ISs must be able to communicate highly technical information clearly to callers who come from all demographic groups and who differ considerably in their levels of knowledge; and they must have access to the most current cancer information (Davis and Fleisher, 1998; Morra, 1998). Performance standards for telephone calls are set nationally. The *Policy and Procedures Manual*, typifying the high levels of formalization within the CIS, clearly specified the responsibilities and limitations of this role (NCI, 1996). Most importantly, ISs were charged by policy #4002 with 'identifying the information needs of the caller' and then 'answering all cancer–related questions' … 'by providing accurate and current information in accordance with CIS policies and procedures'. They were expressly forbidden from using the word 'counsellor' to describe their function and were required to refrain from any form of therapeutic counselling. Further, they also had to provide a medical disclaimer that they were not doctors and could not provide medical advice, recommendations or endorsements, supporting the current doctor–patient relationship a caller might have. They were to provide complete citation for any information resources provided recognizing that most information available to the CIS is supplied by other divisions of the NCI. They needed to recognize the limits of their personal knowledge and skill, obtaining 'assistance as needed to ensure accuracy and appropriateness of all responses'. They also were cautioned to recognize that 'not every question has a clear–cut answer' and that it is possible to tell callers the CIS could not answer some queries. Specific protocols were also established for consulting databases and other NCI personnel if information was not available at the level of a RO with a rank order of authoritativeness of sources starting with PDQ. They were charged to establish and to maintain a dialogue with callers providing 'information in a clear, concise, appropriately paced, non–rushed manner, giving the caller ample opportunity to speak and ask questions'. In short, ISs were clearly constrained to be information providers within strict protocols, not to interfere with existing medical relationships, to refrain from counselling, and to provide callers with quality assurances of the information they provided (for example 'this is consensus scientific information').

OMs were responsible for disseminating health messages through networking with other organizations such as the local ACS, state health departments and so on. All possessed a bachelors degree and some had a masters degree in public health education, social work or communication (Morra, Van Nevel et al., 1993). Their primary activities were directed at developing relationships with community organizations, sharing their expertise in the development of communication programmes. OMs in these ROs form partnerships with local organizations and the media to disseminate cancer information to the public, although their role had fluctuated during the course of the CIS (Morra, Van Nevel and Stengle, 1993). In doing this they served a strategic multiplier function within the CIS. In many ways OMs act as change agents in classic diffusion of innovation frameworks who identified intermediaries who served as opinion leaders for their groups (Rogers, 1983).

3.5 INTERNAL COMMUNICATION MECHANISMS

Effective network organizations also require the kind of rich, multidimensional, robust relationships that can be developed only through face–to–face interaction. (Nohria and Eccles, 1992, p. 290)

Effective integration has become a considerable source of concern in response to increased organizational diversity that is a product of greater technological and environmental challenges facing contemporary organizations (Katz and Kahn, 1978; Galbraith, 1995). It is also essential for the development of consensus–based knowledge in organizations. Among other effects, increased differentiation into more and more specialized subunits decreases system effectiveness, impedes coordination, hinders the development of strong values and appropriate climates, and slows the diffusion of innovations within the firm, unless there is also a concomitant increase in integration (Rogers and Agarwala–Rogers, 1976). As a result of the organization's increasing complexity, integration can no longer be handled by a single individual or by top management alone (Lawrence and Lorsch, 1967b; Galbraith, 1995) and knowledge becomes more tacit and diffused.

The principal mechanisms employed by traditional organizations to achieve integration have included line management structure, cross–organizational teams and committees, individual coordinators, coordinating departments and plans and procedures, all of which communicatively link organizational groupings together for the purposes of achieving coordination toward common organizational goals (Lawrence and Lorsch, 1967a, b, c; Moynihan, 1982; Galbraith, 1995). All of these integrating mechanisms are used by the CIS in one form or another (Morra, Van Nevel et al., 1993).

The concepts of match, fit, congruence and contingency have been used rather loosely in the literature to capture an essential idea related to structures; there is some optimal arrangement of structural elements that promotes the accomplishment of particular functions. For example Tushman (1979) found in an R&D laboratory that effectiveness is a function of matching communication patterns to the nature of a project's work, particularly at the subunit level. Specifically, high–performing research projects need more intra–project communication than high–performing technical service projects (Tushman, 1978). Given the complex information environment of the CIS and the increasing external challenges it faced during this period, it might be expected that it would have a rich array of integrating mechanisms, especially ones relating to KM.

Perhaps the most well–known research study done relating to the contingency perspective is the classic research of Lawrence and Lorsch (1967c) relating to differentiation and integration. In this study, companies that varied in their level of performance in three different industries – plastics, food processing and container – were examined to determine which factor led to high performance. In general Lawrence and Lorsch (1967a, b, c) found that high performers matched their levels of differentiation and integration to the demands of their environment. Differentiation is often a response to environmental pressures, with some groups (for example public relations) reflecting new environmental relationships of the organization (Katz and Kahn, 1978). In this connection, at the start of the contract period that was the focus of this study, the CIS formally introduced the role of OM to specifically relate to external publics at the various ROs. In addition new elements were added to OCC to deal with information technology and to relate to various interest groups.

As the organization becomes more and more divided into functional subgroups, a corresponding pressure arises to integrate these groups to common organizational goals. Depending on the imperative an organization feels to control the activities of its members, integration may put a limit on the extent to which an organization can grow, since it represents increased administrative costs, information processing demands and complexities related to coordination. It also contributes greatly to how widely knowledge can be shared. Thus integration is an area where improved communication can make a substantial difference to an organization:

> The capacity of an organization to maintain a complex, highly interdependent pattern of activity is limited in part by its capacity to handle the communication required for coordination. The greater the *efficiency of communication* within

the organization, the greater the tolerance for interdependence. (March and Simon, 1958, p. 162)

Differentiation of organizations in Lawrence and Lorsch's (1967c) view is associated with four major dimensions that distinguish subgroups in organizations: formality of structure, which as we have seen is very important to the CIS; goal orientation, with a high normative commitment to serving callers at the CIS RO; interpersonal relations, with high levels of trust; and time pressures characterized by increasingly short turnarounds. These are all factors that also play a role in effective KM.

Integration is accomplished by various linking mechanisms. Lawrence and Lorsch (1967c) identified the following integrating mechanisms: the use of teams, direct managerial contact, the managerial hierarchy and the paper system of the organization. What they found is that organizations that were the most successful matched their levels of differentiation and integration to their environments. Organizations in the container industry, which had the most stable environment, had the lowest level of differentiation and only used three integrating mechanisms: direct managerial contact, managerial hierarchy and the paper system. On the other hand, organizations in the plastics industry that had the most competitive environment, had in addition to these three integrating mechanisms, integrative departments and permanent cross–functional teams at different levels of management. Most interestingly, they found that organizations that had too many integrating mechanisms in the container industry were lower performers, because of increased conflict, delays and waste of resources.

For the unique organizational form represented by the CIS, with the additional strains represented by geographic dispersion and multiple institutional affiliations, the operation of various integrating mechanism becomes critical. In this chapter I will review the rich variety of mechanisms used by the CIS to accomplish integration. I will especially focus on the role of conferences, perhaps the most complex face–to–face integrating mechanism in an organization's arsenal, to illustrate the various purposes integrating mechanisms serve in organizing for KM.

Rich Variety of Integrating Mechanisms

Early in the project, we began to realize the richness of the CIS's communication structure, especially in terms of the variety of methods that were used to communicate with its geographically diverse members. Besides using various integrating mechanisms already in place (for example CIS network meetings, CIS task forces) the CISRC programme project, as we will see in Chapter 4, added another rich, coexisting set of communication mechanisms designed to implement trials of various innovative intervention strategies. In this section I will briefly describe some of the more important integrating mechanisms in the CIS that we did not explicitly study over the whole course of this project because of the limits of time and resources; and their direct relevance to the implementation of intervention strategies.

Circular calls

Circular calls were one of the primary means the CIS used to regularly communicate operational information to its members. These telephone conferences could involve only a few members (for example talking about specific ad hoc topics for a few minutes) or over 30 participants who discussed a variety of topics for a couple of hours. Monthly calls were typically scheduled for the various functional roles (for example PD) and for the CISRC during this period. In addition, circular calls were used by Project Officers to communicate with ROs.

Weekly packages

The 'Weekly Package' was distributed to all the ROs on a weekly basis. It contained a variety of documents (for example memorandum, news clips, news releases, standard mailings) that were often heavily laden with information. Coincident with each quarterly data collection, we performed a content analysis of that week's package during the first two years of the project. Most of the communication in the Weekly Package was concerned with providing members of the CIS with background information about cancer primarily by means of current news clips (see Johnson, Berkowitz et al., 1994b; Johnson, Chang et al., 1994; Johnson, Chang, LaFrance et al., 1995; Johnson, Chang, Meyer et al., 1995; Johnson, Chang et al., 1996). With a few notable exceptions (for example the distribution of the *CISRC News* in the 9 June 1994 package), most of the information in the Weekly Package was background information or operational and it was being de–emphasized by the OCC as a means of communicating as the Internet developed. Accordingly we stopped coding this data midway through the project. This points to the rapidly evolving internal communication mechanisms in KM organizations during this period.

Ad hoc meetings

Ad hoc meetings, bringing together many CIS members in one location, occurred regularly during this period and focused on several topics (for example outreach, quality control). These meetings were usually associated with training sessions, especially the ones related to intervention strategies.

The CIS follows a train–the–trainers model, which was adopted by the CISRC for its intervention strategies training sessions. This model further served to increase 'ownership' of members of the CIS of innovations and to increase their familiarity with formal procedures.

Task forces as communities of practice

> Within a CoP, people collaborate directly; teach each other; and share experiences and knowledge in ways that foster innovation. (Smith and McKeen, 2003, p. 395)

With a limited staff at the OCC due to attrition, attributable to the hiring freeze at the NCI that lasted most of this period, task forces within the CIS were delegated increasingly important roles in the implementation of policy. These task forces also represented communities of practice (CoPs) within the CIS, formed around areas of common interest and exchanging information that resulted in improvements in the whole (Huysman and van Baalen, 2002; Kuhn, 2002). CoPs are formed by groups of people who share tacit knowledge and/or learn through experimentation focusing on central organizational processes or problems (Tidd, 2000; Lesser and Prusak, 2004). They represent the people side of KM and how it is often negotiated communicatively (Iverson and McPhee, 2002). These communities are particularly important for geographically dispersed, virtual organizations, like the CIS (Scarbrough and Swan, 2002).

In effect, OCC staff had an agenda–setting function (Rogers, 2003) for major strategic initiatives, leaving the details of implementation to task forces. This set of complementary functions obviated some of the problematic relationships that develop between CoPs and management in other contexts (Smith and McKeen, 2003). These task forces supplemented circular calls with face–to–face meetings periodically and involved the numbers of people characteristic of mini–conferences. It is critical in these contexts that CoPs meet periodically to synchronously share tacit information (Sarmento et al., 2003). Chapter 6, which focuses in part on the implementation of computerization within the CIS, provides a detailed case study of part of the activities of one task force, the Computerization Advisory Group (CAG).

Task force membership was diverse, following established KM practice, including representatives from various functional roles in ROs, NCI–OCC liaisons, and outside expert advisory members and/or other interested parties (for example outreach partners). The Policy and Procedures Task Force and the Training Task Force both played a critical role in formalization processes within the CIS. The Outreach and Promotion Task Force had an especially central role because of the introduction of the OM role in the new contract. The Evaluation Task Force was especially active in this period, implementing a new Call Record Form and Outreach Contact Form procedures which improved the CIS database on these activities.

The Information Resources Task Force (IRTF) provided critical support for providing quality information for callers. It established KM strategies for the essential knowledge distribution function of the CIS identifying both core and optional resources that could be used in ROs. Central to this task force's functions was the IRTF's prior approval of any non–NCI resources provided to clients. The IRTF also developed protocols for rank ordering the quality of information to be provided.

'The strength of user innovation communities lies in the free revealing of detailed information about the innovation among members of the community' (Huysman and van Baalen, 2002, p. 4). This was especially true for the computerization innovations described in detail in Chapter 6. The CAG was an exemplary task force in this regard. In general, there was a tension in the CIS between ROs positioning themselves for unique strategic advantages in the periodic contract renewals and the need to cooperate on larger goals. In this instance, the need for a critical mass of users and the outside institutional pressures, resulted in a most effective innovation process.

3.6 CIS NATIONAL CONFERENCES

Although stormy at times and difficult for NCI to control, the semiannual get–togethers (c.f., conferences) solidified the feeling of network, as individuals from around the country worked in teams with the NCI staff to solve common problems in carrying out difficult tasks embodied in the contract. (Morra, Van Nevel et al., 1993, p. 12)

The conference can be seen as a key strategic tool to be used in linking a diverse array of participants, through communicative processes, to achieve the level of integration required by new organizational forms, such as the contractual network represented by the CIS. Since knowledge sharing requires trust, face–to–face meetings are essential to relationship building (Davenport and Prusak, 1998). Conferences were the primary venue for face–to–face interaction related to innovation within the CIS. The conference represents perhaps the most complex integrating mechanism available to management for moving tacit knowledge to explicit knowledge. For example 'search conferences' have been viewed as an instrument for organization learning by creating consensus, commitment to goals and continued interaction (via newly forged partnerships) (Axelrod, 1992; Bailey and Dupré, 1992; Lawson and Ventriss, 1992). For use in the present discussion, a conference is defined as a formal meeting of individuals from various organizational groupings, temporarily called together away from the organizational setting, for the purposes of increasing understanding, agreement and interaction related to common organizational goals. Conferences can be seen as being analogous to the traditional integrating mechanisms of temporary committees and work teams (Lawrence and Lorsch, 1967a, b, c), although at a much higher level of complexity and expense.

Beginning in the 1970s, the CIS has held conferences for members of the network. These conferences not only discussed day–to–day business matters but they also communicated about major issues faced by the CIS network (Morra, Van Nevel et al., 1993). These annual meetings allowed for the discussion of problems and provided a structure for forging solutions (Morra, Van Nevel et al., 1993). In the course of this project we analysed two national conferences: the four–day Atlanta conference in the first year, which was the initial conference under the new contract, and the five–day Denver conference in the third year, where pressing issues related to the future of the CIS were discussed. In this section we will discuss conference evaluation in terms of a model of factors predicting conference success, which included the necessary prior conditions for conference success, and conference process variables which determine conference outcomes, which then determine long–term consequences. This model was successfully tested empirically with the Atlanta conference data (Johnson, Meyer et al., 1995; 1996). Feedback based on the research results from the Atlanta conference was also used in the planning of the Denver conference demonstrating the learning capacity of the CIS.

Factors Predicting Conference Success

Necessary prior conditions

Four conditions that have a direct impact on conference success must be considered in conference planning: homophily, interest, participative climate and clear conference goals. Homophily, or the similarity between people (see more complete discussion of this concept in Chapter 5), is necessary for a successful conference for a variety of reasons. Firstly individuals tend to interact with similar individuals in situations of choice (Tsui and O'Reilly, 1989; Zenger and Lawrence, 1989). Secondly when source and receiver share common meanings, beliefs, attitudes, values and a mutual language, communication is more likely to be effective (Farace et al., 1978). However homophily will only be a positive attribute up to a certain point, because too great a level of homophily inhibits the exchange of new ideas and reduces the requisite variety needed for innovations to occur. In fact the positive benefits of increased differentiation and heterophily are often overlooked (see Chapter 5). The crucial area where homophily is needed in communication is in shared codes that promote understanding and knowledge sharing, especially for tacit knowledge, and in shared perspectives on appropriate organizational goals and means of attaining them (Tsui and O'Reilly, 1989; Zenger and Lawrence, 1989).

Interest, the second condition likely to affect conference success, can encompass such broad concepts as curiosity, fascination and concern. A conferee with little or no interest would bring few insights based on their tacit knowledge, a lack of enthusiasm and little participation to the conference. It would even be possible for such a conferee to interfere with the efforts of interested conferees, through the expression of negative attitudes and actions. On the other hand, a highly interested conferee would most likely be an avid and enthusiastic participant working toward attaining conference goals.

The third factor necessary for conference success is a participative climate. Climate generally can be used to express the overall gestalt of an organization, characterizing the internal environment of the organization as experienced by an insider (Tagiuri, 1968). For the purposes at hand, a participative climate will be defined as an individual's perception of how receptive the organization is to employee involvement in formal and informal interactions within his or her normal work environment. An individual's perception of climate will affect his or her willingness to participate. One goal of the conference is to bring together as much diversity of opinion and perspective as possible (Bailey and Dupré, 1992). Because of this, it is important to get everyone to participate. Participant involvement can lead to effective integration within the organization.

Perceived low receptivity will ultimately interfere with the success of the conference by inhibiting attendance, and by carrying over into the climate of the conference. Perceived high receptivity to employee participation should increase willingness and motivation to become involved and interact during the conference (Gibb, 1974), resulting in greater tolerance for conflict, more individual responsibility, and greater tolerance for risk taking (Ireland et al., 1978).

The fourth and final variable critical to conference success is clear conference goals. These goals must be identified by the organization as the first step in developing the conference. Clear and attainable conference goals, which relate meaningfully to overarching organizational goals (or a few well-developed cultural themes) pave the way for a successful conference that meets the organization's expectations. Clear goals are also easily relayed to those organizational members who attend the conference, giving them an advantage in preparation and guiding their interaction and activities throughout the conference.

These four variables – homophily, interest, participative climate and clear conference goals – establish the foundations for a successful conference. The planning process and activities before the conference determine their level and set a framework in which it is possible to have successful outcomes for the conference.

Conference process variables

Once the conference is under way, key process variables such as effective communication and involvement will also determine its ultimate success. In general, effective communication is considered to be the degree to which a receiver's response is consonant with the overall objectives of the sender (Farace et al., 1978). For a conference, effective communication becomes associated with the goals established by the conference planners. For example some conference planners may choose to follow the practice of most successful companies and focus on a few well–developed themes relating to their strong organizational cultures (Peters and Waterman, 1982). With regard to the specific messages presented at the conference, care must also be taken to reduce vocabulary differences and the semantic information distance, which refers to differences in education, vocabulary, training and so on, between conferees, which is crucial to reducing communication problems in interpersonal relations generally (Jablin, 1979), and this is particularly important to KM. It is also useful to follow other principles for effective communication during actual conference sessions, such as promoting feedback and using credible speakers.

There must also be ample opportunity for informal interaction to occur, both during the formal sessions and during designated 'freetime.' It is during this time that conferees get to discuss ideas, attitudes and issues, and also become better acquainted with each other. An atmosphere favouring intense informal communication and a free flow of information characteristic of successful innovative companies (Goldhar et al., 1976; Peters and Waterman, 1982; Galbraith, 1995) and innovation implementation generally (Fidler and Johnson, 1984; Johnson, 1993; Johnson et al., 1995b), must be established. To the greatest extent possible, formal sessions should also have the low structure necessary for an achievement–oriented organizational climate (Ireland et al., 1978). This low structure should promote accessibility, thus reducing distortion, involving people more fully in decision–making, and increasing the timeliness of information transfer (Farace et al., 1978). This sort of formal involvement produces a number of beneficial effects, such as an increased commitment to decisions or to goals expressed in the conference (Fidler and Johnson, 1984).

Crucial outcomes

Conference success serves as a moderator to the effectiveness of a conference as an integrating mechanism. In this section, three direct outcomes of conference success crucial to its effectiveness as an integrating mechanism will be discussed: understanding, agreement and interaction. Understanding reflects an individual's comprehension of the central issues focused on at the conference and is a crucial step in making knowledge explicit. Increased understanding is one crucial outcome of a conference that affects the maintenance of organizational cultures, the effective flow of information, and successful control and coordination of day–to–day organizational activities. Indeed more generally it has been argued that meetings are sites where organizational meanings are created (Eisenberg et al., 1998). The very act of calling a conference on a particular theme heightens its salience and re–emphasizes the understanding of organizational members as to its importance.

Understanding in turn lays the groundwork for agreement between conferees. Through the exchange of views inherent in conference activities, conferees can develop a more empathic understanding of others. They can also see where conferees can benefit from mutual, rather than purely selfish, courses of action. Of course some conferences may want to heighten this particular outcome by focusing on developing mutual agreements between all concerned conferees that are officially adopted at the conclusion of the conference. Any resulting peer group consensus will be a major factor in determining willingness to change and later acceptance of change (Deal and Kennedy, 1982). Thus a conference can produce a feeling among conferees of heightened involvement in decision–making, which is usually directly related to decreased resistance to organizational change efforts (Fidler and Johnson, 1984; Johnson, 1993).

To maintain understanding and agreement once the conference is over, a continual pattern of interaction between the conferees must be an additional outcome of the conference. The conference itself legitimates interaction between the conferees, often a critical step in knowledge transfer (Davenport and Prusak, 1998), demonstrating that the organization sees relationships between them as important. The conference will also produce a feeling in conferees that collective action is crucial to organizational success. Thus individuals will see there is a possibility of organizational rewards attached to continued interaction. Finally, the conferees should feel that the recognition often provided by the conference, and their involvement in important organizational activities, enhances their feelings of perceived influence within the organization. All of these factors have been identified as crucial to the success of more traditional integrating mechanisms (Lawrence and Lorsch, 1967a).

Organizational consequences

The long–term consequences of effective integration include systemic effects, climate impacts and enhanced information flow. At the systemic level, one measure of integrating mechanism effectiveness is the degree to which the mechanism provides for greater cooperation, coordination and control associated with organizational goals. If there is to be increased coordination within the organization, there must first be increased understanding of the goal itself, increased agreement as to its feasibility and worthiness as a goal, and increased interaction among organizational members toward that goal. All of these factors are associated with successful conferences.

With regard to the effects upon the human side of the organization, one could view a conference as a maintenance structure similar to those described by Katz and Kahn (1978), useful in creating stability and predictability in the organization. It provides a greater feeling of involvement for employees and a potential for recognition of their achievements. The increased conferee involvement characteristic of successful conferences also should result in more favourable attitudes toward the organization and individual perceptions of an improved organizational climate.

A further benefit of a successful conference is its implications for diffusion of information, particularly its implications for loose coupling (Weick, 1976) and the notion of the strength of weak ties (Granovetter, 1973). Weak ties provide for a greater exchange of knowledge and ideas because of the novel nature of these contacts. Conferees can form contacts in other departments which will allow them to obtain information they need in their normal organizational positions. Organizational members will also have clearer ideas of the perspectives of other units and their roles in the larger organization and, thus, will be able to co–act with them more successfully, resulting in enhanced information flow within the organization.

Results for the Atlanta conference

The Atlanta national conference was the first since the advent of the new five–year contracts. We asked participants a number of questions relating to both their communication at the conference and their perceptions of the conference, as well as follow–up questions on organizational consequences two months later. (For more detail see Johnson, Meyer et al., 1995, and Johnson, Meyer et al., 1996). Data indicated conference participants looked forward to attending the conference, agreed that it was going to be productive, felt it addressed important agenda items and felt that the goals of the conference were clear (Johnson et al., 1994b). Respondents agreed that they were involved in formal sessions and that the presenters at the conference were effective. Conference participants left the meeting with a better understanding of the goals of the CIS, greater agreement with them, and with a commitment to continue interacting with others in the network about what was discussed at the conference. Conference attenders reported enhanced information flow related to many of the issues discussed at the Atlanta conference. Very positive climate and systemic effects within the CIS appeared to develop as a result of the conference.

However results related to the informal participation variables were not as positive. This may have been partially attributable to the scheduling of the conference for Atlanta, which essentially used up every available minute. In addition to the formal sessions which ran from 8 a.m. to 5 p.m. most participants also had formally scheduled breakfast, lunch, and dinner meetings. In the end, almost all of participant's time was formally scheduled. Because of their expense there is constant temptation to over schedule conferences, which can directly effect 'hidden', intangible outcomes, such as informal participation.

Planning and evaluation and the Denver conference

The planning for the Atlanta conference was unique in recent CIS history. It was decided several months before the conference to delegate to the three major groups of conference attendees, PDs, OMs, and TSMs, the planning and development of the relevant conference sessions. This decision in part emerged from a concern over the top–down organization of recent ad hoc group meetings. As might be expected then, for most participants, their most frequent informal communication contacts were with individuals who had similar functional roles (Johnson et al., 1994b). The responses to most of the scales indicated that this decision resulted in the sort of very positive outcomes and long–term organizational consequences which the organizational literature on participation discussed earlier would have predicted. In essence, it appears that individuals get out of conferences what they put into them; old–timers were very active in the planning of the conference and had very positive reactions to it. Thus one way of enhancing conferences for all participants would be involving more people in their planning and execution.

Before the Denver conference took place in 1995, conference planners received written and verbal feedback about the Atlanta conference. Written feedback was obtained from surveys the participants filled out at the Atlanta conference and also from a report prepared by TEAM that included an evaluation of that conference (Johnson et al., 1994a). Verbal feedback was given to the conference planners by some of the participants who attended the Atlanta conference. The conference planners also received open–ended comments from an evaluation report separately sponsored by OCC.

Because of the feedback received, three major changes took place in the design and implementation of the Denver conference. The first change involved the planning process. The planning process began earlier, starting in 1994 when three committees involving different functional roles were formed to create an agenda for the conference. The committees included people from 13 of the 19 regions within the CIS. Each committee consisted of six people and one chairperson and one overall conference chairperson coordinating the process. Furthermore committee members sought input from other network members, within their specific region, in terms of how the conference agenda should look. The committee chairpersons communicated by monthly telephone conference calls and had a face–to–face meeting in Washington prior to the conference.

The second change was how sessions were scheduled. Schedules were arranged to permit more interactive sessions and more informal communication. The previous conference essentially had formal meetings from seven in the morning to well into the evening.

The third change increased the number of sessions attended by persons from different roles within the CIS. In the previous conference most sessions were segregated by functional roles.

One way of involving people in planning is a commitment to evaluation efforts such as this one. The CIS has a long history of evaluation of conferences. One of the reasons for the generally positive reactions to conferences noted earlier is the commitment of the CIS to incorporating feedback in future conference planning. The Denver conference involved CIS participants to a higher degree than other recent ones because of the feedback resulting from the conference immediately preceding it. In turn, the results of this evaluation led to starting the planning process earlier, involving people representing different groups more in break–out discussions associated with formal sessions, and cutting back on the scheduling of formal sessions in the next conference. This cycle of continuous feedback and implementation results in an overall perception of participation that increases receptivity to conferences and makes their success more likely as well as increasing organizational learning.

Comparison of the Atlanta and Denver conferences

Tests were conducted to determine if there were significant differences between the Atlanta conference and the Denver conference for each of the factors identified in the conference model. In general, the Denver conference was evaluated slightly more favourably than the Atlanta conference. This is especially interesting because the Denver conference focused on some very sensitive issues, including various scenarios for reorganizing the CIS (Johnson, Berkowitz et al., 1994b; Johnson, Chang, Meyer et al., 1995a: Pobocik et al., 1997).

For the necessary prior conditions, homophily was found to be higher in the Atlanta conference and clear goals was found to be higher in the Denver conference. By increasing the group break–out sessions so that they overlapped with different functional roles, participants interacted more across different roles in formal sessions in the Denver conference than they did in the Atlanta conference. This suggests that conference planners efforts to increase communication across functional roles was effective. Another effective change made by the conference planners was to start the planning process early and to include members from all levels of the organization. By doing this, members of the CIS were well informed on what to expect at the conference. Participants evaluated interest the same for both conferences. This may have occurred because of the traditional importance of the annual conference within the CIS. Members look forward to attending these conferences because it brings them together as a network and allows them to interact with different members of the organization about issues facing the CIS. CIS members evaluated participative climate higher in the Atlanta conference than they did in the Denver conference. This was an interesting finding because specific strategies were employed to encourage participant involvement at the Denver conference (that is having CIS members facilitate various discussion and brainstorming groups). Perhaps CIS members felt less able to participate in groups that included all functional roles compared to groups of their peers.

For the process variables, participants evaluated effective communication higher for the Denver conference than they did for the Atlanta conference. Because the planning of the Denver conference started earlier than the Atlanta conference and more members of the organization were included in the planning, it may be that the outcomes of the conference reflected more of the original intent of the planners. Participants also evaluated involvement higher in the Denver conference than they did in the Atlanta conference.

For the outcome variables, participants evaluated understanding the same for both conferences. This finding was surprising because the CIS members received a completed agenda a few months ahead of time for the Denver conference. They also received detailed planning documents on the topics to be discussed at the conference. It may have been the case that the participants who attended the Atlanta conference were clear about the general content of the meeting based on previous attendance at CIS annual meetings. Unlike the Denver meeting, the Atlanta meeting was more similar to previous meeting formats. Therefore preparation ahead of time may not have been necessary for the participants' understanding at the Atlanta conference.

Participants evaluated agreement higher in the Denver conference than they did in the Atlanta conference. Agreement may not have been a necessary outcome in the Atlanta conference, but was more important in the Denver conference. As mentioned before, the Denver conference included members from all levels of the CIS on discussions regarding the future of the CIS. Even though the issues covered in the Denver conference were difficult and complex, participants were given the opportunity to share ideas and concerns and to reach consensus. Participants evaluated continued interaction the same for both conferences. However this result could be due to the traditional nature of CIS annual meetings. The conference is planned so that the content of discussions directly relates to the work of the CIS and what they want to implement after the conference is over. Therefore continued interaction is essential for implementation after every conference.

For the organizational consequence variables, participants evaluated systemic effects the same for both conferences and they evaluated the flow of communication higher for the Denver than the Atlanta conference. In general, conferences are a way to enhance coordination and control within the organization by bringing together members of the organization to discuss organizational goals. Because of the nature of the Denver conference and the topics discussed, a continuous flow of communication was essential. How the CIS would operate in the next contract renewal and how to computerize the entire CIS programme affected the organization then and would play an important role in the future of the CIS. The primary goal of the CIS in the year 2000 was to continue to offer high–quality CIS services in the face of a changing health care system and decreasing resources, both human and financial. To do this the CIS network had begun to evaluate the impact of the programme and the degree to which the CIS was meeting its goal. Any reorganization of the CIS network would necessitate ongoing discussions and programme refinements.

Participants evaluated climate effects the same for both conferences. This was an interesting finding because even though numerous members of the CIS were included in the planning of the Denver conference, the issues of organizational change and reorganizing might have mediated the reactions of the participants to the overall organizational climate after the Denver conference. Because it was made clear to the members of the CIS that the future was uncertain, a great deal of tension could have built up during the conference. Thus the conference planning process may have mitigated countervailing forces which could have easily led to negative outcomes.

In general the informal communication across different functional roles within the CIS was not found to be significantly different between the Atlanta and the Denver conference (Pobocik et al., 1996). This finding was very surprising because one of the changes made to the Denver conference involved increasing discussions among CIS staff from different functional roles. Even though participants were encouraged to communicate more across different functional roles, they may have not felt comfortable doing so outside of formal sessions. Once the sessions were over, they resumed communicating informally with people who performed similar roles in the CIS.

Summary

Conferences are exceedingly expensive and only in special circumstances will their use as integrating mechanisms be justified. As Lawrence and Lorsch (1967a, b, c) have established, there are circumstances where too much integration has a negative impact for organizations. Not all conferences will be effective integrating mechanisms. While members of the CIS would prefer more face–to–face meetings of task forces and national conferences, which follows from their general preference for interpersonal communication (Johnson, Berkowitz et al., 1994b), often conference calls and other forms of electronic communication must be substituted as less time–consuming and costly (Wooldridge et al., 1993).

A conference can be a very positive experience for an organization. It provides rewards (for example travel) for organizational members while performing a crucial communicative function for the organization. Generally, organizations which could successfully utilize a conference will be faced with one or another of the following circumstances which confronted the CIS during this period: a high level of differentiation, with many functional subunits; a high need to maintain an organizational culture; a high need to reach consensus; thus making explicit that which was formerly tacit; and a highly dynamic environment (Lawrence and Lorsch, 1967a, b, c).

3.7 LESSONS LEARNED

As the CIS has grown to meet a variety of environmental demands it has added more ROs and functions. The CIS, as we have seen, represents a new organizational form operating in a very complex, highly changeable environment. Traditionally it has focused on an interpersonally driven, knowledge broker strategy for providing service to the public. The development of a rich variety of integrating mechanisms (for example task forces) to insure the high levels of coordination needed for its successful operation has always been characteristic of its operation.

At the outset of this contract cycle many enhanced means of communicating, particularly a variety of circular telephone calls, were implemented. The changes in communication over the life of this research provided unique opportunities for natural experiments, such as the conference evaluation reported in this chapter. Close observation of this unique new organizational form also led us to the sad conclusion that it may be impossible to inventory the rich variety of communication mechanisms characteristic of the modern KM organization; rather the researcher must strategically choose those mechanisms to study that most closely relate to the phenomenon of interest.

A constant struggle within the CIS has been related to the need to balance formalization and centralization from the OCC, with the flexibility needed to operate new organizational forms. However with the limited staff at the OCC during this period, much of this work had to be delegated, primarily to PDs and task forces representing CoPs. It should come as no surprise, given its basic organizational strategy for providing service to the public, that the two major tactics it adopted for facilitating organizational change rested on the sharing of often tacit knowledge through the rich, interpersonal integrating mechanisms of CoPs and periodic national conferences.

CoPs

Organizations experimenting with CoPs understand the learning needed in the flexible structures of new organization forms (Smith and McKeen, 2003). The CIS had a rich tradition of work with CoPs primarily in the form of task forces. These task forces then represented the major sites of organizational learning and the generative mechanisms for change with the CIS. They prepared the CIS for what would become its most complex CoP to date, the CISRC consortium that was designed to address a major strategic objective of the CIS to demonstrate that it could perform higher–end knowledge generation functions.

Conferences

The CIS as a new organizational form was very complex, but as we will see in the next chapter, during this time period the CIS was also developing a CoP with a consortium of researchers and reaching out to its various publics that underlined the importance of rich integrating mechanisms. I have focused especially on one vital mechanism, the national conference, in this chapter, detailing the variety of issues that must be considered in planning for a conference and how this planning process ultimately determines conference success. This process is one key indicator of the CIS's constructive approach to organizational learning: it exhibited an admirable ability to voice concerns, engage in self–criticism, provide appropriate feedback, and then develop innovative approaches to problems identified.

In sum, the sources of CIS competitive advantage traditionally had rested on translating authoritative, government–based scientific information to the public. The CIS had been very successful in fulfilling this mission; however it was not enough to just provide this basic knowledge delivery service within the context of the NCI. Developing a state–of–the–science communication laboratory would give the CIS a unique role that could not be easily replicated for cost and proprietary reasons by private contractors, and cost and expertise reasons by non–profit competitors. Thus 'the capacity to develop organizational capability may be more important in creating sustainable competitive advantage than the specific knowledge gained' (Schendel, 1996, p. 3). The CIS, with the addition of the CoP of the CISRC, would have a complex mix of KM assets that would more likely lead to its sustainability and maintenance (Schendel, 1996).

4. Organizing for knowledge generation: the Cancer Information Service Research Consortium

4.1 INTRODUCTION

We view innovation as an organizational process that may come about as a strategic response to changing circumstances in the external environment (i.e., opportunities and threats). (Lozada and Calantone, 1996, p. 311)

One of the central issues in the organizational innovation literature is the different types of structures necessary for different outcomes. For example at different phases of the innovation process different structures may be emphasized. Zaltman et al. (1973) have argued that organizations need one type of structure to generate ideas (low formalization, decentralization and high complexity), which reflects the market–driven forces necessary for informally generated innovations. Papa (1989) has found that network size and diversity were related to how quickly employees became productive after the implementation of a new computer system. This is also reflected in the work of Aiken and Hage (1971) which suggests that organic organizations, with decentralized decision–making, a number of occupations, slack resources and a history of innovation are more likely to be innovative.

However implementation, such as the elements of the CIS covered in Chapter 3, requires high formalization, centralization and low complexity, the sorts of structure characteristic of classic bureaucracies. These very conditions also reflect the general historical trend of research studies related to innovation. In the 1960s and 1970s researchers focused on formal approaches and the implementation of innovation sanctioned by top management (Rogers, 1983). More recently research has focused on more informal approaches and the initiation of innovations. These informal processes, in effect, add to the capacity of the organization to innovate by increasing the volumes of information that can be handled (Fidler and Johnson, 1984).

Accomplishing both innovation and productivity poses a difficult problem for an organization since both appear to require different structures (Kanter, 1983). Some organizations choose to emphasize either innovation or productivity, recognizing the inherent difficulties in trying to accomplish both. For example organizational efficiency can be improved not by producing more information, but by reducing the amount of information any one subsystem must handle (Johnson, 1993). However this strategy will be deleterious to the development of innovations within the organization, with Hage and Aiken (1970) arguing that the greater emphasis on efficiency, the slower the rate of change.

The CIS developed an alternative strategy, one that has become increasingly popular, of developing coalitions with key external partners both to develop higher–end KM functions and to broaden its market, which not so coincidentally had considerable potential political pay–offs. By developing partnerships with its outreach partners through coalition building it was both addressing a major criticism, related to its use by underserved populations, as well as expanding the number of stakeholders who would speak on its behalf. I will focus on these issues first in the chapter. I will then address how these issues were 'sold' to internal staff members to create a more positive internal climate for innovations. Finally, I will focus on the development of what is essentially a 'franchise' operation for research, the CISRC, that 'bought' the needed research talent essential to satisfying key groups within the NCI that the CIS considered was essential to the institute's research mission. External relations were inherently a strategic and a political process aimed at satisfying key stakeholders. I will conclude this chapter with discussions of its lessons for the development of consortia and for the human side of new organizational forms.

4.2 COALITION BUILDING

Who proposes innovative ideas for adoption? Most new ideas probably originate with organizational members who span the boundary between organizations and technological environments. (Daft, 1978, p. 195)

While the primary focus of this book is on innovation within the CIS, naturally the information environment represented in the world outside the CIS was also important, especially since it effected internal innovation processes and knowledge transfer. Firstly the world outside the organization is often the primary source of highly technical, specialized information, such as that related to computerization. For example a general finding in the innovation literature is that a high level of external communication is important for work team effectiveness in R&D laboratories (Katz and Allen, 1982). Secondly environments create imperatives for organizations to innovate in certain ways as I discussed in detail in Chapter 2. Thirdly knowledge sharing is increasingly viewed as vital for public sector organizations that have a focus on service delivery (Wright and Taylor, 2003).

The CIS has always had critical relationships with key stakeholders in its environment. Most of these relationships have been more politically oriented than focused on knowledge gathering or sharing. There has been a tradition of one–way knowledge transfer, especially focused on getting NCI messages (for example screening, 5–a–day) out to the public. This new contract period, partly in response to concerns about the narrow demographic range of CIS clientele, also saw a specific attempt to reach out to regional community partners in the form of a newly configured outreach programme.

While it has been commonplace to categorize government agencies as operating in placid information environments (Emery and Trist, 1965), recent events suggest they often operate in turbulent fields. As I have detailed in Chapter 2, the CIS during this time period had significant threats in its environment. It also created a new role in the current contract of OM which was designed to routinize some boundary–spanning communication. In addition to the traditional representational and gatekeeping functions of boundary spanners, OMs in the CIS also focus on developing community coalitions as a way of building political support from various stakeholders for their ongoing efforts, and also as a way of increasing the reach and impact of the CIS. So increasingly the CIS realized the importance of its environment, that it directly impinged on its operations, and that changes in its formal organizational structure were needed to enhance its adaptation to a changing world.

OMs were often called on to perform opinion leadership roles. In many ways they acted as change agents in classic diffusion of innovation frameworks who identified intermediaries who served as opinion leaders for their groups (Katz, 1957; Katz and Lazersfeld, 1955; Rogers, 1983; Valente and Davis, 1999). Opinion leadership originally suggested ideas flow from the media to opinion leaders to those less active segments of the population (Katz, 1957). Opinion leaders not only serve a relay function, they also provide social support information to individuals (Katz, 1957), reinforce messages by their social influence over them (Katz and Lazarsfeld, 1955), and validate the authoritativeness of the information (Paisley, 1994). So not only do opinion leaders serve to disseminate ideas but they also, because of the interpersonal nature of their ties, provide additional pressure to conform as well (Katz, 1957; Rogers, 2003; Valente and Davis, 1999).

Increasingly more formal groups are also serving as opinion leaders and information seekers for individuals. It was exactly with these groups that OMs were charged with developing coalitions. For those individuals who cannot get past denial or the emotional problems associated with a diagnosis of cancer, support groups can often provide critical information on such deeply personal issues as who is the most caring physician in the community, who is the best physical therapist, who is the most supportive in providing reconstructive breast surgery, where is the best place to get a wig for the bald head I have because of chemotherapy, and so on (Johnson, 1997a).

Advocacy groups for cancer (Breast Cancer Action, CAN ACT, PAACT, and so on) serve as increasingly important lobbyists for the provision of information. These groups have been very successful in increasing research funds for breast cancer research. They actively seek more money for research that leads to information for databases, for enhanced access to and availability of information, and so on. In short, they lobby for an information infrastructure (Johnson, 1997a). Recognizing the importance of community groups in disseminating cancer–related information, the formal organizational structure of the CIS changed during this period to include an OM role designed to formally manage these relationships.

Boundary Spanning

Organizations, as open systems, need to sustain themselves by communicating with diverse and dynamic environments (Farace et al., 1977). The external communication transferred across organizational boundaries interacts with the internal flow, affecting structures, procedures and control within organizations (Brown, 1966). The interaction with the external environments, often cast as boundary–spanning activities, has been demonstrated to be an indispensable element for modern organizations ability to survive and to succeed (Aldrich and Herker, 1977; Church and Spiceland, 1987; Dollinger, 1984; Jemison, 1984; Grover et al., 1993; Kotter, 1979; Seabright et al., 1992).

Boundary spanners are individuals 'who operate at the periphery or boundary of an organization, performing organizational relevant tasks, relating the organization with elements outside it' (Leifer and Delbecq, 1978, pp. 40–41). They are responsible for making communication contacts with external information sources and supplying their colleagues with information to cope with the outside environment. In general, two levels of activities have been examined. Firstly boundary–spanning activities occurred across working units within an organization. Past research has studied boundary spanners across different product teams (Ancona and Caldwell, 1992), departments (Jemison, 1984) and project groups (Tushman and Scanlan, 1981a, b). Secondly boundary–spanning activities, in a more traditional sense, were between an organization and its environment. Adams (1976) has identified the following organizational roles as boundary spanners: marketing and sales personnel, purchasing agents, dispatchers and traffic men, personnel recruiters, admission and placement staffs, advertising and public relations workers, information and intelligence gatherers and purveyors, legislative representatives, negotiators and bargaining agents, and so on.

Since organizations must adapt to their environments, a number of formal structures and associated functional roles are created explicitly to deal with them (Galbraith, 1984). So for example boundary spanners (such as department heads, customer service representatives) maintain external communication because of their formally assigned roles (At–Twaijri and Montanari, 1987; Burk, 1994; Friedman and Podolny, 1992; Grover et al., 1993; Keller et al., 1976; Lysonski and Johnson, 1983; Schwab et al., 1985; Singh et al., 1994; Stevenson, 1990). They are responsible for making communication contacts with external information sources and supplying their colleagues with information concerning the outside environment, all while maintaining an organization's autonomy (Aldrich and Herker, 1977).

Thus depending on the unit of analysis, boundary spanners can be interpreted differently. For our research, we examined both internal and external boundary spanners. That is the communication occurring between units within the CIS, discussed in Chapter 5, were internal boundary–spanning activities, while the communication taking place between the CIS and its outside environment were external boundary–spanning activities, and are the primary focus of this chapter.

Past research has focused on boundary functions in terms of the information flowing in inter–organizational relationships. Boundary spanners filter and facilitate information flow at an organization's boundary, and they cope with environmental constraints to maintain an organization's autonomy (Aldrich and Herker, 1977). They 'represent an organization to its environments, and the environment to the organization' (Eisenberg et al., 1985, p. 240). Thus they play two distinct structural roles: 'a gatekeeper, who is a conduit for inflows to the group of which the boundary spanner is a member, and a representative, who is a transmitter of outflows from the group of which the boundary spanner is a member' (Friedman and Podolny, 1992, p. 32). In fact Allen (1977) made this distinction between the two roles when he applied the two–step information flow to study boundary–spanning activities. Also Tushman and his colleagues (Tushman and Scanlan, 1981a, b; Katz and Tushman, 1981) through their extensive research reinforce the distinction between gatekeeping and representational roles.

The integration and commitment of boundary–spanning personnel has always been problematic for organizations. Boundary spanners are individuals who while members of one social system, have links to another. Usually these linkages are discussed in terms of individuals who have communication ties to people outside their organization because of their formal organizational position. Central to the definition of boundary spanning is the idea that these individuals process information from diverse sources and they represent the organization externally (Womack, 1984). Professionals in different organizations share information with each other informally (for example TGIFs, association meetings) and formally (for example trade journals). The most productive scientists are often those who communicate most outside the boundary of the organization (Allen, 1966). These positions are critical to innovations, especially in health care organizations (Robertson and Wind, 1983), and the diffusion of ideas between and within organizations (Czepiel, 1975; Daft, 1978; Ghosal and Bartlett, 1987). These boundary spanners become the mechanism that operationalizes environmental cues to the internal organizational structure and accumulate power in organizations because of their ability to absorb uncertainty (Spekman, 1979).

In addition the nature of information processed by various functional specialties also differs, with production–based information more certain and quantifiable than the typical mix of marketing and sales information for example (McKinnon and Bruns, 1992). This specialization, which can be augmented and enhanced by information technology, makes it much harder for differing groups to communicate across their boundaries (Hoffman, 1994).

Various studies have examined the behavioural and psychological consequences of boundary spanning. Boundary spanners appear to be more influential (Allen, 1989; Jemison, 1984; Tushman and Scanlan, 1981b), and yet at the same time they experience more role stress than non–boundary spanners (Katz and Kahn, 1978; Miles, 1976; Singh et al., 1994). These consequences have been associated with job outcomes. Research has shown that boundary spanners associate positively with project performance (Katz and Tushman, 1981) and with promotion (Tushman and Katz, 1980). However research has also demonstrated the negative correlations between role stressors and turnover and low job satisfaction (Singh et al., 1994).

Formal Boundary Spanning Roles in the CIS

The outreach programme of the CIS serves as a catalyst and focal point for cancer education at the state and regional level. As the NCI's primary outreach network, the 19 ROs of the CIS serve as field offices in a nationwide effort to facilitate the adoption and use of OCC programmes and materials to priority audiences. At the outset of the new contract cycle each RO was asked to choose one of four priority audiences – African Americans, Hispanics, older Americans and persons with low literacy skills – for special attention.

Particularly interesting is the reintroduction of the OM role in the current contract cycle of the CIS. OMs were specially charged with enhancing local implementation of NCI national campaigns. OMs in the RO form partnerships with local organizations and the media to disseminate cancer information to the public, although their role has fluctuated during the course of the CIS (Morra, Van Nevel and Stengle, 1993). In this contract cycle OMs were primarily charged with coordinating intermediary development, materials distribution, and media relations in their regions.

Since the mid–1980s the NCI had primarily focused on developing relationships with intermediaries who are in direct contact with the public, patients and health professionals. The NCI, through the OMs, suggests project areas, primary target audiences, appropriate messages and communication channels, and distributes materials. The intermediary organizations in turn help the NCI by providing access to organizational members, enhancing the credibility of messages, providing additional resources and expertise and co–sponsoring programmes.

An interesting new twist for this role is the strategic use and extension of the classic representation role of boundary spanners to purposively increase the capacity of the CIS to reach various audiences with its message both directly and indirectly, thus taking a more proactive role in resource dependence issues (Mizruchi and Galaskiewicz, 1993). This role is intended to produce a 'multiplier effect' for NCI efforts by developing community coalitions designed to address various cancer–related issues. One way this approach is 'sold' to community coalitions is in terms of capacity building with the pooling of resources from various community organizations creating a whole that is more than the sum of its parts. In this approach the CIS provides technical assistance (for example training, public education materials) in the creation of campaigns, serves as a facilitator for coalitions, and provides access to resources (Ballard, 1996). It was felt that it was better to lodge the responsibility for this outreach function at the regional level, so that national initiatives could best be adopted to local needs.

The CIS outreach network is an example of a system that needs to balance conflicting goals. For example the CIS operates in many diverse environments (comprehensive cancer centres, consortium centres, university settings, hospitals and so on) with diverse staff members and it is responsible to more than one master (under contract to the NCI and formally a part of individual institutions). The CIS must adhere to the policies and procedures mandated by the NCI that may be at odds with the objectives of the individual institutions who could potentially form a community coalition. The CIS also has diverse components in its mandated statement of work. While many of its organizational elements must be centralized, they must be adaptable to local circumstances and conditions. The CIS is charged with carrying out NCI national initiatives that need to also address the concerns of local communities. As such, it operates as a boundary spanner for the NCI to a variety of interested publics. All of these pressures, which act to decrease the level of uniformity and integration within the CIS, point to the need for special efforts to integrate its communication system and the unique role that the OM must perform.

The radial network of the CIS system is composed of individuals who relate to the CIS and who are concerned with its operations, but who are not involved in its day–to–day operations. For example the NCI relates to national and local ACS offices, other science organizations and Congress. The radial network requires different analysis procedures than the CIS system data which focuses on all the linkages within the CIS network. Essentially the radial network data is a focal network composed of one individual's overall pattern of relationships with others. In Table 4.1 we summarize the major categories (for more detail see the technical reports) of radial communication contacts of CIS members during three annual data collection periods.

Table 4.1 Radial communication contacts for regional offices

Type	Time 1		Time 2		Time 3	
	Cont-acts	%	Cont-acts	%	Cont-acts	%
ACS	57	8.3	57	12.1	57	12.4
Cancer Center	94	13.7	66	14.0	67	14.5
Government	132	19.3	84	17.8	78	16.9
Other intermediaries	130	19.0	92	19.5	91	19.7
Local media	77	11.2	21	4.5	21	4.6
Medical community	88	12.8	41	8.7	29	6.3
Public at large	67	9.8	81	17.2	94	20.4
Other	40	5.8	29	6.2	24	5.2
Total	685	99.9	471	100.0	61	100.0

Note: Respondents were asked to estimate the number of times they communicated with members representing the various groups about intervention strategies by any means of communication.

The frequency of contacts with the ACS, 57 at each time point, were remarkably stable over time and the percentage of contacts with other Cancer Center personnel, government agencies (for example health departments) and intermediary organizations were stable in overall percentage terms. Local media and medical community contacts declined during this time period, while the proportion of contacts with the public at large grew substantially. Overall contacts declined substantially from the first to the second year, then stabilized, perhaps reflecting an initial wide–ranging array of contacts, which then focused on those that were most rewarding.

As would be expected the number of external contacts differed substantially by functional groups within the CIS. Except for TSMs, there was a general decline across all groups in external communication (Chang, 1996; Chang et al., 1997). OMs had by far the most external contacts, with PDs the next most numerous group. These patterns reflected what would be expected of members of the CIS given their formal role requirements. OCCs were in charge of coordinating and supervising the activities of the regional CIS network. PDs engaged in a mixture of internal and external communication coordinating work with OCCs, other regional offices, or their local cancer centres. TSMs mainly focused on the internal telephone and referral services. OMs were active in the external network because they were responsible for developing relationships with community organizations.

The Relationship between Internal and External Boundary–Spanning Communication

Three models were tested based on this data that might explain how boundary–spanning communication develops over time (for more detail see Johnson and Chang, 2000). Firstly in the functional specialization model individuals are posited to focus on either internal or external networks depending on their formal functional positions. In new organizational forms all individuals engage in some boundary spanning and traditional organizational boundaries become increasingly arbitrary (Starbuck, 1976).

Contrary to the functional specialization explanation, another portion of the boundary–spanning literature suggests that the two distinctive external and internal communication roles can be played by the same individual (Aldrich and Herker, 1977; Allen, 1989; Friedman and Podolny, 1992; Katz and Tushman, 1981; Tushman and Scanlan, 1981a, b). Thus a variety of research studies have focused on boundary spanners who have extensive external as well as internal communication activities (Nagpaul and Pruthi, 1979; Tushman and Scanlan, 1981b; Mintzberg, 1973; Manev and Stevenson, 1996).

While it would seem obvious that there are finite limits to the amount of communication one can engage in (Baker, 1992), several empirical studies suggest that individuals who are high communicators in one setting are also high in others; that heavy users of one information medium related to work are likely to be users of other media that also carry this same information (Caroll and Teo, 1996; Paisley, 1980; Weedman, 1992), which is also a finding of more general media use studies (Berelson and Steiner, 1964).

Thus based on the preceding discussion it seems reasonable to suggest that boundary spanners focus on both internal and external activities simultaneously. They acquire relevant information from their extensive external contacts and filter and feed the information inwardly within the organization. Consequently they are perceived as influential by their peers, who seek them out for information (Paisley, 1980; Reynolds and Johnson, 1982).

While the literature suggests various types of boundary--spanning communication activities, few studies have simultaneously examined internal (between organizational units) and external (with other organizations) communication patterns over time, especially in relation to innovation processes (Goes and Park, 1997). The second model was the communication stars explanation where individuals were predisposed to the same levels of communication in both internal and external networks. While the first model stresses the formal side of an organization, the second model underlines the informal side of an organization and individual predispositions.

A third model offers a cyclical explanation of individuals rotating their internal and external communication in a dynamic pattern because of inevitable systemic, behavioural and psychological consequences of boundary–spanning. Individuals may shift due to the systemic consequences resulting from the boundary–spanning activities and dynamic organizational requirements which, fortunately, we could examine given the longitudinal nature of our data. Strategically, boundary spanners might actively select one network (internal or external) to focus on instead of both networks, to avoid role conflict and to focus their work efforts. So as suggested by the R&D literature, the importation of external ideas might result in considerable internal communication relating to generating internal innovations, which in turn are then exported to other organizations through external communication.

Our results suggested a lagged effect for a communication stars explanation, with high levels of internal communication at the preceding time period producing high levels of lagged external communication. The finding of a significant path from internal to external communication but not vice versa, at consecutive time periods, fits perfectly with the CIS's plans for external communication. In addition to their traditional representational and gatekeeping functions, boundary spanners in the CIS also focus on developing community coalitions as a way of building political support from various stakeholders for their ongoing innovation efforts and also as a way of increasing the reach and impact of the CIS, thus taking a more proactive role in resource dependence issues (Mizruchi and Galaskiewicz, 1993).

Thus the CIS recognizes a central tenet of organizations in competitive environments – it must seek cooperative relationships with other organizations (Kumar et al., 1993). It is also interesting to note, as the research findings suggest, that these external relationships flow from the CIS, based on centralized internal planning, with little explicit feedback from community organizations.

One early concern related to the operation of the CISRC internal intervention strategies was that they might detract, given the press of work and the finite resources of the CIS, from other intervention strategy efforts. However there appeared to be more involvement by CIS members in external intervention strategy efforts in their communities than internal ones. This may be attributable to CIS members' greater control, influence, sympathy and understanding of these efforts (Chang et al., 1997). In the CIS there was a clear difference between internally and externally oriented innovation–related communication, with external communication much more frequent. This pattern of external communication is typical of organizations that want to maintain their relative autonomy within a community (Oliver, 1991).

4.3 INNOVATION CLIMATE

... effective absorption of new knowledge or innovations is a function of the strength of an organization's climate for implementation of that innovation and the fit of that innovation to targeted users' values. (Fiol, 1996, p. 1017)

Perceptions of innovativeness can impact upon perceptions of overall climate of an organization, members' satisfaction and the likelihood of members initiating innovations (Hurt and Teigen, 1977). Perceptions of innovativeness within an organization have also been directly linked to employee satisfaction and willingness to participate in innovation processes generally (Hurt and Teigen, 1977). In effect, the perceived climate for innovativeness can lead to intentions to act that may result in actual innovative behaviours. This climate for innovativeness may reflect the extent to which the underlying cultural value for innovativeness is realized in actual accomplishments in an organization (Fiol, 1996). An organization's perceived innovativeness provides a viewpoint from those most intimately aware and knowledgeable of the organization's overall approach to innovation, its members. For innovation to flourish the organization's climate must be supportive of it (Kanter, 1983) and conducive to a willingness to change (Hurt et al., 1977). Climate and culture are often seen as intertwined macro concepts that capture a more holistic view of an organization's reaction to innovations. An innovative culture is one where people are receptive to new approaches and motivated to develop them to improve the organization (Wright and Taylor, 2003). In the CIS during this time period, a number of innovation projects supported by the formal structure of the CIS came to fruition in part because of a generally receptive climate to innovations of all sorts.

To evaluate the CIS's perceptions of innovativeness we gathered data annually for three years. Scales were created for each of the key constructs (for example formalization, slack resources, decentralization, persuasion, communication quality and perceptions of innovativeness) (see Johnson, Meyer et al., 1997 for more detail on their psychometric properties and procedures). Means for representative items, which reflect a Likert–type scale with 0 indicating 'total disagreement' and 10 indicating 'total agreement', are shown in Table 4.2.

Communication Environment

Communication is the primary tool used to secure the participation of others in innovations (Kanter, 1983). As we will detail in Chapter 5, communication channels are crucial to the formation of internal coalitions that support an innovation. But it is not only the structure of communication relationships that is important; the nature of the communication plays a key role in overcoming resistance to innovations and in the reduction of uncertainty. The very complexity of most innovations may require more intensive interpersonal interaction to arrive at high–quality decisions (Tushman, 1978). In essence it is not only the number of ideas dispersed within an organization, but also the perceived quality of innovation–related communication that determines how innovative organizational members perceive their institution to be. Thus in the manner first suggested by Indik (1965), the communication environment may mediate the impact of structural variables on perceived organizational innovativeness.

Enhanced communication quality is positively related to innovation because individuals with a broader awareness of the consequences and implications of an innovation are more likely to facilitate innovation (Monge et al., 1992). This facilitation is largely a function of uncertainty reduction, a process by which communication can break down barriers to innovation caused by fear or lack of knowledge (Johnson, 1990).

Organizational members who are generally pleased with the quantity and quality of information that they receive about an innovation are more likely to perceive that they work in an innovative environment. Thus perceptions of innovativeness can be enhanced by an effective communication system.

Table 4.2 Mean perceptions of the CIS as an innovating organization

Items	Time 1 (n = 86)	Time 2 (n = 85)	Time 3 (n = 83)
Communication quality			
I am satisfied with the quality of communication within the CIS.	6.4	5.8	6.5
CIS's formal communication system is efficient.	6.7	5.2	6.7
I am pleased with the quality of information that I receive from people at higher levels of the CIS.	7.2	6.8	7.2
The CIS maintains good communication between its members.	6.9	6.6	7.2
Acceptance			
I fully understand the importance of new interventions at the CIS.	6.8	7.1	7.6
I am convinced by what I am told that new interventions are worthwhile projects.	6.4	6.3	6.8
The CIS provides me with a rationale as to how the new intervention strategies fit its goals and objectives.	6.5	6.0	6.5
Decisions about new CIS intervention strategies are made by those who best understand the work.	5.5	5.7	6.4
Decentralization			
I have a reasonable amount of input into the creation of new intervention strategies at the CIS	4.9	5.7	5.7
I feel I can initiate ideas for new intervention strategies	6.1	6.3	6.5

Items	Time 1 (n = 86)	Time 2 (n = 85)	Time 3 (n = 83)
Formalization			
The policy and procedures manual for the CIS covers what happens in a typical day.	6.7	6.8	6.9
Policies and procedures are strictly enforced at CIS.	7.5	7.1	7.5
I follow established procedures exactly.	7.2	6.9	7.2
Slack resources			
There is a reliable source of funding for new intervention strategies at the national level	3.7	3.2	4.0
New intervention strategies can easily be added to what we are already doing.	5.3	5.2	5.7
I have the time to pursue new approaches to intervention strategies.	4.0	3.8	4.1
Perceived organizational innovativeness			
Most people who work for the CIS are very creative in how they go about implementing new intervention strategies.	6.5	7.0	7.3
The CIS is creative in its method of operation.	6.4	6.1	7.0
The CIS seeks out new ways to do things.	6.7	6.7	7.3
The CIS frequently tries out new ideas.	5.8	6.3	7.2

Note: On a scale of 0 to 10 where 0 indicates 'total disagreement' and 10 indicates 'total agreement'.

Over this time period in the CIS considerable effort was expended on improving the communication system, through enhancements in computer systems and supplanting of electronic mail systems. In addition, new CIS members were becoming more familiar with procedures, and various training programmes were introduced. Items on this scale received moderately high scores, with a uniform dip at Time 2, reflecting general uncertainties in the CIS and changes in their communication channels detailed in Chapter 3 and 5.

Involvement reflects the active participation in innovation processes resulting from a psychological acceptance of the importance of the innovation to the individual and to the organization. It has been found to be a critical factor in the receptivity of organizational members to innovations (Leonard–Barton and Sinha, 1993). The various types of power used to overcome resistance to innovations are crucial in determining the success of innovative processes generally, since acceptance can be hindered by both passive and active resistance (Zaltman et al., 1973). Influence is the primary means available to secure participation in an innovation. It is the 'capacity of an individual to cause changes in another's behavior by the use of more subtle, informal, and often cognitively oriented means than those associated with sanction or authority' (Fidler and Johnson, 1984, p. 707). Communication scholars argue that influence modes are key factors in employees' acceptance of organizational change (Poole, Gioia and Gray, 1989). For informal channels, influence is the primary means available to secure participation in an innovation (Johnson, 1993). Influence is positively related to innovation because individuals who are exposed to evidence, arguments and a rationale advocating acceptance of an innovation are more likely to accept it (Johnson, 1990; Weenig and Midden, 1991). Since effective influence results in greater participation in the implementation of innovations, it usually entails less resistance to the eventual implementation of innovations as well (Kelman, 1961) and is more likely to insure active involvement (Bennis, 1965).

The results of Johnson's (1990) study on informal and bottom–up innovation processes suggested that persuasion had a paramount impact on innovation adoption, reinforcing the notion that communication is central to innovative processes within organizations. Both participation and persuasion have been positively related to the implementation of change efforts in organizations (Nutt, 1986). In a similar manner, organizational members who accept an innovation are more likely to perceive their organization to be innovative. Given the number of meetings (see Chapter 3) devoted to training and explaining innovations programmes in the CIS and the successful implementation of a number of them, we expected that levels of acceptance would increase over the three–year study period. As Table 4.2 reveals, acceptance initially had moderate scores that increased slightly over time.

Formal indices

Formal structural variables are usually cast as indices that provide researchers with a systematic way of describing an organizational property in terms of a precise combination of other attributes (Johnson, 1993). These indices are derived from the vertical and hierarchical differentiation of the organization (Jablin, 1987). Many studies concerned with formal structural variables, such as slack resources, tend to downplay or to treat only superficially the role of informal communication in the innovation process (Johnson, 1993). In this research we focused on formal structural variables that were both salient to contractual networks and which had been identified as central in the literature. In a meta–analysis of the traditional literature, Damanpour (1991) identified several formal structural determinants of innovation. He found that slack resources was positively correlated with innovation, while centralization and formalization had an inverse relationship with it.

Centralization has been conceptualized as the degree to which authority for decision–making is concentrated at higher levels of management (Thompson, 1967; Jablin, 1987), and has been argued to be perhaps the most salient structural variable to the study of organizations (Marsden et al., 1994). Because there are many dimensions of authority, it can be operationalized in several different and potentially conflicting ways. Jablin (1987) makes a distinction between operationalizing decentralization as: (1) the hierarchical level at which decision–making takes place, and (2) the extent to which subordinates participate in decision–making.

If we consider centralization as the extent to which decision–making is concentrated in an organization, it follows that decentralization, the inverse of centralization, is the degree to which decision–making is dispersed (that is delegated) in an organization (Pfeffer, 1982). For the purpose of this study, we will focus on decentralization, the organizational members' perceived level of participation in decision–making (Aiken and Hage, 1971), a critical issue in new organizational forms where levels of the hierarchy may not be clearly ordered. In this case, decentralization has been found to be positively associated with involvement or active participation in innovation processes (Johnson, Donohue, Atkin and Johnson, 1994). One could logically posit that decentralization should be positively correlated with innovation because participatory work environments facilitate innovation by increasing organizational members' awareness, commitment and involvement (Damanpour, 1991). In turn, this heightened involvement leads organizational members to make positive attributions about communication quality.

It seems reasonable to posit that decentralization is also positively correlated with acceptance of innovations, because participatory decision–making processes should increase the degree to which an organizational member is convinced that an innovation is salient or worthwhile. The relatively formalized innovation process and the lack of involvement, represented by low volumes of communication, of CIS members in innovations, should have resulted in a decrease over the three time periods in perceptions of decentralization. However in actuality, perceptions of decentralization increased over time, although they were only in the moderate range. This may have reflected the declining staff at the OCC that led to more work being delegated to task forces and other groups in the CIS as I have discussed in Chapter 3 and as I will also detail in Chapter 6.

Pierce and Delbecq (1977) conceptualized formalization as 'a form of control employed by bureaucratic organizations ... the degree to which a codified body of rules, procedures or behavior prescriptions is developed to handle decisions and work processing' (p. 31). Jablin (1987) defines formalization as 'the degree to which the behaviors and requirements of jobs are explicit – that is codified into policies, rules, regulations, customs, and so forth' (p. 405). Formalization may be manifested in many ways, for example in the presence of rules manuals, job descriptions or the degree to which rules are enforced (Aiken and Hage, 1971). As a result of its importance as an index of organizational structure, formalization has recently been included in the National Organization Study (Marsden et al., 1994). For the purpose of this investigation, formalization is seen as the perceived degree of freedom available to organizational members as they pursue their functions and responsibilities versus the extent to which rules precisely define their activities. Damanpour (1991) suggests that formalization should be negatively correlated with innovation because its opposite, flexibility and low emphasis on work rules, may lead to a climate of openness that promotes a favourable evaluation of communication quality and encourages new ideas and behaviours. During this time period, increased training, the operation of the various task forces and CISTERS should result in an increase in perceptions of formalization. Formalization items had the highest means and were the most stable across the three time periods.

Damanpour (1991) defines slack resources as what an organization has beyond what it minimally requires to maintain operations. Traditionally this construct has been viewed in an economic sense, often measured in terms of financial resources (Aiken and Hage, 1971) or human resources slack (Miller and Friesen, 1982). On the basis of Damanpour's meta–analysis (1991), we expected that slack resources would be positively correlated with innovation because adequate resources allow an increased capacity for purchasing innovations, advocating innovations, implementing innovations, absorbing failure and exploring new ideas (Mohr, 1969). Innovative organizations are also more likely to expand their resources by creating joint programmes with others, thereby increasing their resources (Aiken and Hage, 1971), a factor underlying the coalition–building efforts of the CIS. In a more recent look at slack resources, Nohria and Gulati (1996) have found an inverse u–shaped relationship, arguing that too many slack resources may lead to a lack of discipline, with organizations embarking on innovations of dubious effectiveness.

For organizations such as the contractual network examined here that depend on contract renewal for fiscal security, the construct of slack resources may be especially relevant to the innovation process. Thus slack resources, such as reliable sources of funding, and sufficient time, should enable organizational members to participate in the creation and adoption of innovations. The increased call volume (and length of calls), budget reductions, furloughs, disbandment threats and computerization investments should result in a decrease in perceptions of the availability of slack resources during this time period. However this mean actually was relatively stable between Times 1 and 3 with a slight decrease at Time 2, perhaps reflecting the uncertainty concerning the contract renewal at Time 2. This factor had the lowest means of any of the factors.

For the perceived organizational innovativeness items there was a general increase, demonstrating a more positive climate for innovations in the CIS near the end of the study period, with Time 3 item means at or above 7 on the 11–point scales. Interestingly, members who had higher positions within the CIS (for example PIs and PDs) perceived higher levels of decentralization and persuasion than those at lower levels (for example OMs and TSMs) (Johnson, Chang, LaFrance, et al., 1995; Johnson, Chang, Ethington, LaFrance, Meyer, and Pobocik, 1996; Johnson, LaFrance, Chang, Kiyoma, and Ethington, 1997).

At a formal level, management can effect innovation by setting goals and priorities (Daft, 1978) and a cultural emphasis on innovativeness helps (Hoffman and Roman, 1984). Perhaps the most direct assessment of the role that organizational culture plays is in issues related to the compatibility of the innovation with existing values, past experience, and the needs of adopters (Rogers, 1983; Klein and Sorra, 1996). As we will examine in more detail in Chapter 6, the more compatible an innovation is along these dimensions, the more likely it is to be adopted and effectively implemented (Klein and Sorra, 1996).

4.4 THE CANCER INFORMATION SERVICES RESEARCH CONSORTIUM

Companies seek to acquire knowledge from the outside when there is a capability gap – that is, when strategically important technical expertise is unavailable or inadequate internally. (Leonard, 1995, p. 138)

Over time, the CIS had become a community–based laboratory for state–of–the–science communication research (Marcus, Woodworth and Strickland,

1993) and had conducted more research on cancer–related information seeking than any other site (for example Arkin et al., 1993; Freimuth et al., 1989), while simultaneously meeting its service goals (Marcus, 1998a). The most recent example of this tradition is the Cancer Information Service Research Consortium (CISRC), a series of programme project grants funded by NCI (Marcus, 1998b). The creation of this consortium was in part a response to the lack of slack resources within the CIS and also to the reality that creating a new semi–autonomous structure is often necessary when embarking on a new, innovative organizational activity (March and Simon, 1958).

The CISRC projects and the outreach programme, which partners with community organizations, have broadened the services of the CIS to reach out to traditionally underserved, special populations (Morra, 1998, p. vii): 'The telephone continues to be an essential health information source for medically underserved populations.' In general, telephone–delivered interventions have been found to be cost effective in achieving various health behaviour changes (McBride and Rimer, 1999).

The CISRC in part grew out of a one–time Request for Applications released by NCI in 1986 that solicited proposals specifically focused on communication issues in the context of the CIS (Morra, Bettinghaus et al., 1993). The PIs of the funded proposals, and others who submitted them, formed a nascent core of researchers and practitioners that eventually coalesced into the CISRC. One of these investigators started to see the possibility for a broader, comprehensive, enduring funding programme for communications research based on the CIS (Marcus, Bastani et al., 1993). He had already formed strong, if regionally limited, contacts with practitioners and started to reach out to a national group through the various ad hoc committees the CIS forms to solve specific problems (Pobocik et al., 1997). His major opportunity came in the early 1990s when the AMC Cancer Centre decided to invest in prevention programmes as its major strategic focus. At this time AMC hired a former CIS project officer and his division chief, a solid group of researchers in prevention, and it placed the Dean of the College of Communication Arts and Sciences at Michigan State University who was a member of the National Cancer Advisory Board on the AMC board.

The CIS through the development of the CISRC constructed a knowledge network with key research partners outside of its formal structure (Nonaka and Takeuchi, 1995). This provided a strong formal base for relationships, with many associated informal contacts, that could be used to build an even broader coalition, combining with key PDs to form a CoP.

Once funded, to ensure appropriate collaboration, several committees in addition to the formal AMC core served as means for the various groups to interact with each other including the Executive Committee, the Steering Committee, the Publications Subcommittee, Members' Council and advisory committees for each of the projects (Marcus, Morra et al., 1998). One unique feature of programme projects of this sort is that they have shared resources that all of the projects can draw on, including in this case Administration, Cost Effectiveness Analysis, Survey Research, and Biostatistics Cores. There was considerable complexity involved in the CISRC which was further enhanced by four out of the six major components being spread across the country at different host institutions. This consortia was designed to become a basic structure within which a number of innovations could be developed, thus turning the CIS into an 'innovation factory' (Hargadon and Sutton, 2000).

The major focus of the CISRC during this time period focused on the piloting of three new intervention strategies to facilitate the dissemination of cancer information to the public. The first and third innovations were connected to the CIS 1–800–4–CANCER telephone service, utilizing the toll–free number as a nexus from which to disseminate cancer information to targeted populations. The second and third projects are tailored to the health information needs of traditionally underserved sectors of the American public. These interventions were designed to address 'performance gaps' of the CIS that have been seen more generally to be important triggers for innovation in organizations (Hage, 1999). Each of these innovations was piloted on a different set of ROs. The following project descriptions were drawn from the first issue of *CISRC NEWS*, a newsletter initiated by the CISRC (see also Meyer, Johnson and Ethington, 1997).

Project 1 (5–A–Day for Better Health) involves the use of proactive counselling in the CIS to offer information about fruit and vegetable consumption to callers who would not ordinarily receive this information as part of the usual service. Proactive counselling is delivered at the end of a regular call, no matter what the caller had initially contacted the CIS about, in order to encourage callers to increase their fruit and vegetable consumption. Project 1, which was piloted in 13 ROs, added an additional component, proactive counselling, to the routine service that IS provided to callers.

A study of proactive counselling (Marcus, Bastani et al., 1993), which concerned mammography, the initial focus of Project 1, had been previously conducted in one of the regional CIS offices. This study resulted in several encouraging findings. Firstly callers and ISs alike gave a strong endorsement of proactive counselling for mammography screening. Secondly the interactive counselling protocol exposed participants to substantially higher levels of information and counselling about mammography screening, resulting in higher screening mammography rates among those callers who received the intervention. These findings lend credence to Project 1 in that successful recent intervention efforts of a similar nature in the CIS would tend to reinforce a climate of acceptance for

Project 1 among CIS members. Marcus, Heimendinger et al. (1998) describe the results for this project and Marcus et al. (2001) describe a replication of it.

Project 2 was concerned with encouraging women to receive regular mammograms. This new intervention strategy reached out to women by making cold calls from the CIS to low–income and minority women in targeted communities in Colorado. This intervention strategy was unique in that it focused on making outcalls from the CIS, an activity that was substantially different from the traditional role of a telephone service that responds to calls placed by people in the community to a toll–free number. The procedure of making outcalls was foreign to ISs, who were trained to give information in response to callers' inquiries. Because of its unique approach this project was only piloted in one RO (see Crane et al., 1998, and Crane et al., 2000, for follow–on study).

Project 3 ('Quit Today!' Smoking Programme for African Americans) was a tailored, multichannel media campaign designed to increase the CIS call volume of low–income African American smokers and recent quitters. This project involved two interrelated studies. Study 1 focused on a paid advertising campaign designed to motivate adult African American smokers to stop smoking and to call the CIS for help in doing so. This campaign developed six radio advertisements and tailored the messages to three radio listening formats (two ads each for jazz, gospel and black contemporary). One television spot was also produced. Outreach materials included a revision of the *Pathways to Freedom* videotape which was disseminated as *Quit Today!*.

Study 2 tested the efficacy of newly developed self–help smoking cessation materials and targeted CIS counselling tailored to the quitting barriers and concerns of African American smokers in motivating themselves to quit compared with standard non–tailored CIS smoking cessation materials and counselling (for more details see Boyd et al., 1998). Study 1 paid advertisements were strategically placed on radio and television stations with high African American listenership and viewership. African American smokers who called the CIS in response to the ads and who met Study 2 eligibility requirements were randomly assigned to either the newly tailored cessation programme or the standard CIS cessation protocol. To ISs, Project 3 was the usual service, providing accurate, up–to–date information in response to caller requests.

A review of 15 years of media promotion of the CIS (Arkin et al., 1993) concluded that mass media campaigns can increase the number of calls to the CIS. In addition, promotions targeted to specific segments of the population can have an impact on the types of callers who contact the CIS. Further, paid advertising can result in substantial increases in call volume. The CIS, when adequately promoted, can be a key resource in stimulating interest and action among targeted populations. Arkin et al.'s (1993) findings lend credence to Project 3 efforts, suggesting that mass media campaigns, when combined with counselling via the CIS telephone service, are a viable way to promote smoking cessation in targeted populations. Successful past intervention efforts of a similar nature in the CIS would tend to reinforce a climate of acceptance for Project 3. A prior study by the principal investigator had demonstrated telephone counselling increased adherence to quitting protocols and enhanced quit rates (Orleans et al., 1991). In addition, another CIS–based study of a randomized mass media smoking–cessation intervention designed for blue–collar workers had positive results (Thompson et al., 1993). Initial positive outcome evaluations and additional funding may contribute to acceptance of the project across the CIS network; initially four ROs agreed to participate in it.

TEAM, the Network Analysis Project

The Michigan State University TEAM was part of the Administrative Shared Resource of the CISRC. The TEAM sought to evaluate the impact of the programme project on CIS operations and to develop recommendations that would enhance the effectiveness of the consortium of researchers and of practitioners who compose the CISRC (Marcus, Morra et al., 1998). In a sense, it operated as a bridge between the disparate entities of the researchers evaluating projects and the practitioners who were implementing them.

While generically this project was labelled network analysis within the CISRC, its design was much richer and more complex than the typical network analysis project. Essentially it combined the classic features of an organizational audit, including a complete list of self–report questionnaires, with network analysis communication logs (Downs and Adrian, 2004; LaFrance et al., 1997). In addition to assessing how members of the CIS were reacting to the programme project (Meyer, Johnson and Ethington, 1997), the TEAM provided a portion of the information on project implementation used by the Administrative Core as part of the Quality Control Monitoring System (QCMS) (Marcus, Morra et al., 1998).

The TEAM also examined issues at multiple points in time over the four–year course of the project (for example Johnson and Chang, 2000), assessing the impact of temporal communication events on the implementation, dissemination, reinvention and adoption of the three proposed interventions within the CIS (for example Meyer, 1996a). Naturally occurring experiments were strategically selected that permitted the TEAM to investigate in more detail specific issues (for example conferences: Johnson et al., 1996), and implementation of information technologies (Johnson et al., 1998). So the data presented in this book are the result of the TEAM's work.

4.5 LESSONS LEARNED

Collaboration has been called an 'unnatural act between unconsenting adults.' (Wandersman et al., 1997, p. 274)

The common thread running through all of these alliances is the need to manage based on shared vision, a commitment to common values, and an accountability exacted through communication and information. (McKinney et al., 1996, p. 33)

We collaborate to gain some advantage. We can achieve something which would be more difficult or less likely to occur without collaboration. (Cullen et al., 1999, p. 132)

Maximizing the full research potential of the CIS was viewed by many as helping the CIS become even more closely aligned with the primary mission of NCI which, like all of the National Institutes of Health, is primarily dedicated to research. (Marcus, Morra et al., 1998, p. S13)

Consortial relationships are increasingly important because: (1) they can lead to the development, implementation and evaluation of useful new ideas; (2) they can enhance the policy relevance of ideas that are tested; and (3) there is a greater likelihood of successful implementation if practitioners have input early in the development of pilot research projects. The question of what promotes cooperative relationships in social systems has been one of the central issues for social scientists in this century. Symbolic interactionists (Mead, 1934; Fine, 1993), sociologists (Parsons, 1960), dramatists (Littlejohn, 1992), economists (Coase, 1937; Hollander, 1990), management scholars (Smith et al., 1995), organizational communication researchers (Harter and Krone, 2001) and others have all grappled with this problem.

As we have seen, this was an exciting time period for the CIS. Simultaneously it reached out to two key groups of stakeholders: community partners that would enhance its capacity for reaching underserved populations, and research partners that would demonstrate that it could be a laboratory for community–based communication research, thus satisfying key stakeholders within the NCI. Building coalitions is an inherently political activity: it has also been observed that KM is also highly political (Davenport and Prusak, 1998).

Here we will focus on the issues that resulted from the CISRC that could be applied to the future operation of organizations interested in KM and innovations. The CISRC changes occurred in an organization whose members had a strong normative commitment to its basic, traditional mission. The resulting uncertainties and ambiguities pointed to the human side of KM and innovation, issues that typically are not confronted directly in the vast literatures on this area.

Lessons for Consortia

Nevertheless, I would say that Structure is a defining characteristic of an organization — *it* is what brings about or makes possible that quality of atmosphere, that sustained, routine purposiveness that distinguishes work in an organization from activities in a group, a mob, a society, and so forth. (McPhee, 1985, p. 150)

Given the general findings in unitary organizations that slack resources are necessary for achieving innovative outcomes, it is interesting to note that the item means for slack resources were low in the CIS, while the overall level of perceived innovativeness was high. One would anticipate that a perceived scarcity of resources would have a negative impact on innovative behaviour. The availability of slack resources plays a critical role in how organizations respond to environmental changes: whether they reach out to others or develop innovations internally (March, 1988). Aiken and Hage (1971) suggest that organizations like the CIS with a history of innovativeness find ways of expanding resources by developing joint programmes with others, such as the coalitions we focused on in the last parts of this chapter.

Decentralization, information exchange and a strong persuasive rationale for new intervention strategies can apparently mitigate the potential negative impact of scarce resources on innovativeness. In addition, in an interesting way, innovation has been formalized in the CIS since it was specifically mandated in the five–year contract that ROs would participate in research programmes like the ones developed by the CISRC. It is increasingly the norm of modern organizations and new organizational forms that members find that they must innovate in difficult circumstances.

In these new forms organizational members must often innovate without access to the time, financial resources and quality communication often viewed as necessary conditions for innovations. Geographic, economic and political barriers to coordination and integration create unique challenges for them. In these conditions, it is not surprising that decentralization, or participation in innovation decisions, enhances communication quality and acceptance. In more decentralized environments, messages from a wide range of sources may actually be more effective and less costly for an organization than exclusively relying on a top–down approach to innovation (Leonard–Barton and Deschamps, 1988).

However some structure, as represented by formalization, contrary to recent trends in the literature related to unitary organizations (Damanpour, 1991; Krackhardt, 1994), must also be present to manage uncertainty. To achieve some balance when innovating within confederations, consideration should be given to reintroducing the stability and framework provided by formalization. So even though theorists have advocated organic forms of organizations for innovation processes (for example Aiken and Hage, 1971), it must be recognized that these forms existed in the presence of the formal structure of unitary organizations in their original formulations.

In the end all organizational innovation processes must confront these factors, balancing the everyday press of operational issues against the needs of organizations to adjust to ever–changing environmental circumstances (Van de Ven, 1986), with individual coping responses determined by balancing concerns for performance with culturally based normative responses and environmentally induced uncertainties (Lewis and Seibold, 1996). Somehow organizations must achieve a balance between stability and flexibility (Weick, 1969): how to strike that balance is still very much open to question.In this regard, culture plays a significant role in innovation processes. All cultures develop rules that shape them. Strong cultures can improve organizational effectiveness by clearly delineating roles, relationships and contexts within which individuals can innovate. Innovative cultures also focus on end–users or customers, searching for new ways of improving service delivery, such as the CISRC projects (Wright and Taylor, 2003).

Implementation often requires high formalization, centralization and low complexity. One compromise strategy organizations adopt is to compartmentalize these processes with very rigid structures in production processes and more flexible ones in R&D labs. In some ways, this became the approach taken by the CISRC, with new intervention strategies developed by research partners. The ignorance resulting from this sort of compartmentalization is often essential to the maintenance of system equilibrium (Schneider, 1962; Smithson, 1989).

The classic findings about the structuring of small group networks (Shaw, 1971) suggest that when left to their own devices organizational members will create the structures most appropriate to the task at hand (Pacanowsky, 1989). The decline in overall levels of external communication during this period may reflect this sort of process, with the drop between Time 1 and Time 2 fairly dramatic. This result might reflect an initial exploration of a range of community–based organizations by the relatively new OMs at Time 1, followed by a more steady state reliance on partners who have demonstrated their usefulness at Times 2 and 3. This pattern of declining communication was also found in various types of internal communication, and will be discussed in detail in Chapter 5. This decline might also reflect the opportunity costs to the CIS of not having a truly reciprocal relationship with partners, especially when controversies developed like that over mammography screening. The CIS was also missing the chance to capture the tacit knowledge of these groups. However this focus on information dissemination rather than true collaboration is common for non–profit organizations (Lewis et al., 2003).

Lessons for the Human Side of Organizations

A more realistic view of innovation should begin with an appreciation of the physiological limitations of human beings to pay attention to nonroutine issues, and the corresponding inertial forces of organizational life. (Van de Ven, 1986, p. 594)

A critical role of management in innovation process is that of managing attention (Van de Ven, 1986). While exposure is the first step to persuasion (McGuire, 1989), the audience members most likely to attend to messages related to management's interests are those organizational members already committed to them. Dervin (1989), in this connection, has suggested that the most appropriate strategy might be to change the institutions delivering the message, rather than to expect the audience to change deeply seated behaviour patterns. In effect, management campaigns may be reaching the already converted. While this might have a beneficial effect of further reinforcing beliefs, the organizational members who are most in need of being reached are precisely those members who are least likely to attend to management's message. Even more telling in new organizational forms is that members, especially boundary spanners like OMs, are confronted with multiple, often conflicting messages about their role performance. New organizational forms often mean de–skilling and offshoring except for a few highly talented knowledge workers. They 'thrust a large number of its citizens into a condition of permanent survival oriented tension' (Child and McGrath, 2001, p. 145).

During much of this project there was a real question as to whether this basic precondition for cooperative relationships was established, especially on a system–wide basis. While there were certainly examples of temporally focused attention during national meetings and local foci surrounding the implementation of trials, the overall pattern of research findings, especially related to innovation communication (Johnson, Bettinghaus et al., 1997) and the pattern of 'don't knows' in response to questions dealing with specific innovation attributes of the various projects (Meyer, Johnson and Ethington, 1997), suggested that this basic precondition for cooperative relationships was not established.

While attentive listening or reading is also a form of cooperation (Browning et al., 1995), here the various parties were not fully implicated in each other's work. While it is not necessary that parties continuously attend to each other (Couch, 1987), there was a real question whether there was enough attention to each other throughout the project for cooperative action to occur. Indeed, the various parties went about their business with a minimal amount of direct communication (Johnson, Bettinghaus et al., 1997), although there were substantial formal mechanisms established for it (Marcus, Morra et al., 1998).

Role Conflict, Role Ambiguity and Innovativeness within the CIS

The many changes the CIS was experiencing occurred in an organization with a core of members that had a strong normative commitment to its basic, traditional mission, but which also had some new ROs, as well as many new occupants of the OM role. One way that literature has approached the human side of organizational roles is through a focus on role conflict and role ambiguity. We empirically tested a model of the impact of formalization, role ambiguity, role conflict, and communication quality on perceived organizational innovativeness with a subset of our data (Johnson et al., 1998), because of the likelihood of problems in these areas. These data suggested that formalization makes an important contribution to innovation with the human side of consortia in the highly uncertain world of new organizational forms. Stress and resulting turnover is a key problem for call centres generally (Downing, 2004).

Comparatively little research has looked at role stressors and communication quality together as they mediate formal structural variables and perceived organizational innovativeness. As with much of the role stress literature, role conflict and role ambiguity, as well as their relationships with other variables, have received much attention from organizational scholars (see Fisher and Gitelson, 1983; Jackson and Schuler, 1985 for a comprehensive list). Several antecedents of role conflict and ambiguity have been hypothesized, including many structural variables such as: formalization, participation in decision–making, span of subordination, size and organizational position level (Greene, 1978; Kahn et al., 1964; Morris et al., 1979; Nicholson and Goh, 1983; Organ and Greene, 1981). Many negative psychological, emotional and behavioural outcomes have been associated with both role conflict and ambiguity, including: tension, burnout, anxiety, dissatisfaction, absenteeism, as well as lack of commitment, low performance, low involvement and reduced levels of autonomy (Brief and Aldag, 1976; Fisher and Gitelson, 1983; Jackson and Schuler, 1985; Miller, 1995; Van Sell et al., 1981).

Role conflict can be defined as, the 'incongruity of the expectations associated with a role' (Van Sell et al., 1981). The source or sender of these expectations may vary. Perhaps an organizational member receives contradictory expectations from the same sender or they may receive conflicting expectations from more than one supervisor or in this case outreach partner. In their seminal work, Kahn et al. (1964), theorized that the relationship between formalization and role conflict would be negative. However research on the relationship between formalization and role conflict has demonstrated somewhat inconclusive results (Organ and Greene, 1981; Morris et al., 1979) A meta–analysis investigating the antecedents and outcomes of role conflict and role ambiguity found a *negative* but weak mean correlation between formalization and role conflict (Fisher and Gitelson, 1983; Jackson and Schuler, 1985).

Our research served to clarify the relationship between formalization and role conflict within a larger model that predicts perceived organizational innovativeness. Following the original hypothesis of Kahn et al. (1964), we too hypothesized a negative relationship between formalization and role conflict. If an organization is highly formalized (for example written policies and procedures exist), then the expectations of an individual working under those policies are known. Therefore the chance that conflict may arise between individuals' expectations and the organization decreases considerably.

The second role stressor, role ambiguity, has often been conceptualized as the degree to which information is either vague or lacking regarding a person's role expectations, means of performing organizational duties, or the outcomes of organizational behaviour associated with her or his role (Van Sell et al., 1981). In keeping with previous research, we proposed that formalization will also be negatively correlated with role ambiguity; that clear policies and procedures for organization members' duties will diminish uncertainty.

In support of the hypotheses asserted above, the following relationships were found. Firstly perceived organizational innovativeness was strongly predicted by communication quality. Secondly formalization was a substantial predictor of communication quality. Thirdly role ambiguity and role conflict were predicted by formalization (Johnson et al., 1998). Contrary to the hypothesized relationships, role conflict had little impact on CIS members' level of communication quality. In addition, the relationship between role ambiguity and communication quality was in the *opposite* of the predicted direction. Firstly there seemed to be a minimal relationship between role conflict and communication quality. One possible explanation for this was that individuals might have differential reactions to role conflict as a psychological stressor. For instance seeking out more information in an attempt to alleviate role conflict can backfire, if the new information further complicates messages sent by the role set. Alternatively the new information may clarify messages, depending upon the individual's relationship with various members of the set or one's ability to interpret other types of communication (for example non–verbal).

Secondly perhaps some organizational members expect to experience role ambiguity while performing the duties associated with their role. This expectation may be particularly important in new organizational forms. Thus individuals develop the skills necessary to function and even thrive regardless of their levels of role ambiguity. For example it may be the case that one uses the ambiguity to find creative solutions in situations where ambiguity allows for more autonomy. In this way, role ambiguity empowers individuals to perform daily tasks without clearly contradicting their role prescriptions and therefore enabling communication rather than hindering it. In fact CIS members who resided at higher levels of the organizational hierarchy reported significantly lower levels of role ambiguity than those members at the lower levels. A key finding of another of the empirical studies in our research stream was that formalization is positively related to communication quality (Johnson, Meyer et al., 1997). This may be explained by the logic of Organ and Greene's (1981) rationale for the effects of formalization on professional involvement. The authors argued that formalization may be negatively related to professional involvement because high levels of formalization increase the probability of role conflict. However they caution that this effect of formalization on involvement may be mediated or even reversed by the extent to which formalization decreases role ambiguity. In fact in their study the authors found that the net effect of formalization is a tendency to reduce the alienation of professionals, thus increasing their level of involvement.

If formalization increases involvement by reducing role ambiguity and alienation, it may also lead to favourable impressions of communication climate. Specifically, one could posit that increased levels of perceived organizational innovativeness could logically be an outgrowth of participation in decision–making, If organizational members experience a reduction in uncertainty by experiencing adequate levels of formalization about their job role, they may be more inclined to report high levels of communication quality. Overall, organizational members' perceptions that they have a stake in the decision–making process and are involved in the active exchange of ideas with other organizational members promotes an awareness of organizational–wide innovation.

Contrary to recent trends in the literature related to unitary organizations (Damanpour, 1991; Johnson, 1990; Johnson, Meyer et al., 1997), some structure, as represented by formalization, must also be present to manage uncertainty. In this study, formalization had positive direct and indirect impacts on innovativeness when examined in a system of other variables. Managing the tensions inherent in the paradoxes of stability and change is critical to the operation of alternative organizational forms (Harter and Krone, 2001). Indeed managing the process of uncertainty reduction, rather than necessarily achieving it, may be the critical issue (Harter and Krone, 2001; Babrow, 1992, 2001).

Somewhat relatedly, perhaps to reduce role conflict, there was a clear specialization of communication functions for internal and external communication, with very little association between external intervention strategies, primarily driven by community coalition–building concerns, and internal communication, primarily driven by the implementation of trial projects associated with the CISRC. One early concern related to the operation of the CISRC was that it might detract, given the press of work and finite resources of the CIS, from other intervention strategy efforts. However there appeared to be more involvement by CIS members in external intervention strategy efforts than in CISRC ones. This might have been attributable to their greater control, influence, sympathy and understanding of these efforts. I will return to this cluster of issues when I compare the internally generated computerization effort perceptions with those related to the three CISRC projects in Chapter 6.

Still, in spite of these barriers, in today's environment, organizations and their members may have no other choice; if they are to survive in the long term they must pay the price of innovating. The real question may be strategically what innovations are in their best interest to pursue, and to what end. The 'costs' of innovation in the CIS, psychological, temporal and material, compared to the value or benefit of potential innovations are quite real. Working on an innovation may result in delaying opportunities, complicating decision–making and increasing information load. There are also additional psychological costs, such as the loss of self–esteem and frustration, that result from unsuccessful innovations. I will return to these issues in the final chapter when I discuss success.

5. Organizing informally for innovation

5.1 INTRODUCTION

While we will consider various knowledge transfer issues and strategies ... many of them come down to finding effective ways to let people talk and listen to one another. (Davenport and Prusak, 1998, p. 88)

The organizations producing more innovations have more complex structures that link people in multiple ways and encourages them to 'do what needs to be done' within strategically guided limits ... (Kanter, 1988b, p. 95)

Research has shown that social integration is associated with the early adoption of normative innovations. (Burt, 1980, p. 329)

Innovations are not only adopted, implemented, and confirmed through social relations among people; they are also created, understood, and defined socially. (Dearing et al., 1994, p. 17)

Innovation theory suggests that the close communication linkages among cooperative group members and between scientific committees will allow new ideas to flow easily and rapidly, resulting in a fast rate of innovation adoption ... In addition, member 'homophily' created by shared beliefs and backgrounds should lead to more effective communication of information on cancer control research and a stronger diffusion effect. (McKinney et al., 1992, p. 277)

The information context of the modern organization is rapidly evolving. Information technologies, including databases, new telecommunications systems and software for synthesizing information, make a vast array of information available to an ever–expanding number of organizational members. Management's exclusive control over information resources is steadily declining, in part because of the downsizing of organizations and the decline of the number of layers in an organizational hierarchy. This is particularly true in new organizational forms like the CIS that are made possible by new forms of electronic communication, but which need especially rich forms of interpersonal communication for integration. These trends make our knowledge of informal communication channels, particularly those focusing on interpersonal relationships, the human side of KM, increasingly critical for understanding of innovation and KM.

5.2 COMPARING FORMAL AND INFORMAL COMMUNICATION STRUCTURES

Communication structure research, which encompasses hierarchies, markets and networks, has traditionally been viewed as a central area of organizational communication theory (Jablin, 1980; Jablin et al., 1987; Redding, 1979). There are many different approaches to communication structure (see Johnson, 1993). The two used most frequently to analyse organizational communication systems are the formal approach (see Chapter 3), the primary focus of most traditional KM, and the informal approaches, especially network analysis, that I will focus on in this chapter. An organization's communication structure consists of both formal and informal elements, as well as other ingredients, and is not reducible to either (March and Simon, 1958). However to most organizational researchers this fundamental distinction captures two different worlds within the organization, worlds that have different premises and outlooks and most importantly, different fundamental assumptions about the nature of interaction (Allen, 1977; Dow, 1988).

Early approaches to studying communication structure in organizations concentrated on the organizational chart and the flow of messages vertically and horizontally within it. Traditionally, control in organizations has been viewed as occurring within the formal communication structure. The formal organizational chart is embedded in the assumptions of the classical approach to rational management (Astley and Zajac, 1991; Morgan, 1986). They act to 'constrain some actors' abilities to form ties, or specific types of ties, and therefore confine the extent to which actors can shape or reshape their networks so as to "optimize" their returns ...' (Lazega and van Duijn, 1997, p. 375). Formal approaches focus on the following characteristics of structure: formal authority relationships represented in the organizational hierarchy; differentiation of labour; and formal mechanisms for coordination (Dow, 1988). These characteristics, along with the notion of goal or purpose, have been seen by some to represent the very essence of what an organization is (Schein, 1965). In some theorists' view, these structures also constituted an information technology, with formal hierarchies constituting a primitive computer (Beninger, 1990; Contractor and Monge, 2002).

Formal approaches started to break down with the increasing uncertainty facing the modern organization (Galbraith, 1995) and concomitant increases in information load (Fidler and Johnson, 1984) leading to a focus on informal coordination as a means of processing ever–increasing volumes of information. Knowledge networks are likely to be more fluid in terms of both agents and linkages, with changes in patterns based on evolving tasks, knowledge distribution and agents' cognitive knowledge (Monge and Contractor, 2003). Horizontal flows through informal channels facilitate dissemination of incremental knowledge to relevant parties and its adaptive exploitation (Schulz, 2001). Informal, fluid structures characterized by individual autonomy are the key to creating knowledge (Nonaka and Takeuchi, 1995).

Certainly with a highly risky and complex innovation, which requires high volumes of communication to effect, the chances of successful implementation become problematic. These contingent situations suggest that there is a practical upper bound to formally implementing innovations within organizations, unless some parallel processing system is created to increase capacity (Fidler and Johnson, 1984). In recent years, it has become obvious that innovation adoption does not occur solely at the level of top management (Johnson, 1993). Indeed the very limitations on communication and information processing capacity outlined here entail that if innovation is to flourish it cannot be limited to management, or to the planned network and centralized administration historically characteristic of the CIS system. In fact there is some evidence that formal communication has a negative effect on technological innovation (Ebadi and Utterback, 1984). In general, informal coalition–building is critical to the development of innovations (Albrecht and Hall, 1989; Kanter, 1983). Face–to–face channels, such as the network linkages examined in this project, are also crucial to the formations of coalitions which support an innovation (Valente, 1995).

Considerable research attention in the 1960s and 1970s was devoted to the relationship between formal structure and innovations, with a disheartening array of mixed findings (see also Rogers, 1983; Monge and Contractor, 2003). For example the contradictory findings related to organizational size and innovation have been attributed to two offsetting processes. While size increases occupational diversity, it stifles innovation through the institution of more bureaucratic controls (Daft, 1978; Kim, 1980). There does appear to be support, with some cross–cultural verification in Korea, for the hypotheses that complexity and integration are positively related to innovation, and formalization and centralization are negatively related (Kim, 1980). Thus adoption of technological innovations is more prevalent in organizations which are large, specialized, functionally differentiated and decentralized (Kimberly and Evanisko, 1981; Rogers, 1983), factors which have also been found to relate to innovation adoption by lower–level decision–makers in organizations (Moch and Morse, 1977). For KM, formal approaches do offer some advantages: vertical flows can promote faster, more comprehensive examination of the relevance of new knowledge and facilitate widespread exposure of new knowledge to remote distant knowledge (Schulz, 2001).

Informal approaches recognize that a variety of needs, including social ones, underlie communication in organizations, and that as a result the actual communication relationships in an organization may be less rational than formal systems (Johnson, 1993). Informal structures function to facilitate communication, maintain cohesiveness in the organization as a whole, and maintain a sense of personal integrity or autonomy (Smelser, 1963).

Network analysis represents a very systematic means of examining the overall configuration of communication relationships, both formal and informal, within an organization. The most common form of graphic portrayal of networks contains nodes, which represent social units, and relationships, often measured by the communication channel used to express them, of various sorts between them. Because of its generality, network analysis is used by almost every social science to study specific problems (Johnson, 1993) and has become the preferred mode for representing informal, emergent communication (Monge and Contractor, 2003). Recent years have seen a resurgence of interest in network analysis in the social (Monge and Contractor, 2003; Biggart and Delbridge, 2004; Pescosolido and Rubin, 2000) and even natural sciences (Barabasi, 2003; Buchanan, 2002; Newman, 2003; Watts, 2003), in part because of the development of such heuristic concepts as social capital (Coleman, 1988; Putnam, 2000; Seibert et al., 2001; Kadushin, 2004) and structural holes (Burt, 1992, 2000; Finlay and Coverdill, 2000; Taylor and Doerful, 2003). Indeed social networking represented by such sites as Friendster is argued to be the next 'big thing' on the Web (Waters, 2003).

Network analysis and the diffusion of innovation literature have been intimately intertwined with each other for decades (Rogers and Kincaid, 1981; Rogers, 1983, 1995; Valente, 1995; Wallace, 2001). Most prior research has focused on the implementation by management of innovations through formal channels (see Rogers, 1983), rather than the informal communication processes that are linked to the initiation of innovations in more contemporary organizations (Kanter, 1983). Formally generated innovations are ones originating in upper management, using the traditional authority structure as the primary impetus underlying adoption.

However Rogers concluded that 'in all cases it seems that social systems whose members are more closely linked by communication networks have a stronger diffusion effect and a faster rate of adoption of innovations' (1983, p. 235). Further, someone's positioning within the social structure is particularly important, with Becker (1970) for example finding for public health officers that their centrality in communication networks was positively related to the adoption of innovations. A variety of network factors are associated with the adoption of innovations. Classically, the typical scenario for facilitating the adoption of innovations painted in the diffusion of innovations literature is: (1) identify the opinion leaders of a system; (2) expose them to sources of information they value; (3) increase the prestige value of the innovation; and (4) reduce risks associated with adoption (Becker, 1970). More recent empirical studies have found similar processes at work. Firstly the more multiplex someone's relationship, the more likely an individual is to be an early adopter (Bach, 1989). Secondly the more central they are the more likely they are to adopt (Czepiel, 1975; Ebadi and Utterback, 1984). If early adopters are central then the diffusion of innovations is more rapid throughout the system (Valente, 1995). Thirdly the more frequent and important their communication the more likely they are to adopt (Ebadi and Utterback, 1984). Fourthly the more diverse their communication, the more positive the effects on technical innovation (Ebadi and Utterback, 1984).

Valente (1995) in his systematic review of the diffusion of innovations literature adds threshold and critical mass as central generating mechanisms to diffusion processes. Threshold models of collective behaviour suggest that individuals engage in behaviours when a sufficient proportion of others do, with individual thresholds varying. Critical mass represents the number of individuals needed before an innovation can spread to others. One problem for the diffusion of communication technologies is that a certain number of users is required to make them useful. These two variables can interact with each other, since once an individual adopts an innovation it lowers other thresholds because of decreased risk. The more individuals who adopt, the lower the levels of risk, setting in motion a snowball effect.

Johnson (1990) tested a model of the effects of persuasiveness, salience, and uncertainty on participation in innovations. This research focused on the role of informal communication channels in the transmission of influence attempts related to a new component of an existing programme. This research examined the initial stages of the development of innovations at lower levels in an organization. The communication channel typically used in this phase is primarily interpersonal, and these sub–formal channels reflect the informal authority structure of an organization (Downs, 1967). Typically these more personal channels are more likely to be effective, since they meet the specific needs and questions of the receivers because of the immediacy of feedback and the situation specificity of the channel. As a result there is an inherent reduction of uncertainty involved in the use of these channels, since they lead to increased understanding of a proposed innovation, which may in part account for the somewhat more moderate impact of uncertainty in the model. Indeed the very complexity of most innovations may require more intensive interaction to arrive at high–quality decisions (Tushman, 1978). Johnson's (1990) model was tested on data gathered from a large financial institution and the results suggested that the classic communicative variable of persuasion had a paramount impact on participation, reinforcing the notion that communication is central to innovative processes within organizations.

Generally, persuasive strategies have been found to be the most effective means of ensuring the successful implementation of innovations, especially highly risky and complex ones (Bennis, 1965; Zaltman and Duncan, 1977). Effective persuasion can best overcome resistance attributable both to lack of understanding and to fear; in addition, the use of persuasion results in a higher level of involvement (Bennis, 1965). The path between uncertainty and willingness to participate showed a moderate negative relationship, which confirms the view that firms must build in an ethos of risk taking (Johnson, 1990), a system of rewards for accepting and adapting to change, for innovation to prosper (Goldhar et al., 1976). Nohria and Eccles (1992) suggest that several factors related to new technologies make entirely new organizational forms, such as networked organizations, possible. Firstly they increase the possibilities for control and decrease the need for vertical processing (for example condensation) of information. Secondly new technologies facilitate communication across time and space. Thirdly they increase external communication thus blurring traditional lines of authority within the firm. Fourthly information technologies enhance flexibility within the firm by decreasing the reliance on particular individuals for specialized information.

On the other hand, recently a market approach that shares much with both network and formal approaches and rests on economic and exchange assumptions, has begun to emerge (Nohria and Eccles, 1992). 'Markets are arrangements which coordinate the actions of large numbers of people automatically, and on a lateral basis, through the operation of the price mechanism, without infringing their freedom or requiring inequalities of status' (Beetham, 1987, p. 136). While markets have been viewed as occurring outside the context of formal organizations, they have been recognized as containing many authority properties found in organizations, and organizations with complex, multidivisional structures take on market characteristics (Eccles and White, 1988). 'The internal operations of real–world firms are controlled by a blend of authority and market–like mechanisms' (McGuinness, 1991, p. 66).

5.3 INNOVATION AND COMMUNICATION CHANNELS

Effective network organizations also require the kind of rich multidimensonal, robust relationships that can only be developed through face to face interaction. (Nohria and Eccles, 1992, p. 290)

One of the primary structural features associated with the diffusion and the implementation of innovations within systems is the number and arrangement of recurring communication channels. The heuristic value of any network analysis is determined by how the relationships between nodes or links are defined (Monge and Eisenberg, 1987; Rogers and Kincaid, 1981), with one critical issue reflecting the communication channels involved. Links can be conceptualized in a variety of ways. It very important however that any conceptualization be systematic and that it fully capture various relational properties (Richards, 1985).

Channels have been variously defined: 'an information transmission system' (Goldenson, 1984, p. 137) or '... the means by which the message gets from the source to the receiver' (Rogers and Shoemaker, 1971, p. 24). Channels are also often seen as constraints, as in the conduit metaphor; thus a message has to stay within channels (Axley, 1984). As the preceding illustrates, and as Berlo (1960) has noted, channels have become one of the more ephemeral communication concepts. Relying on the metaphor of a person on one shore trying to reach another on the opposite shore, Berlo distinguishes between three senses in which channels are used: 'modes of encoding and decoding messages (boat docks), message–vehicles (boats), and vehicle–carriers (water)' (p. 64). Here I will stress mainly the sense of channels as message–vehicles, the contrivances by which messages are delivered to an individual. Thus 'a channel is a medium, a carrier of messages' (Berlo, 1960, p. 31).

General properties of channels can impact on individuals' relative evaluations of them as disseminators of information. Mass–mediated channels tend to provide information of a fairly general nature with considerable efficiencies in reaching large audiences quickly with a message (Schramm, 1973). Interpersonal channels are viewed as more effective in reducing uncertainty because they provide social support, enhance confidence in suggested outcomes, and are more tailored to individual needs and questions because of their immediacy of feedback and the situation specificity of their communication (Schramm, 1973). For these reasons interpersonal channels are seen as more useful in presenting complex, serious information and most influential in the diffusion of innovations. Because of the geographic dispersion of the CIS, interpersonal channels consisted of telephone as well as face–to–face communication, with the telephone the primary means of accomplishing relationships between national meetings.

Setting the Stage

During our first data collection we gathered data on the perceptions of CIS members of their communication channels using a battery of questions containing scales reflecting the major theoretical perspectives of channel selection (Johnson et al., 1994b; Johnson, Chang et al., 1995; Johnson, Chang et al., 2000). While respondents reported that they used all of the channels frequently, they differed dramatically in how they evaluated three channels that are particularly important to the CIS. In terms of their ability to provide information, from richest to leanest, the following continuum of channels was examined: interpersonal (primarily telephone), e–mail, and facsimile or written (Schmitz and Fulk, 1991; Trevino et al., 1990). An additional complicating factor within the CIS (and elsewhere) was the clear functional role differences and individual predispositions toward different channels. It has been suggested that perceptions of channels should differ by an individual's functional role in an organization, because particular positions have media associated with job performance and because members of a particular profession may come to develop similar norms of media usage (Rice, 1993; Rice and Aydin, 1991; Markus, 1994). For example higher–level organizational positions typically focus more on uncertainty reduction and thus use more interpersonally–oriented channels (Rice and Shook, 1990; Daft and Lengel, 1986; Pondy and Mitroff, 1979; Sullivan, 1995). Indeed in a meta–analysis of over 40 studies, Rice and Shook (1990) found that usage of media was different for management versus others and was highly correlated with organizational level. Each role in the CIS seems to have its own preferred mix of channels (Johnson, Chang et al., 1994; Johnson, Chang et al., 2000). In addition there were clear individual differences, with some laggard Luddites teased at national meetings for their unwillingness to use e–mail. All in all these results suggested a need for the maintenance of a very diverse communication system to support different functions and individual preferences.

Differing Perspectives

Channel, or media, selection models in organizations have captured increasing attention (Fulk and Boyd, 1991; Markus, 1994; Johnson, 1997c). One of the major reasons for the interest in this area is the assumption that there is an optimal match between channels and organizational tasks which will lead to more effective organizational performance (Rice, 1993; Steinfield et al., 1987), a traditional theme in communication research (Rogers, 1962). Most of this research has focused on the technological attributes of channels, especially the cutting–edge electronic channels, which have received such labels as the 'new media' (Rice and Associates, 1984). As a result of the presumed revolutionary impacts of these new information processing technologies on organizational life, several major theoretical approaches have emerged to explain the underlying bases for channel selection.

In our research we examined six major competing approaches: social information processing, decision–making, cost minimization, social presence, uncertainty reduction and appraisal.

Social information processing

One competing school for explaining channel selection is the social information processing approach, which shares many assumptions with cultural approaches, but most closely follows the work of Salancik and Pfeffer focusing on formal work groups (1977, 1978). The key tenet of a social information processing approach is that workers jointly construct their own interpretations of the workplace and that an individual's social environment affects media selection (Schmitz and Fulk, 1991).

Decision making

Another general approach to channel selection is to evaluate the appropriateness of the media for various organizational tasks. Decision making thus focuses on rational explanations of channel selection (Fulk & Boyd, 1991).

Cost minimization

Reinsch and Beswick (1990) have developed a systematic approach to cost minimization with research focusing on voice mail in an organizational setting. Based on prior work by Marschak (1968), they argue there are three areas in which organizational members might analyse costs and associated probabilities of use: access, errors and delays. Access costs relate to the actual dollar cost of channel use. Relatedly, effort costs can be associated with such factors as the amount of physical space between two potential interactants (Conrath, 1973; Dutton et al., 1982; Hiltz and Kerr, 1980; Klauss and Bass, 1982; Trevino et al., 1987), familiarity with technology (Steinfield et al. 1987), length of message, and complexity (Daft and Lengel, 1986). Error costs reflect possibilities of discrepancies in signals. Blame can be attached to the user of any media which results in these discrepancies. Relatedly, a channels capacity to produce documentation may be important for its selection. A preference for avoiding blame can result in preferences for media which promote the delivery of messages even in asynchronous situations and with multiple channels, since they enhance the likelihood that the intended party will receive a message.

Social presence

Because face–to–face communication uses all of the senses, has immediate feedback, and is more spontaneous, it has become the 'standard' against which other channels are evaluated (Durlak, 1987). This emphasis on face–to–face communication is related to the notion of social presence of a particular medium. Social presence refers to the degree to which a channel approximates to the personal characteristics of face–to–face interaction (Durlak, 1987), and has its roots in the work of Short et al. (1976) on teleconferencing. Social presence approaches generally argue that mediated channels filter out non–verbal cues that make more salient the presence of other interactants (Walther, 1994). Social presence has been found to predict the perceived utility of media by managers (Ruchinskas, 1983) and it is generally accepted that people will be most receptive to communication channels that reveal the presence of others (Sullivan, 1995).

Uncertainty reduction

Researchers concerned with technological impacts on communication have come to classify both social presence arguments and media richness as two representatives of the media characteristics school (Fulk et al., 1987; Steinfield et al., 1987). These approaches argue that individuals make rational decisions concerning the most appropriate media for any one particular communication task (Fulk et al., 1987). Media richness approaches argue that the information processing requirements of individuals are a function of equivocality and/or uncertainty, terms that are frequently used interchangeably in the literature. As equivocality increases, more personal, 'rich' forms of communication are sought to substitute for more impersonal modes (Daft and Lengel, 1986; Lengel and Daft, 1988).

In general it has been argued that complex, non–routine tasks require more information processing than simple, routine tasks (Daft and Macintosh, 1981). As task uncertainty increases, more personal, 'rich' forms of communication substitute for more impersonal modes (Hiemstra, 1982; Picot et al., 1982; Van de Ven et al., 1976). Communication media or channels differ in their inherent capacity to process rich information. 'Information richness is defined as the ability of information to change understanding within a time interval' (Daft and Lengel, 1986, p. 560). Thus media of low richness (for example impersonal written documents) are effective for processing well–understood messages and standardized data, while media of high richness (for example face–to–face meetings) are necessary to process information high in equivocality and uncertainty. So individuals will ultimately choose channels which match the level of uncertainty reduction they feel is required in any one information processing task (Sitkin et al., 1992). If a problem is extremely complex, then face–to–face discussions may be the only way to address it.

Appraisal

A model of Media Exposure and Appraisal (MEA) that has been tested on a variety of channels and in a variety of international settings (Johnson and Meischke, 1993b; Johnson, Donohue et al., 1995a) suggests that receiver appraisals predict media usage. Appraisal factors such as editorial tone and communication potential primarily relate to message content attributes. Editorial tone reflects an individual's perception of the credibility and intentions of a source. If individuals perceive that a source has motives other than the mere provision of information, then this will weigh heavily in their exposure decisions. Communication potential refers to an individual's perception of the manner in which information is presented. This dimension relates to issues of style and comprehension. For example is an article in a company newsletter visually stimulating and well written? Comprehension has been found to be a critical factor in determining the selection of technical reading material by engineers (Allen, 1977).

Summary

Empirical research directly comparing these contrasting perspectives has not been unequivocally supportive of any of the above positions (for example Contractor et al., 1996; Fulk and Boyd, 1991; Markus, 1994; Rice, 1993). Media richness perspectives have often been faced with contradictory findings in empirical research, in part attributable to the unexpected impacts of new media of communication (Fulk and Boyd, 1991). Steinfield et al. (1987), in reviewing the literature on social presence, have found some moderate support in laboratory contexts, but in general they found that social presence only accounts for a small proportion of the variance in media behaviour. Social information processing has also been subject to contradictory empirical findings (Rice and Aydin, 1991). Theoretical work is still evolving in this area, demonstrating a commendable capacity to incorporate new research findings and theoretical arguments, with recent arguments that these different theoretical perspectives are complementary rather than competing (Webster and Trevino, 1995).

Interpersonal Channels

While there may be an infinite variety of communication channels that could be used to transmit information, the literature has given clear primacy to interpersonal communication in social networks (Rogers, 2003). The capacity of interpersonal channels to provide social support and enhanced confidence in the outcomes of an innovation can be crucial to the ultimate adoption of innovations (Fidler and Johnson, 1984; Valente, 1995). Interpersonal channels generally have been found to be more useful in transmitting highly complex subject matter (Picot et al., 1982; Tushman, 1978). They are more flexible than mediated channels, they can activate more senses, and they can be more attuned to the specific problems of receivers (Picot et al., 1982; Rogers and Shoemaker, 1971; Tushman, 1978). Interpersonal channels also can carry more information through a variety of codes; as a result of this 'richness' of channel, they are in a better position to reduce uncertainty caused by the complexity of organizational settings (Picot et al., 1982). In addition the more modalities an innovation is communicated through, the more likely it is to be diffused by managers to workers (Fidler and Johnson, 1984).

Typically more personal channels are more likely to be effective in the diffusion of information, since they meet the specific needs and questions of the receivers because of the immediacy of feedback and the situation specificity of the channel (Johnson, 1993). Indeed the very complexity of most innovations may require more intensive interaction to arrive at high-quality decisions (Tushman, 1978). As a result there is an inherent reduction of uncertainty involved in the use of these channels, since they lead to increased understanding of a proposed innovation.

Advocating change necessarily results in increased uncertainty, which can lead to resistance to innovation by adoption units (Katz and Kahn, 1978). Communication plays a key role in overcoming resistance to innovations and in the reduction of uncertainty (Nyblom et al., 2003). Complexity and risk are elements of uncertainty that are crucial to the ultimate implementation of innovations. Complexity in this context relates to the number of potential alternatives perceived in an innovation adoption. Risk is the perceived consequences to the adoption unit associated with the implementation of an innovation (Fidler and Johnson, 1984). The perception of risk is often a result of a lack of knowledge concerning the implications of an innovation (Fidler and Johnson, 1984), which necessitates additional information transfer to reduce uncertainty. The more risky the adoption of an innovation, the more likely it is that an adoption unit will be resistant, requiring more rewards or influence attempts by the decision unit before the acquiescing of the adoption unit in the implementation of an innovation (Zaltman and Duncan, 1977).

Across all of the theoretical perspectives the results (see Table 5.1) revealed generally high evaluations, with slightly lower ones for cost minimization and characteristics, with little differences across PDs, OMs and TSMs for interpersonal channels (for more detail see Johnson et al., 2000; Chang and Johnson, 2001). For example social presence, a key factor in interpersonal communication, was essentially rated 9 on an 11–point scale by all functional groups.

Table 5.1 Means for interpersonal channel

Perspective	Functional groups		
	Project directors (n = 8)	Outreach Managers (n = 17)	Telephone service managers (n = 18)
Social information processing	8.2	8.2	8.2
Decision-making	8.3	7.0	7.8
Cost minimization	7.5	7.6	7.2
Social presence	9.0	9.0	8.9
Uncertainty reduction	8.0	7.3	7.8
Characteristics	6.5	7.9	7.4

Note: N = 43

Table 5.2 Means for e-mail channel

Perspective	Functional groups		
	Project directors (n = 9)	Outreach managers (n = 14)	Telephone service managers (n = 18)
Social information processing	7.3	6.7	6.7
Decision-making	5.3	4.0	4.8
Cost minimization	6.9	6.2	7.5
Social presence	4.6	3.8	4.0
Uncertainty reduction	7.4	6.9	7.6
Characteristics	6.8	7.5	7.3

Note: N = 41

E-mail

In this time period, there was generally one computer shared in each RO devoted to the FTS–2000 e–mail system. The PDs and TSMs used this channel the most often because they had greater access and occasion to use it. PDs relied on e–mail for operational and coordination matters and TSMs were often alerted to breaking news stories that might stimulate calls to the CIS through FTS–2000 e–mail (Johnson et al., 1994b). OMs often did not have easy access to it because they were often off–site, travelling to intermediary organizations. Similar to other findings, the OCC staff could employ e–mail, even though it is a lean medium, because of the high volumes of messages it enables them to send efficiently (Schmitz, 1988; Markus, 1994). Interestingly, e–mail can be used to increase control by organizations of outlying branches, which can also lead to conflict (Garton and Wellman, 1995). Like many other organizations during this period (Markus, 1994), FTS–2000 e–mail, which by contract must be downloaded twice each day in the RO, was initially accessible only through one terminal in most offices, which was also used for other, often more pressing purposes (Wooldridge et al., 1993). The level of computerization of the various offices also differed substantially, with some offices having LAN systems that somewhat ameliorated this problem.

As a result of these difficulties, evaluations for the FTS–2000 e–mail channel were generally lower than interpersonal, especially for social presence and decision–making perspectives (see Table 5.2), with many individual items having modal responses of 0 (Johnson et al., 1994a). When respondents were asked in an open–ended question which communication mode needed improvement, the most frequent response was FTS–2000 e–mail, followed by other e–mail systems (Johnson et al., 1995). Some members of the CIS, because of these various difficulties, turned to public carrier e–mail systems (for example Prodigy, Compuserve). Eventually, because of the continued pattern of problems with the FTS–2000 e–mail system, it was abandoned in favour of Internet hook–ups.

Table 5.3 Means for written and facsimile channel

Perspective	Functional groups		
	Project directors (n = 9)	Outreach managers (n = 17)	Telephone service managers (n = 18)
Social information processing	7.0	6.4	6.5
Decision-making	5.8	4.7	4.6
Cost minimization	8.4	7.6	7.4
Social presence	5.3	4.7	3.9
Uncertainty reduction	7.7	6.4	6.9
Characteristics	7.3	7.2	7.3

Note: (N = 44)

Written and Facsimile Communication

Documentary research essentially focuses on the operations of a formal communication system within an organization. Written documents (for example memorandums, news clips, news releases, standard mailings such as the Weekly Package) (see Chapter 3) constituted formal communication. During this period there was rapid diffusion of fax communication for written messages in the CIS system. In addition during this time period the Weekly Package and other authoritative written documents were increasingly placed on the Internet. It quickly came to supplant some forms of written communication and was used to convey traditional written forms such as memos more rapidly.

Respondents also had differences in perceptions of how they evaluated written (including formal memoranda, the Weekly Package and fax) channels of communication (Johnson, Berkowitz et al., 1994b). Again the means for the decision–making and social presence perspectives especially were lower than for interpersonal channels (see Table 5.3). However as could be expected, these channels received the highest evaluation for cost minimization. Reflecting the new roles defined in the new contract, for both written and e–mail, lower evaluations were reported for uncertainty reduction for OMs than for the other functional groups (Johnson et al., 2000).

5.3 KNOWLEDGE NETWORKS

Needless to say, there are considerable overlaps between innovation processes and KM ones for network analysis, with knowledge sharing and creation critical to both. Social networking technology is viewed as a key feature of modern business approaches to how knowledge spreads within a company (Cross et al., 2003; Waters, 2004). However as one moves towards implementation, with similar moves from tacit to explicit knowledge, the characteristics of the essential networks needs to change as well. In this section, I will discuss these parallels in much more detail, focusing on the relation of key network concepts to knowledge transfer, particularly in reference to the distinction between tacit and explicit knowledge, and the classic innovation stages of creation, adoption and implementation (See Table 5.4).

Knowledge transfer has been a compelling issue in a variety of areas including technology transfer between developed and developing nations, between organizations, and within organizations. Here I will primarily focus on internal organizational transfer, given our focus on intraorganizational networks. Since knowledge transfer among organizational units can provide opportunities for learning, cooperation and creativity, it has been directly related to organizational innovation (Tsai, 2001). To be effective, transfer implies a level of understanding that enables action (Jensen and Meckling,

1995).

Tacit versus Explicit

Fundamentally two types of knowledge may be spread in communication networks (Nonaka, 1991). Explicit knowledge is easily transferred because it can be encoded in a widely recognized symbol system. In the network literature this has also been referred to as migratory knowledge since it refers to information in books, designs, blueprints and so on that can be easily moved from one location to another (Monge and Contractor, 2003). In economics similar notions underlie the concept of general knowledge which is relatively inexpensive to transfer (Jensen and Meckling, 1995).

Tacit knowledge presents special challenges and can only be spread under exceptional conditions. This has also been referred to as embedded knowledge that is associated with craftsmanship and unique talents and skills that are particularly difficult to transfer across organizational or group boundaries (Monge and Contractor, 2003) or in economics – specific knowledge (Jensen and Meckling, 1995). This type of knowledge has been described as 'sticky' because it is difficult to spread (Tsai, 2001) due to such issues as causal ambiguity, absorptive capacity, retentive capacity, and the arduousness (for example maintaining it over a distance) of the relationship (Szulanski, 1996).

Key Relational Issues

Since network analysis is essentially a means of representing patterns of linkages, the quality of these relationships become important determinants of the patterns of linkages for individuals. So the overall satisfaction of an individual with his or her linkages with others can affect their frequency, duration and ultimately the possibilities of knowledge transfer. Here I will focus on how such fundamental issues as trust, codification, redundancy, social contagion and influence related to knowledge sharing and innovation stage (see Table 5.4).

Trust

Trust is an essential ingredient of long–term collaborative relationships in collectivities (Amabile et al., 2001; Davenport and Prusak, 1998; Goodman et al., 1998; Monge and Contractor, 2003; Powell, 1990; Smith et al., 1995), and may be the most important attribute of network relations, at least in market terms (Burt, 1992, 2000; DeBresson and Amesse, 1991; Finlay and Coverdill, 2000; Frances et al., 1991; Gulati, 1995; Hakansson and Sharma,

1996). Many have argued it is the key ingredient for successful KM (for example Abrams et al., 2003; Wallace, 2001; Ford, 2003; Lesser and Prusak, 2004; Prusak and Cohen, 2004). It is especially important in spreading tacit knowledge because of its often private character.

Table 5.4 Network analysis parallels between knowledge transfer and innovation stage

Network	Knowledge transfer			Innovation stage	
Concept	Tacit	Explicit	Creative	Adoption	Imple–mentation
Key relational issue	Trust	Codifi–cation	Non–redundant	Contagion	Influence
Homophily	High	Low	Low	Mediated	High
Multiplexity	High	Low	Low	Low	High
Differentiation	High	Low	High	Mediated	Low
Integration	Low	High	Low	Weak ties	High

The classic network analysis research results summarized in Reynolds and Johnson (1982) suggested that liaisons were more open in their communication with other organizational members, with liaisons being more receptive to differing types of communication encounters, and often sought out by others in their communication networks. Indeed liaisons may emerge because others initiate contact with them, partly because they perceive liaisons as more open and trustworthy. As a result liaisons become sources of scarce and valuable information, which results from the wide diversity of their contacts.

Of course trust may have many bases (Ford, 2003; Levin et al., 2004): process–based trust results from recurrent transactions, characteristic–based trust results from social similarity, and institutionally–based trust is tied to formal social structures (Bradach and Eccles, 1989). Thus people would be more likely to trust individuals with whom they have had past successful relationships, who are homophilous, key figures then in knowledge networks, within an institutional framework that has strong norms of conduct and associated penalties. Trust emerges in reciprocal relationships, with reciprocity norms encouraging symmetrical relations needed to clarify new knowledge (Schulz, 2001). Relational and identity–based trust have been argued to be particularly important for CoPs (Ford, 2003).

Codification

Knowledge codification represents the translation of explicit knowledge into some written or visual format (Ford, 2003). It can increase the quality and speed of knowledge creation and distribution (Kayworth and Leidner, 2003). While much attention has been paid to content in network analysis, the degree to which network members share similar meaning has received somewhat less attention, although some of the work on semantic networks touches on this issue and the distinction made between manifest and latent link properties discussed by Johnson (1993) also addresses the issue. Fundamentally, for explicit knowledge to be transferred, there must be a shared symbol system with common meanings for the same symbols among network members. This codification can take many forms: maps, documents, diagrams and so on (Ford, 2003).

Redundancy

Highly redundant linkages impair creativity, in part, because clique members have the same knowledge base that results in similar world–views. Non–redundant linkages have often been associated with weak ties and the spread of novel information in social systems. The strength of weak ties is perhaps the most well–known concept related to network analysis. It refers to our less–developed relationships that are more limited in geographic range, time commitments and depth of emotional bonds (Adelman et al., 1987; Weimann, 1983). This concept has been intimately tied to the flow of information within organizations and by definition is removed from stronger social bonds, such as influence and multiplex relations (Weimann, 1983). Weak ties notions are derived from the work of Granovetter (1973) on how people acquire information related to potential jobs. It turns out that the most useful information comes from individuals in a person's extended networks; casual acquaintances and friends of friends. This information is the most useful precisely because it comes from infrequent or weak contacts. Strong contacts are likely to be people with whom there is a constant sharing of the same information; as a result individuals within these groupings have come to have the same information base. However information from outside this base gives unique perspectives and, in some instances, strategic advantages over competitors in a person's immediate network.

Weak ties are also crucial to integrating larger social systems, especially in terms of the nature of communication linkages between disparate groups (Friedkin, 1980, 1982; Weimann, 1983). Granovetter (1982) now maintains that this bridging function between different groups is a limiting condition necessary for the effects of weak ties to be evidenced. In highly differentiated networks like the CIS, weak ties are critical for the diffusion of innovations (Valente, 1995). Because new ideas are risky, workers initially share their ideas first with members of their immediate network, which can provide the support an individual needs to reach individuals with whom they do not have strong ties (Ray, 1987). The number of messages that an individual is exposed to in their interpersonal communication network can reduce uncertainty, which in turn increases their willingness to participate in innovation processes and the ultimate likelihood that an innovation will be successfully implemented.

However weak ties may be discouraged in organizations because of concerns over loyalty to one's immediate work unit and questions of control of organizational members. Strong ties may also be preferred because they are more likely to be stable and because, as a result of the depth of their relationship, individuals may be willing to delay immediate gratifications from the other person associated with equity demands (Albrecht and Adelman, 1987c). Individuals to whom an individual is strongly tied may also be more readily accessible and more willing to be of assistance (Granovetter, 1982). Strong ties are also essential for the sharing of tacit knowledge.

Weak ties provide critical informational support because they transcend the limitations of our strong ties, and because, as often happens in organizations, our strong ties can be disrupted or unavailable (Adelman et al., 1987). Thus weak ties may be useful for discussing things you do not want to reveal to your close work associates, providing a place for an individual to experiment, extending access to information, promoting social comparison and fostering a sense of community (Adelman et al., 1987).

Generally it has been argued that diversity in perspective is a necessary precondition for innovation and creativity (Albrecht and Hall, 1989). Individuals with many weak ties are exposed to information about innovation from a variety of sources. They are likely to perceive that they work in an innovative environment and be exposed to innovation–related knowledge. Information from diverse sources gives unique perspectives and is thus often a source of creative ideas (see Table 5.4). Interestingly, while weak ties are necessary for innovation, individuals may be less willing to share novel ideas with someone whom they know only casually because they are uncertain about the other's reaction (Albrecht and Hall, 1989).

Social Contagion

Over the last several years a major debate has developed within the innovation literature about whether direct communication or forces related to competition are the major motive forces for innovation adoption within social systems (see Table 5.4). Burt (1980) has argued that one motive force for innovation is the presence of competitors who occupy structurally similar positions. If competitors adopt an innovation and it is successful, this would put another individual at a competitive disadvantage. Thus the other has a structural interest in adopting innovations. This entails an individual will adopt an innovation when a structurally similar alter does even if they are not in direct communication contact. From this theoretical framework, members of the CIS systems may adopt and implement innovations because they perceive there is a competitive advantage vis–a–vis other ROs in doing so. An interesting twist to these arguments is that a prominent person may be even more compelled to adopt normative innovations because they want to remain prominent (Burt, 1980).

In contrast, a cohesion perspective, perhaps best represented in the work of Rogers and his colleagues (Rogers, 1983; Rogers and Kincaid, 1981), would suggest that direct communication results in changes in the individual that result in the adoption of innovations. Thus enthusiastic supporters of an innovation, such as those in CoPs, may directly communicate with members of other ROs who were not involved in its development. This enthusiasm is contagious and the members of the other ROs decide to adopt the innovation because of the credibility and persuasiveness of their colleagues.

Cohesion and structural equivalence serve as competing theoretical explanations of the impact of social context (the structural configuration of communication relationships) on social contagion processes. Cohesion perspectives essentially argue that communication contacts determine the development of norms. Thus cohesion focuses on the socializing effect of discussions. The central assumption of the cohesion perspective is that the more frequent and empathetic the communication between individuals, the more likely their opinions and behaviours will resemble each other's (Burt, 1987).

Structural equivalence focuses on competition. In this view, supervisors could be expected to hold views similar to other supervisors because of their potential competitive roles in the network. This position requires that they maintain certain attitudes and behaviours. Thus individuals may be the focus of similar information, requests and demands from members of their role set, creating an information field which when internalized creates even more powerful pressures to conform than direct discussions with others. Thus two OMs at different ROs may come to hold similar views of the world, even though they never actually discuss them directly with each other, which may impact upon overall volumes of communication in a network.

Social contagion suggests an individual reaches evaluations about ambiguous objects, such as communication media, through a social process in which the evaluations of all the proximate others in the system are weighed (Burt, 1982; Rice and Aydin, 1991). As a result, people who are proximate with each other (in terms of their communication linkages) in the social structure tend to develop 'consensual standards' (Burt, 1982, p. 110) toward ambiguous objects. These consensual standards will trigger a homogeneous attitude. What one person says or does is contagious for other people within the same group. Thus this theory suggests that ambiguous objects stimulate the contagion process which in turn leads to a social norm regarding a particular practice within social groups.

However the contagion process, the social mechanism, can operate in two conceptually related yet distinctive ways: cohesion and structural equivalence. The first proximate mechanism that brings homogeneity is cohesion (Burt and Doreian, 1982; Burt, 1987; Burt and Uchiyama, 1989; Friedkin, 1984). The cohesion model has a long history of being used as a predictor of attitudes and beliefs in the social sciences (see a brief review by Burt, 1987, pp. 1289–90). The model posits that homophily between ego (the focal individual, the object of influence) and the alter (others in a network who may influence the ego) can be predicted by the strength of their intense and mutual relations with one another. 'By communicating their uncertainties to one another regarding some empirically ambiguous object, people socialize one another so as to arrive at a consensual evaluation of the object' (Burt and Doreian, 1982, p. 112). Thus the more frequent and empathic the bond is between ego and alter, the more likely they come to share attitudinal and behavioural tendencies. As summarized in Hartman and Johnson (1989), 'The ego is able to come to a normative understanding of the costs and benefits of specific actions and opinions in terms of the people with whom the discussions are held and thus reduce the ego's level of uncertainty' (p. 524). Where cohesion concerns influential relations among individuals within a primary group, structural equivalence concerns relational patterns among individuals who occupy particular positions (Burt, 1982, 1987). In the structural equivalence model, the driving force for similarity in perceptions is competition between ego and alter. The more the alter is able to substitute for the ego in the ego's role relations, the more pressure the ego feels to conform to the alter's attitudes or behaviours. 'The ego comes to a normative understanding of the costs and benefits of the alter filling his or her role and a social understanding that is shared by others in similar roles' (Hartman and Johnson, 1989, p. 525). From a structural equivalence perspective, direct communication contacts between individuals are not necessary for the development of a shared frame of reference (Burt, 1982, 1987). Hartman and Johnson (1989) further explained that structurally equivalent individuals may experience more pressure toward uniformity because they 'may be the focus of similar information, requests, and demands from members of their role set, creating an information field in which they are embedded, which, when internalized, creates even more powerful pressures to conform than discussions with similar alters' (p. 525). Employees in different functional roles rely on structurally equivalent referents for job–related information and on cohesive referents for general organizational information (Shah, 1998). In sum, both cohesion and structural equivalence approaches to social contagion have been linked to innovation adoption, with the former the traditional approach and the latter offering important new insights (see Table 5.4).

Influence

Fidler and Johnson (1984) described systematically the consequences of using various types of influence processes in innovation implementation, a key relational issue in Table 5.4. Using the classic framework of French and Raven (1959), they discussed the relatively high communication costs of the use of sanction and persuasion and the low costs of using legitimate and referent power. They also contrasted the higher levels of involvement induced by classic influence types of power represented by persuasion, expert and referent power, with the lower levels of involvement resulting from sanction and legitimate power. Expert power is obviously particularly important for KM and represents some special problems for the person exercising it. If every step leading to a judgement must be explained to the other party, especially in situations of high tacit knowledge, than very high communication costs may be involved. On the other hand, if just a summative answer is needed, then its costs may be as low as those of legitimate power. Paradoxically the more an expert needs to explain, the less power they may ultimately have since they are transferring their basis of influence to the other.

Homophily

Homophily has generally been considered a central communication variable (Monge and Contractor, 2003; Rogers, 2003; McCrosky et al., 1975). More specifically it has been suggested it enhances diffusion effects and leads to more effective communication in cancer control consortia (McKinney et al., 1992). It has traditionally been defined as the degree to which parties 'are similar in certain attributes, such as beliefs, education, socio–economic status and the like' (Rogers, 2003, p. 19). The degree of similarity between parties, which relates directly to perceived social distance, has been a central issue in both intercultural (for example Sarbaugh, 1979) and organizational (Johnson, 1993) communication theory, since there appears to be a natural tendency for people to communicate mostly with others like themselves

(Rogers, 2003; Tsui and O'Reilly, 1989; Zenger and Lawrence, 1989). It has been argued that effective communication, which results in fewer misunderstandings, is more likely to occur between homophilous communicators (McCrosky et al., 1975; Rogers, 2003), suggesting high levels of homophily are necessary for tacit knowledge transfer (See Table 5.4).

Homophilous communicators are also more likely to be willing to accept information (Berscheid, 1966) and thus be subject to the greater influence necessary for implementation. Generally it has been found that increases in perceived similarity lead to closer relationships cross–culturally and that the communication in these relationships tends to be more effective (Gudykunst and Kim, 1984; Rogers, 2003). Or stated in another way, 'People's perception of other people determine to a major extent whether there is a communication attempt made' (McCrosky et al., 1975, p. 323). This in turn is a major stumbling block for the exchange of information between diverse parties essential to creativity (Kanter, 1988b).

Multiplexity

Multiplexity refers to the nature of overlap, or correspondence, between differing networks (for example friendship as opposed to work) (Farace and Mabee, 1980; Rogers and Kincaid, 1981) which obviously has direct connections to homophily. 'The relation of one person to another is multiplex to the extent that there is more than one type of relation between the first person and the second' (Burt, 1983, pp. 37). The nature of these overlaps is of great pragmatic concern, since it can suggest the inherent capabilities of individual actors within systems, and it also has rich implications for the understanding of social systems generally (Reynolds and Johnson, 1982; Roberts and O'Reilly, 1979). Organizations are actually composed of a variety of overlapping and interrelated networks of differing functions (Jablin, 1980); however functional dimensions are but one of the many dimensions along which network linkages can be multiplexed (see Eisenberg et al., 1985; Minor, 1983; Tichy et al., 1979).

The degree of multiplexity has been related to such issues as the intimacy of relationships (Minor, 1983), temporal stability of relationships (Minor, 1983; Mitchell, 1969; Rogers and Kincaid, 1981), reduction of uncertainty (Albrecht and Ropp, 1984), status (Albrecht and Ropp, 1984), the degree of control of a clique over its members (Rogers and Agarwala–Rogers, 1976), performance (Roberts and O'Reilly, 1979), redundancy of channels (Mitchell, 1969) and the diffusion of information within networks (Minor, 1983). High levels of multiplexity promote deep relations of the sort necessary for tacit knowledge transfer (see Table 5.4).

Multiplexity is also crucial to processes of social contagion, since it can be expected that individuals with a high degree of participation across different types of networks might be more affected by contagion–related influence processes than those individuals involved in only one type of network (Hartman and Johnson, 1990). The breadth of someone's linkages might serve to provide an individual with a variety of information sources, as well as repetition of certain effects, which determine such contagion–related processes as attitude change. Thus the high relationship posited between multiplexity and implementation in Table 5.4 (Foray, 2001). Conversely low levels of multiplexity, associated with strength of weak ties perspectives, are associated with creativity and the diffusion processes associated with adoption. Interestingly the balance needed between cohesion within groups associated with high levels of work interdependence and associated cooperation, and the structural holes that need to be bridged by managers through weak ties, often determine the relative adaptability of organizations to change (Gargiulo and Benassi, 2000).

Differentiation and Integration

Kanter (1983) has offered compelling arguments that organizations which are segmented into different functional groups with strong barriers, especially informal rule structures, between them are not going to be capable of generating or diffusing innovations. Differentiation is necessary for the synergy essential to the creation of ideas, partly through the creation of requisite variety (Van de Ven, 1986), but it also makes it difficult to insure the system–wide consensus necessary for their implementation. However Hage (1999) has suggested that a complex division of labour is the key overlooked factor in promoting organizational innovation. Differentiation refers to the tendency of organizations to divide into more and more groups in order to specialize their labour, become more sophisticated, larger and competitive (Katz and Kahn, 1978). We discussed this concept in particular detail, especially in regard to integrating mechanisms, in Chapter 3. Unfortunately the differentiation of skills required by complex modern organizations makes it increasingly unlikely that differing functional specialties will have similarities in outlooks (Lawrence and Lorsch, 1967a, b, c) which also means there are relatively simple explicit code systems (for example numbers) across groups in contemporary organizations. Differentiation also entails that implementation is more likely to be successful within the confines of a particular specialized unit, which implies widely varying implementation stories for the same innovation across units.

As the organization becomes more and more divided into functional subgroups, a corresponding pressure arises to integrate all of these groups with common organizational goals. The principal mechanisms employed by traditional organizations to achieve integration have included line management structure, cross–organizational teams and committees, individual coordinators, coordinating departments, and formalized plans and procedures, all of which communicatively link organizational groups together for the purposes of achieving coordination toward common organizational goals (Lawrence and Lorsch, 1967a, b, c; Galbraith, 1995). However as Lawrence and Lorsch also argued, 'an indiscriminate increase in connectedness can be a drag on productivity, as people get bogged down in maintaining all their relationships' (Cross et al., 2004, p. 51). Indeed dense communication within organizations has been found to be related to low production, low morale and an experience of chaos (Krackhardt, 1994). Network analysis research has shown considerable interest in the integration related to bridging groups over the years, particularly in relationship to network linking roles, centrality, brokerage and range.

Bridging Gaps in Social Structures

Network analysis, which focuses on relationships between entities, such as the researchers and practitioners in the CISRC, is one approach to examining how separate parties are brought together in social structures. Classical network approaches focus on linking roles such as liaisons, with often explicit connections to formal structures, while more modern approaches have emphasized market–driven behaviours (Johnson, 2004). Ron Burt (1992, 2000) argues that much market–oriented competitive behaviour, which is endemic in new organizational forms, can be understood in terms of the access of individuals to 'holes' in network structures. Structural holes are gaps or separations in communication network relationships and are framed as 'disconnections or nonequivalencies between players in an arena' (Burt, 1992, pp. 1–2). These holes are discontinuities in a social structure that create opportunities for information access to certain actors. Individuals can turn such relationships into 'social capital' that gives them strategic advantage in the competition for scarce resources (Burt, 1992, 2000).

A structural hole separates two entities with dissimilar network relationships who are not connected to each other, but could be. Structural holes normally exist in a functioning network since network members do not share equal access to information or resources (Burt, 1992). They provide opportunities for brokerage since actors can pursue their autonomous interests, free of the constraints imposed by cohesive groupings (Burt, 1991). The information benefits of structural positioning revolve around the classic question of who knows about opportunities, who participates and when they participate. Individuals who are correctly positioned know about key pieces of information earlier than others because of their unique pattern of ties. They can also gatekeep (or at least slow the progress of) the distribution of this information to others, and they may have an idea of when and how the information is likely to diffuse to others in the social system (Burt, 2000). A special case of brokerage comes when a person brokers relationships between asymmetrical groups. So someone who controls access to authority in an organization (Wellman, 1988), or to resources in more informal coalitions, has additional possibilities for influence. Thus brokers have 'betweenness' centrality and therefore can facilitate, impede or bias the transmission of messages from different groups (Freeman, 1977).

Perhaps the most interesting application to date of structural hole arguments comes in its implication for promotion. Burt (1992, 2000) has found that managers with networks rich in structural holes get promoted faster and at a younger age than their competitors. This is partially because the higher you go in organizations, the more promotion is based on what you can accomplish with other people. More recently Burt (2003) has also found an association between innovative ideas and the structural holes of managers. Others have extended Burt's work, highlighting its importance as a 'starting point for conceptualizing the strategic use of network building to advance a given set of interests' (Pollock et al., 2004, p. 50).

Predating the structural hole and related weak ties literatures is one that focused specifically on linking roles in organizations that operated in systems frameworks. The liaison communication network role by definition occupies a structural hole, since it links two or more groups, while not being a member of any one of them (Johnson, 1993). An individual's network communication role is determined by the overall pattern of his or her communication relationships (or linkages) with others. Reynolds and Johnson (1982) conducted an early, comprehensive review of research related to liaisons. The strategic positioning of liaisons has earned them the label of 'linking pins', which through their promotion of more positive climates and successful coordination of organizational functions, serve to hold a formal organizational hierarchy together (Likert, 1967). The role of the liaison in the coordination and control of organizational activities is closely tied to the concepts of integration and differentiation. That is, as a social system divides into more and more specialized groups, greater efforts have to be made at pulling these groups together through integrating mechanisms (Galbraith, 1973; Lawrence and Lorsch, 1967a, b, c). These integrating mechanisms are crucial to system survival, since without them it would be a collection of groups each going off in its own direction. Typically, liaisons are the most efficient personal integrating mechanism between people, who, because of their strategic positioning, can more easily broker relations between disparate groups. Due to their centrality and their direct linkages with others, liaisons can reduce the probability of message distortion, reduce information load, and increase the timeliness of communication (Reynolds and Johnson, 1982).

Unfortunately however, liaisons are relatively rare in organizations, pointing to dilemmas for individuals who occupy these roles; this is reflected in the generally low level of communication between diverse groups (Farace and Johnson, 1974), and is the fundamental reason why structural holes provide such opportunities for individuals. Given their central role in organizations, it is important to understand the factors that make it more likely that an individual will come to assume this role. These factors also relate directly to the capacity of individuals to broker structural holes.

Relational (for example openness) and cognitive factors (for example uncertainty management) are essential to a liaison's role performance and are necessary for liaison emergence; indeed, they are often 'push' factors that impel others to seek out liaisons, thus drawing them into this role in social systems. Motivational, or 'pull', factors determine whether or not an individual will aspire to such a role and perform effectively within it (Reynolds and Johnson, 1982). This is the major contribution of Burt (1992) who specifically articulates a number of entrepreneurial reasons that pull individuals into brokerage roles. The emergent, voluntary nature of network linkages is in part a picture of the choices that organizational members make in their communication relationships. Thus they may describe, in part, the need fulfilment strategies of members (Reynolds and Johnson, 1982). Both of these approaches blend individual action and structure by focusing on motivations that might drive an actor to fill these structural gaps. SHBs often are the key players in brokering knowledge transfer in organizations.

Linking roles

An individual's communication role is determined by the overall pattern of his or her communication linkages with others. Some individuals, labelled non–participants, are relatively uninvolved in a network. Participants, on the other hand, form intense patterns which represent communication groups and linkages between these groups. Several research studies have found key differences between these two kinds of individuals, with participants being more outgoing, influential, satisfied (Goldhaber et al., 1978) and having more coherent cognitive structures (Albrecht, 1979), and non–participants deliberately withholding information, having lower satisfaction with communication (Roberts and O'Reilly, 1979), and reporting less identification, variety, feedback and required interaction (Moch, 1980).

Classical network approaches focus on linking roles such as liaisons, with often explicit connections to formal structures, while more modern approaches, such as the SHB one, have emphasized market–driven behaviours (Johnson, 2004). The liaison role has also been conceived as playing a key role in differentiation and integration (Reynolds and Johnson, 1982). Indeed integration is a very delicate thing, since groups fairly rapidly come to common perspectives, losing the value of diversity (Kanter, 1988b), increasing the importance of brokers who can maintain diversity while transferring information critical to creative processes. Network position, which relates to access to knowledge, and the absorptive capacity, which relates to capacity to learn, of network entities have been directly related to the success of knowledge transfer (Tsai, 2001). Even in very large networks, a few central information brokers are the fulcrum on which everything depends (Watts, 2003).

Centrality

Individual positioning indices, such as anchorage (see Barnes, 1972) and integrativeness (see Farace and Mabee, 1980; Wigand, 1977), try to mathematically capture an individual's location within the configuration of communication relationships within a network. As with most network indices there are a variety of ways of calculating indices for individual positioning which can have important implications for relationships to non–network variables. For example Brass (1981) reports a study in which three different individual positioning measures were used in a study of a newspaper to examine their impact on job characteristics and such organizational outcome variables as satisfaction. Centrality referred to the extent to which a worker could reach others in the network through a minimum number of links. Criticality revealed the degree to which an individual's position was crucial to the flow of materials in a work–flow network. Transaction alternatives referred to whether or not redundancy was built into the system in terms of inputs to particular individuals and their outputs to others.

While centrality and criticality were strongly related to job characteristics, they had different patterns of associations, and transaction alternatives did not relate strongly to job characteristics. On the other hand, transaction alternatives and criticality had significant relationships to satisfaction, while centrality had non–significant relationships. Brass's findings point to the importance of measures of individual positioning in explaining non–network variables, and also to the importance of carefully considering the wide array of the different possible indicators in this category and carefully conceptualizing their relationships to other variables. Classically, various measures of centrality have been directly related to the strategic control of information flows, since central individuals can withhold information or distort it to suit their purposes (Freeman, 1977).

Indices associated with pathways primarily deal with how easily a message can flow from one node to another node in a network. For example reachability focuses on how many links a message must flow through to get from one node to another, usually expressed in terms of the shortest possible path, an issue which has profound implications for an individual's ultimate influence in a social system (Barnes, 1972; Mitchell, 1969) and the spread of knowledge.

In sum, as Table 5.4 reveals, network analysis has a rich set of contingent relationships with both knowledge sharing and stages of innovation. Different processes are critical in different situations, but there are also key parallels between stage and the type of knowledge sharing facilitated by networks. In the next two sections we explore some of these issues by focusing on the pattern of communication linkages in the CISRC over time and a more holistic examination of the summative pattern of influence relationships.

5.4 OVER TIME RESULTS

As we have seen, the literature suggests that in innovative organizations there should be high volumes of communication associated with participation, influence attempts and reinvention. Indicators of these impacts would include higher volumes of participants and group members, higher density of communication, increases of centrality for key members of the organization, greater redundancy in communication ties and so forth. However the literature is less clear on what the precise 'dosage' is and how often it needs to be applied. As the classic differentiation and integration literature suggests, this may be a critical issue in organizations, since too little communication makes it unlikely the 'medicine' will have its desired effect, while too much is at the very least inefficient and an 'overdose' may have damaging effects (for example opportunity costs in other areas).

We tracked the amount of communication over time for both intervention strategy communication and other work–related communication related to the CISRC innovations. In all there were 14 data collection points, timed at three–monthly intervals, designed to capture the work on the three CISRC projects from beginning to end. We used a log or diary format, focusing on a three–day period as a sampling of communication activities. Much more detail on procedures, methods and results can be found in the separate general appendix to the overall project (Johnson, Berkowitz et al., 1994a) and eight network analysis technical reports (Johnson, Chang, Berkowitz et al., 1995; Johnson, Chang, Ethington et al., 1995; Johnson, Chang, LaFrance and Meyer, 1995; Johnson, Chang, LaFrance, Meyer, Ethington and Pobocik, 1996a; Johnson, Chang, LaFrance, Meyer, Pobocik and Ethington, 1996; Johnson, Chang, Ethington et al., 1996; Johnson, Chang, Kiyoma et al., 1997; Johnson, Kiyomiya et al., 1997), as well as publications that have focused on aspects of this data (for example Johnson, Meyer et al., 1997; Johnson and Chang, 2001). The technical reports draw on basic indicators provided by two traditional network analysis programs: NEGOPY (for example communication roles) (Rice and Richards, 1985) and STRUCTURE (for example density, brokerage) (Burt, 1991).

Since it is the simplest expression of this data, and it is the basis for the calculation of all the other indices, here we will focus on the over time results for the number value of direct links in the intervention strategies interpersonal network. In other words, when a respondent reported that they were linked to someone else by discussing intervention strategy content. Remember that the networks at each time period consisted of approximately 120 people composed of the leadership of the ROs, the OCC and PP. For Time 1, there were 83 direct links, or 0.6 per cent, out of a possible 13 110 linkages. The pattern in Figure 5.1 was clear for intervention strategies direct links, starting with very low volumes of communication that increased slightly, then declined to less than 20 at the fourteenth time period.

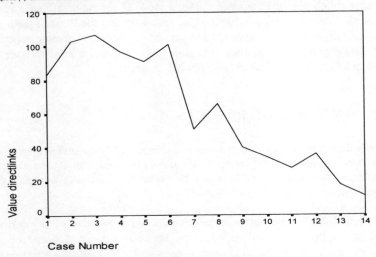

Figure 5.1 Intervention strategies links over time

At the outset, following the diffusion of innovation literature, we focused on interpersonal communication. Because of the relative lack of usage of interpersonal channels and the general perception that facsimile and electronic mail communication were beginning to supplant it, starting at the eighth time period we also gathered information in the communication logs on facsimile and electronic mail, as well as interpersonal communication. This resulted in a slight up–tick in total communication amounts initially, primarily attributable to e–mail, then a reversion to the original pattern.

Some other noteworthy findings were also apparent: (1) other work–related communication was proportionally higher (roughly at a 2:1 ratio for every data period); (2) there was some periodicity to the data, with higher rates in the winter months; and (3) there were some differences among the various network analysis indices, although they all reflect declining communication levels; for average contacts and non–redundant contacts there were more pronounced differences between other work–related and intervention strategies, reflecting the greater penetration in the former network of indirect links, which declined more notably over time. This also implies that weak, diverse links were declining in the network.

Partly because of these surprising results, and the possibility that this sampling, log approach might have missed other types of communication activity and key substantive linkages, we asked respondents for information on their more global advice–seeking during the last of the 14 data collections. In the next section I turn to a more specific examination of these results, which also give a more detailed view of informal influence in the network. We would expect that the CoP members and the PP staff, acting as change agents for their individual projects, would show greater centrality and brokerage. These network indicators are associated with such issues as critical mass, diffusion effects and tipping points.

5.5 SOCIOMETRIC RESULTS

From the outset, the plan was to mobilize and recruit CIS Project Directors to serve as 'idea champions.' ....Fortunately for the CISRC, the CIS Project Directors embraced this challenge and became highly effective idea champions within their organizations. (Marcus et al., 1998, p. S13)

As I established at the outset of this chapter, the foundation of any network analysis is the nature of relationships between entities. I have focused exclusively on communication relationships so far, but now we turn to more classic sociometric relationships to get a more global and perhaps deeper view of what happened within the CISRC. During the last data collection we asked respondents to reflect over the entire course of the project and to: 'Please indicate the individuals that you consider to have most influenced your ideas about **intervention strategies**.' Respondents could then list an unlimited number of names. (More detail on procedures and results can be found in Johnson, 2005.) The data for the sociometric network were analysed by means of UCINET 6 (Borgatti et al., 2002).

If the CISRC was working in the normative pattern described in the literature one could have certain expectations of the nature of these relationships. Firstly there would be key players who linked the consortium's disparate entities, bridging gaps across functional roles representing both researchers and practitioners. Natural candidates for these positions would be individuals in key formal roles such as the leader of the CIS, the PI of the CISRC, members of CoPs, and the PIs of the individual research projects. These key players could be expected to link more informal groups that would emerge around the individual projects, each of which had advisory groups, formal training, periodic face–to–face meetings and continued operational support during implementation, all of which one would expect would lead to the development of influence relationships. Secondly the literature implies, and the strategic importance of this consortium suggests, that this would be an area of broad concern with considerable discussion and influence attempts made during its course.

While there were certain interesting patterns related to the first expectation, again we are left with troubling findings relating to 'dosage' and volume for the second. This network consisted of approximately 185 people composed of the leadership of the ROs, the OCC and PP. Due to turnover, this network had approximately 60 more people in it than the typical quarterly data collection. It also had slightly higher levels of communication with 276 reported links, which still represented only a tiny fraction of those possible. As one might expect, it would appear that the time sampling did not capture all of the influence–related communication events (for example those at national conferences, CoP meetings) that occurred.

The Freeman–Granovetter Groups procedure found no strong ties for this sociometric influence network and 33 900 absent ones. Only 140, or 0.4 per cent of the ties, were weak. Similarly an analysis of weak components, found a 0.86 fragmentation level of nodes that could not reach each other. This entire system was apparently built on weak ties and very fragmented cliques, in fact not unlike the normative findings for innovation networks found elsewhere (Farace and Johnson, 1974). Thus all available evidence pointed to much lower levels of communication than one would expect.

Functional role differences and key players

Organizational innovation requires the fulfilment of specific key roles that guide a new idea through the innovation process. These innovation roles are carried out by members of the organization, and are commonly referred to as idea generators, sponsors and orchestrators (Galbraith, 1984). While critical to the innovation process, these roles are not formal positions, but rather informal roles that can be assumed by individuals throughout the organization.

Idea generators are the creators of the innovative ideas that could be of potential use to the organization. Idea generators initiate innovation by reformulating a particular problem through a creative perspective that they are willing to promote (Brimm, 1988). In effect, the ideas examined here were developed before the data collection period; the primary focus here has been on implementation. The CoP surrounding the CISRC was the primary sources of these ideas.

The sponsor, or idea champion, usually a management–level person, and in this case primarily from the leadership of the OCC, is responsible for recognizing the usefulness of the idea to the organization, and lending authority and resources to the innovation throughout the development and implementation period (Galbraith, 1984). The sponsor of an innovation plays a significant role in gaining organizational acceptance of it. Sponsors are committed to a particular innovation, which is demonstrated through personal identification with the innovation and its outcomes (Brimm, 1988).

The third role needed in the innovation process is that of an orchestrator. Innovations are rarely neutral. Instead they are often disruptive, and may be perceived as impinging upon the territorial rights and personal investments of others. Therefore, orchestrators are needed to manoeuvre the innovation through an organization's political process. The orchestrator must protect the innovation process by supporting idea generators, finding sponsors for innovations, and promoting the trial period and testing of innovative ideas. As the organization's political process is biased toward those who have authority and control resources, orchestrators are typically an organization's top managers.

In the case of the sociometric network it was clear from their centrality scores that there were two orchestrators, who occupied formal leadership roles in the CIS and PP respectively. Both had secondary leaders within their respective units: two middle managers within the CIS and an assistant TEAM leader within the CISRC. The PP leader also had critical linkages to internal sponsors who provided him with legitimacy and access within the CIS (Burt, 2000). A unique role was filled by the only individual who was a research project investigator and who was also a PI for one of the ROs who had an appreciable number of nominations in the sociometric network.

Members of other CoPs and emergent informal leaders were not really evident. This finding, when coupled with the fact that PP research project PIs did not report more ties than other functional roles, may indicate that the orchestrators of innovation have dropped the baton (Meyer and Johnson, 1998). The lack of communication initiated by the orchestrators of innovation to other CISRC members suggests that they are out of the loop, relatively unaware of how practitioners were appropriating their innovations. Alternatively, this finding could indicate that PP staff were primarily idea generators and not orchestrators, perhaps not a surprising finding for researchers.

Also somewhat unexpected, given their key role in implementation of the interventions, was the lack of involvement of TSMs. It would be expected that OMs would not be terribly involved, and also as expected PIs were the least–involved group. The pattern of findings for the various groups suggests the difficulties in arranging communication across them, that was also a problem for programming national conferences as we discussed in Chapter 3.

As we will see in more detail in the next chapter, organizational members who play key roles in the innovation process are likely to have more favourable attitudes toward innovations than other stakeholders. Key players are active participants in innovation who 'buy in' to the innovation process because they have a great deal at stake. Of all the groups, including surprisingly the PPs, PDs had the most cohesive influence linkages among themselves and with other key roles, primarily OCC and PPs, related to this project. In many ways, as a group they filled a crucial structural hole.

In sum, the patterns of linkages found here established one reason for the differential success of the varying types of innovation, which we will return to in more detail in the next chapter. A structure of influence was clearly in place with the formal leadership of the CISRC and CIS for continuation of the CISRC, with a vital link to the larger NCI world essential for continued funding. Not having broadly based ties for individual research projects because of the clear lack of interest of their PIs and the limited impact of their associated PDs makes them vulnerable, as we will see in more detail at the end of the next chapter, to 'tipping points', where opinion turns against them, because they have not achieved threshold and/or critical mass effects (Valente, 1995; Watts, 2003). It should come as no surprise, given these findings, that in spite of their scientific success these knowledge service delivery innovations were not subsequently incorporated more broadly in the operations of the CIS.

5.6 LESSONS LEARNED

This research offered many compelling findings related to informal communication structures impact on innovation within the CIS and the CISRC. As we have seen, these issues also relate directly to the diffusion of knowledge within consortia because of the parallels between KM and innovations. I will follow our discussion of this chapter in elucidating the lessons learned from these findings. Firstly I will focus on the empirical results of a model that attempted to untangle the relationships of formal and informal communication structures on perceived organizational innovativeness. Secondly I will examine the complex mix of communication channels available in contemporary organizations. Finally, I will discuss the most disturbing empirical finding of our research, the relatively low levels of direct communication contacts and influence relationships. I will conclude the next chapter with empirical work focused on Project 2 which brings together innovation climate and attributes with the network analysis themes that are central to this work.

Tests of a Model of Perceived Organizational Innovativeness

A continuing theme of this book has been the tension between formal and informal communication structures. Early on in this research stream we directly tested two competing models of the antecedents of perceived organizational innovativeness, presented in Figure 5.2. The chief distinction between the two models can be understood in terms of the moderator–mediator variable distinction (Baron and Kenny, 1986). Model 1, the traditional model, represents a managerial approach to understanding innovation as a planned outcome of formal structural variables. In this model the exogenous variable, formal structure, is mediated by informal structure. In turn, informal structure is then mediated by communication processes (for example communication quality, persuasiveness) to produce organizational–wide perceptions about innovation.

This general approach to the impact of structural variables, which is implicitly very popular in the literature, is exemplified by Leavitt's (1951) work on the impact of formal communication structure (notably participation in decision–making leads to improved information flow, resulting in increased productivity, and ultimately, increased job satisfaction). While these classic and more recent studies (see also Nadler and Tushman, 1987; Krackhardt, 1990) are concerned with different organizational outcomes, they are joined together by the assumption that the impact of formal structural variables on organizational outcomes is mediated by characteristics of the informal communication structure and communication processes. Model 1 tends to reify formal structures, thus reducing the extent to which the organization is perceived to be adaptable to change; it views communication as an outgrowth of formal structure, with a pattern of information flow that closely mirrors the organizational chart (Johnson, 1993). However an alternative approach has also developed implicitly over the years, especially focusing more on informal communication, that I have developed more fully in this chapter.

Model 2, the coexisting model, suggests that formal and informal structural variables are both exogenous structural variables whose effects are mediated by communication processes. In this model, perceptions about innovation are still predicted by formal structure to a certain extent, but it also recognizes that informal structures exist parallel to formal structures. In Model 2, formal structure and informal structure, as moderator and predictor variables, are at the same level in regard to their role as antecedents to perceived organizational innovativeness (Johnson, 1993). Model 2 thus acknowledges the idiosyncratic nature of informal communication contacts within an organizational network. Finally, and perhaps most salient to this study, Model 2 recognizes that informally generated emergent networks may act as catalysts for innovation, influencing the extent to which the organization is perceived to be adaptable to change (Kanter, 1983).centrality) on organizational outcomes via independence of action. Another classic study, that of Coch and French (1948), found that increased participation in decision–making led to reduced resistance to change via identification. Monge and Miller (1988) present a more recent variation of this model in their discussion of cognitive models of the participation process, in which

We empirically evaluated these two models using the first wave of the perceived organizational innovativeness data discussed in Chapter 4 and the network analysis data discussed in this chapter. Operationally the formal variables were represented by the centralization, formalization and slack resources scales; the informal variables by the prominence and range network indices, and the communication environment by the communication quality and acceptance scale. Tests of Model 2, the clearly superior model, suggested that formal and informal variables are both exogenous structural variables that determine communication environment. In this model, perceptions about innovation are still predicted by formal structure to a certain extent, but it also recognizes that informal structures exist parallel to formal structures. Somewhat similarly to structuration theory (Poole and McPhee, 1983; Riley, 1983), Model 2 suggests that there is a dual process between formal and informal structures, that determines organizational outcomes. Model 2 recognizes that informally generated emergent networks may act as a catalyst for innovation, influencing the extent to which the organization is perceived to be adaptable to change (Kanter, 1983). In short, it recognizes that both formal and informal structures have direct impacts on the communication environment.

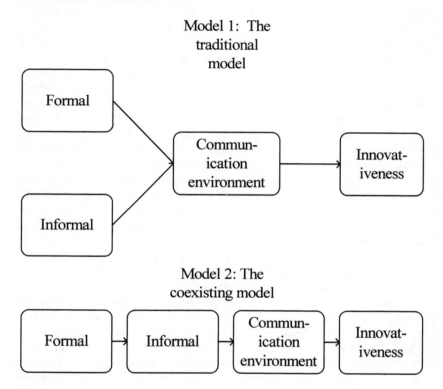

Figure 5.2 Models of perceived organizational innovativeness

Model 2, the coexisting model, accounted for substantial proportions of the variance in innovativeness, acceptance and communication quality, with communication quality and acceptance strong predictors of innovativeness. In addition all of the formal structural variables had significant impacts on acceptance, but only decentralization and formalization had impacts on communication quality. So while informal structure does not appear to mediate formal structure, communication processes do mediate the impact of structural variables on innovativeness. Overall, organizational members' perceptions that they have a stake in the decision–making process and are involved in the active exchange of ideas with other organizational members promotes perceptions of innovativeness.

Perhaps the most disappointing finding of Model 2 was that informal variables played a surprisingly small role in these processes. This result could have reflected some measurement limitations of the informal structural variables, which had surprisingly high standard deviations, reflecting the relatively low levels of communication of most network members. However when an optimal model was evaluated, range did have a direct impact on innovativeness, again emphasizing the importance of being exposed to diverse information sources for innovation to occur.

The presence of complementary structures performing different innovation functions may be essential for organizational success. The most effective strategy in the long term may be to try to adopt a dynamic synergism between formal and informal structures, that sometimes overlap in messy and troublesome ways (Johnson, 1993). In this regard organizational incongruence may be related to overall organizational effectiveness, since it may establish the creative tension necessary to move to more productive organizational systems (Fry and Smith, 1980). Increasingly the academic literature has stressed the market–driven forces characteristic of informal approaches (Johnson, 1996) as being of paramount concern for the contemporary competitive marketplace.

Communication Channels

> This is just the beginning of an exciting new era in communication!! (Steverson, 1995, e–mail within the CIS system)

Managers must carefully match the attributes of the innovation, the social system in which they are embedded, and their goals related to innovation and KM with the communication channels they choose. As we have seen, a whole host of factors have been identified as determining perceptions of an exponentially proliferating array of channels. In many ways there were really several levels of innovation within the CIS during this period. At the same time as the CIS was innovating in a number of substantive areas, which I will turn to in the next chapter, it was also deciding which of a variety of new channels might be best for communicating about them. A number of these experiments, such as voice mail, FTS–2000 e–mail, and the use of bulletin boards ran into problems in implementation. However, while one particular application of e–mail ran into difficulties, one of the things this project captured by happenstance was the evolution of e–mail and its gradual reinvention within the CIS. Serendipitiously, during this time period electronic mail and facsimile communication were increasingly supplanting interpersonal channels for some users. If channels are viewed primarily as a tool, then it is easy to understand how they can be quickly discarded if another channel, more useful for accomplishing the underlying function, comes along. So channel specialization, not equivalence or substitutability, may be the critical issue (Johnson, 1996).

Increasingly there is a blending of functions for sources, messages and channels. One sense of 'multimedia' in fact is to use differing channels to get the same message from the same source across to a greater range of audiences in a variety of ways, thus extending the reach and impact of channels. For most of us, when we initiate an innovation process the issue is the outcome, not the developmental process. There may be an infinite combination of sources and channels that will serve us well in accomplishing our myriad purposes.

Chang and Johnson (2001) analysed social contagion processes on two contrasting theoretical perspectives of communication channel usage with the first wave of data. Their results were strongest for the most narrow functional content networks, intervention strategies, and they did not suggest that biplex networks served as stronger predictors than uniplex ones for either social information processing or media richness. These results suggested future studies need to pay greater attention to the interaction between functional content and media choice. Other studies have suggested that interpersonal and mediated communication are differentially related to these processes, rather than operating in the parallel and reinforcing manner suggested by prior research (Rogers, 1983; Johnson, Donohue et al., 1994, 2001).

Messages in mediated channels, such as written memos, will often need to be reinforced by direct interpersonal contact with consonant messages – the overall role of conferences in the CIS (Johnson, Meyer, Berkowitz et al., 1996). Thus channels can have complementary effects which, while central to traditional diffusion of innovation research, is not often examined in the current institutional environment for communication study (Berger and Chaffee, 1988).

All of this suggests that other organizing schemes or approaches to this area might be strategically more useful than a focus on channels per se, which seem to proliferate in increasing confusion every year. A focus on underlying processes such as equivocality, which was the original impetus for Daft and Lengel's (1986) work, which stimulated much of the interest in this area; with how perceptions of channels are formed (Carlson and Zmud, 1999); or information seeking (for example Johnson, 1997a) might be more fruitful at this particular juncture, especially if we broaden our focus to include users of information in organizations, as well as disseminators of messages.

While communication researchers have generally given primacy to the impacts of emergent, informal, cohesive communication (Johnson, 1990; McPhee and Poole, 2001; Monge and Contractor, 2001), this research implies that structurally equivalent, role–defined communication structures are also important. Interestingly these structurally equivalent peers can exert negative as well as positive influences on channel perceptions (Rice and Aydin, 1991), as reiterated by the negative correlation coefficient between structural equivalence and uncertainty reduction (Chang and Johnson, 2001). The seemingly contradictory results – structurally equivalent respondents have convergent attitudes for social information, yet divergent ones for media richness – actually may reflect the instability of this organization, that was still in the early stages of a new five–year contract cycle when this data was collected. This pattern also emphasizes the importance of the staging and sequencing of innovations in these processes (Gales et al., 1992).

Examining the theoretical streams of media choice and social information processing together allows us to highlight some very interesting potentially reinforcing effects that they may have. While the theories examined here are very useful, much work still needs to be done to unwrap the complexities involved, especially since high–performing managers appear to be more sensitive to them (Gales et al., 1992). As Burt (1982) has noted there are cases where structurally equivalent actors engage in cohesive communication with each other. In these situations there is an additional benefit of homophily between actors that allows them to amplify their social influence over each other. Similarly, as we have seen, it has been argued that in certain situations media richness and social information perspectives can mutually reinforce each other. It is in this unique alignment that we are likely to see very powerful effects. On the other hand, appropriately role–defined, objective channel selection may directly clash with cultural norms about how certain things should be communicated, as often happens in downsizing events in organizations (Susskind et al., 1998), suggesting situations in which these models could produce contradictory predictions.

In conclusion, this research highlights some larger issues for communication theory. Firstly it is curious that such a fundamental question – that is how people choose the means (for example channel) by which they will communicate with others – has received such fragmentary disciplinary responses, with very little cross–fertilization. Social information processing and media richness theories have primarily been limited to organizational applications, while uses and gratifications, one of our few theories that addresses the receiver's needs, has been largely limited to mass media situations. One of the few places these theories come together is in a focus on information seeking, with some interesting possibilities for cross–

fertilization in different contexts (Johnson, 1996, 1997a). Secondly in general, communication theory has favoured cohesion–based explanations, focusing on how communication brings us together. But, and this is borne out in a set of clear findings here, our communication is also driven by socially defined roles and often fragmented in that way.

Communication and Innovation

Perhaps our most convincing over time finding is the most disturbing one – the low and declining intervention strategy communication rates. This consistent empirical finding flies in the face of network models of the diffusion of innovations (for example Rogers and Kincaid, 1981; Valente, 1995). These models privilege direct, interpersonal, cohesive communication as the primary means by which influence related to adoption of particular innovations is diffused through a system by contagion processes. Contagion processes relate to how individuals form opinions that shape their judgements to adopt particular innovations. To explain the classic accelerating S–curve of innovation adoption, concepts of a critical mass of users and thresholds for adoption in individuals have also been suggested as major explanatory factors, although they are still based on the molar unit of interpersonal communication (Valente, 1995).

Most communication theories implicitly paint a picture of the prevalence and paramount importance of communication. Systems theories point to the importance of coordination and interdependence, interpretive theories focus on sharing of perspectives in sense–making activities, and so on. However the empirical work that has been done on actual communication behaviour suggests that especially for innovation–related communication in organizations, people do not talk to each other very much (Farace and Johnson, 1974; Albrecht and Ropp, 1984; Bach, 1989; Monge et al., 1992; Johnson, Donohue et al., 1995). This may be related to a larger failure of mature, large organizations in sustaining product innovation because of the lack of connections between them and resources, process and strategy (Dougherty and Hardy, 1996). More generally, Karl Weick (1996) also has noted a general trend within organizational studies of ignoring empirical findings, which makes the field vulnerable to its external critics and/or competitors.

It has been my experience that when the CISRC network analysis findings are shared with others, the first reaction is to question the quality of the data. It was partly this sort of response from CIS staff that led to our switch midway through the project to include facsimile and electronic mail communication in the communication logs in an attempt to uncover additional communication related to innovation. In the end, the weight of the evidence is compelling: it may be time to look elsewhere for explanations, several of which we discuss below.

Minimalist perspective

Simply put, it could be the case that not much communication is needed to achieve certain effects. In spite of the concerns of persuasion scholars for overcoming resistance, and such shibboleths of communication theory as repetition for getting a message across, in most organizations orders are orders. If my organization says that henceforward all of my communication related to invoices will be by e–mail, as long as the system is minimally intrusive, relatively easy to use and not personally risky (or there are more risks for not going along), I do what is required of me. In most organizations this sort of compliance may not be difficult to achieve and the communication related to it may be minimal (Fidler and Johnson, 1984), especially compared to the winning of hearts and minds assumed by most participation theories.

Thus a key question to be explored in future research is just what 'dosage' is needed to achieve particular impacts. What numbers of people and what amount of communication is needed to achieve threshold and/or critical mass effects (Watts, 2003)? This might have especially disadvantaged Project 2, which was only tested in one RO, thus never achieving the initial critical mass of supporters, especially occupants of key communication roles, to sustain it in the face of initial difficulties. It may be the case that for a number of innovations, minimalist communication strategies, involving some mediated communication and intense interpersonal communication involving only those immediately affected, may be the best approach. Dosage issues related to staging and the management of uncertainty determine how rich and how much information is necessary at different points, especially since acquiring more information can result in delays and increase costs (Gales et al., 1992). Another twist on these questions is perhaps the most interesting unexplored question in structural analysis – why certain relationships do *not* occur (Johnson, 1993).

Structural equivalence

Burt's (1987) introduction of structural equivalence notions to innovation research was perhaps the first systematic attempt to offer an alternate explanation to the classic taken–for–granted assumptions relating to direct interpersonal communication in diffusion theory (Valente, 1995). This approach essentially argues that a person's position exposes them to information that influences their actions regardless of their direct, cohesive communication with others. In addition, competitive motivations may impel individuals to act to maintain or to gain particular advantages. Through structural equivalence factors, organizational roles often bridge individual and organizational levels (Baldridge and Burnham, 1975). From a structural equivalence perspective, it may be the case that *no* cohesive interpersonal communication is required to trigger the appropriate intervention strategies implementation.

Tacit understandings

Another way of approaching this problem is through an individual's understanding of the underlying rules of a game. When I am passed the ball in soccer, I may be well drilled in formalized approaches, and see a pattern that activates a play that is implicitly understood by all of the other players. Thus the high levels of formalization characteristic of the CIS may minimize the need for direct, interpersonal communication (Van de Ven, 1978). Alternatively I may go with the flow of events, reacting spontaneously, and experience the pleasurable sensation of jamming (Eisenberg, 1990), where others react in concert with me and our combined actions achieve our ultimate purpose of scoring a goal. In both of these situations, direct overt communication is not needed; rather, tacit understandings of the rules of the game and what my actions entail within this established framework, are what is required to play.

  In these situations the manager may act as a curious combination of coach and umpire, setting the overall rules framework and then making sure that they are followed. This approach also explains how people deal with so many competing task demands: in effect, some players let others carve out their own turf and delegate to them implicitly (or formally through task forces or CoPs more informally) the accomplishment of particular tasks. (As long as they have the ball, let them run with it; when they pass it off, then we will see what I do.) So players do not become involved until they need to act. Given the preliminary research trials characteristic of the CISRC projects, members of the CIS may not have felt a need to communicate until wide–scale implementation was likely. All parties were relatively busy, committed to different goals, and were in effect willing to have a 'conspiracy of silence' as long as their tacit agreements were not broken. In this sense further communication would only make the everyday working lives of CIS members worse.

Looking in the wrong place at the wrong time

As we have suggested, perhaps the most important communication occurred before the trials of the various interventions even began (Klein and Sorra, 1996), in the initial buy–in phase of the CISRC. After this point, it was just a question of operationalizing original commitments, primarily through the training of ISs, events that we did not specifically measure. Thus it could be the case that the original project ideas were explained so well and commitment was so total that there was not a need for a major ongoing communication effort. This has been termed left–hand censoring, a failure to detect change because it happened before the first data collection (Menard, 1991). Bach (1989) also has suggested that organizational members make their judgements on how to act toward an innovation in the seminal development phase – before it is introduced. Essentially, after this point only a low level of maintenance, fine–tuning, would be needed for the ongoing operation of the project, making the detection of peak, sporadic communication within our sampling intervals more difficult. In addition the projects in the third and fourth year were winding down, which may partially explain the declining levels of communication.

It could also be the case that in the extremely rich, complex communication environment of the CISRC, that we just did not focus on the critical communication events. Perhaps in spite of our societal and academic privileging of interpersonal communication, this may not be the appropriate level of analysis; group communication, in the form of face–to–face national meetings discussed in Chapter 3, may be the best predictor. It was at these meetings that CIS members could get a feel for whether or not a critical mass of their fellows were committed to the projects. With a visible awareness of the actions of their 'competitors', individual thresholds could be reached for their continued involvement in the projects (Valente, 1995).

Summary

Recent years have seen a resurgence of interest in network analysis as a way of portraying informal communication. It offers many compelling advantages in the investigation of organizational communication structure. Firstly it is a very practicable method for examining the overall configurations of communication contacts in a large social system, which can also provide an elegant description of them (Farace et al., 1977; Rogers and Agarwala–Rogers, 1976). Secondly it provides very specific and direct information on the pattern of an individual's linkages, since networks are based fundamentally on the notion of dyadic linkages (Mitchell, 1969). It moves us away from an exclusive focus on the individual to a more conceptually correct focus on the relationship as the unit of analysis (Moch et al. 1983; Monge and Contractor, 1987; Rogers and Agarwala–Rogers, 1976). Thirdly it permits the derivation of a host of other measures from the aggregation of these individual linkages, including clique identification, roles and metrics (for example connectedness), and this data can be aggregated at various levels of analysis including interpersonal, group and whole organization. In this regard it can be used as a systematic means of linking micro and macro perspectives of organizations (Tichy et al., 1979). In sum, network analysis offers the most complete picture of the overall configuration of communication relationships, both formal and informal, yet developed, and certainly a much more complete view than that offered by formal approaches alone (Monge and Eisenberg, 1987). As we have seen in this chapter it can develop very rich descriptions of innovation and KM.

6. Comparing attributes of knowledge delivery and information technology innovations

6.1 INTRODUCTION

> The CIS must remain sturdy yet flexible, stable yet progressive to meet the challenges in the field of cancer communication in the 1990's and to have an impact on that challenge. As the CIS successfully implements the new programme concept, it will continue to be a template for national and international health communications programmes for the 1990s and beyond. (Morra et al., 1993, p. 32)

> Innovations are met with a variety of reactions by potential adopters, from skepticism and derision to excitement and hope. All of us assess innovations on the basis of what we already know, already own, currently use, and currently have invested. (Dearing et al., 1994, p. 17)

Increasingly, innovation must proceed at two levels. Firstly organizations must be simultaneously engaged in a number of innovations, each of which is designed to meet a particular mix of strategic objectives. Secondly organizations must concern themselves with innovation at the meta level, determining how they can best arrange themselves to innovate, a subject that has been a major element of our focus on communication structure in previous chapters and of KM more generally. As this four-year project unfolded, various naturally occurring experiments presented themselves. One was the national conferences, the results of which were described in Chapter 3. Another, discussed here, had to do with the computerization initiative that the CIS began halfway through the project.

While both the CISRC and CAG were very similar to CoPs, they had some important differences. Firstly computerization was primarily developed by champions within the CIS who saw it as both a means of increasing efficiency and of responding to stakeholder pressures; thus they could use it as an opportunity to 'bootleg' changes they had desired all along (Marcus and Weber, 1989). Secondly the computerization effort was primarily implemented by CIS people in a train-the-trainer model. Thirdly intensive internal communication efforts, conferences, site visits and internal training focused on computerization. Fourthly computerization has a central and pervasive effect on organizational functioning, since it often needs to be implemented on a system-wide basis, which makes it qualitatively different than other types of innovation (Sabherwal and Robey, 1993; Crawford, 1996).

In this chapter we focus on the reactions of CIS members to two specific types of innovations that provided interesting contrasts: information technology, or the computerization effort as it was known more colloquially in the CIS, and the three intervention strategies developed by the CISRC related to knowledge delivery. The reactions of CIS members to these two different sets of innovations should provide us with very interesting comparisons and contrasts of how members of the CIS deal with the reality of innovations as opposed to the generalized perceptions of innovation climate we focused on in Chapter 4. This study represents a unique opportunity to examine, within the same setting, whether contrasting dimensions of an innovation are differentially rated depending on the nature of the innovations themselves. If one can sample different innovations, one can get a more realistic picture of an organization's level of innovativeness (Meyer et al., 1995).

6.2 COMPARING THE TWO DIFFERENT SETS OF INNOVATIONS

An *innovation* is an idea, process, or technology that is perceived as being new. An *innovation attribute* is a perceived characteristic of a new idea, process, or technology. (Dearing and Meyer, 1994, p. 47)

While there has been a wealth of research related to innovation processes in organizations (Johnson, 1993), comparatively few studies have directly contrasted innovations within the same organizational setting (Johnson et al., 1995). Historically researchers have described innovations in terms of their attributes or perceived characteristics, which play a significant role in the diffusion of innovations. In some ways these attributes become the content of messages that can be disseminated about an innovation. Early on,

Katz (1963) saw the adoption of an innovation as being contingent upon its compatibility, or the degree to which the attributes of an innovation matched the attributes of potential adopters. Two decades later, Rogers (1983, 1995, 2003) developed the most commonly recognized scheme for examining differing properties of innovations. He identified five perceived attributes: relative advantage, compatibility, trialability, complexity and observability. Innovation attributes provide a useful framework in which to examine the properties of KM innovations.

Previous research indicated that organizational members rate contrasting innovations differentially (Johnson et al., 1995). On the basis of our knowledge about the fit between organizational members' perceptions about innovation attributes and the unique nature of contrasting innovations, we can make policy recommendations about how to manage most effectively the implementation of innovations. They will be used here to diagnose and analyse specific innovation efforts.

Relative Advantage

Relative advantage refers to the degree to which an innovation is perceived as being better than the idea it supersedes. According to Rogers (1983, 1995, 2003), relative advantage can be broken down into two types: economic and social advantage. Economic advantage can be equated with profitability, and social aspects reflect prestige or status to the adopter of any particular innovation. Dearing et al. (1994) isolated three aspects of relative advantage: 'economic advantage', 'effectiveness' and 'reliability'. Effectiveness is the degree to which an innovation is communicated as being relatively more capable in achieving an ideal end-state. Reliability is the degree to which an innovation is communicated as being consistent in its results. Dearing et al.'s (1994) study indicated that more than two-thirds of comments related to relative advantage were non-economic.

In this study we chose not to assess levels of economic relative advantage, since we are focusing on a governmental organization. Additionally we chose not to assess reliability as a part of relative advantage, because we feel that reliability is of such magnitude that it should be treated as a separate construct (see 'riskiness' below). For our purposes, we will frame relative advantage in terms of 'effectiveness', or the degree to which an innovation is capable of achieving an ideal end-state. By focusing on whether or not organizational members perceive that an innovation is a better way of doing things, we can gain an indication of perceived relative advantage that is most relevant to the context of the CIS.

Compatibility

Compatibility is the degree to which an innovation is perceived as consistent with existing values, past experience and needs of adopters. Compatibility is the most important innovation attribute for cancer control research (McKinney et al., 1992) and has also been found to be critical for information technology innovations (Leonard-Barton and Sinha, 1993). The more compatible an innovation is along these dimensions, the more likely it is to be adopted (Rogers, 1983, 1995, 2003). Perhaps the most direct assessment of the role that organizational culture plays is in issues related to the compatibility of an innovation (Rogers, 1983; Klein and Sorra, 1996). The more compatible an innovation is along these dimensions, the more likely it is to be adopted and effectively implemented (Klein and Sorra, 1996). In the organizational context, the degree to which an innovation is compatible with past experience may be especially relevant because the prospect of changing organizational behaviour introduces a great deal of uncertainty for organizational members.

Complexity

Complexity is generally viewed as the degree to which an innovation is perceived as relatively difficult to understand and to use (Rogers, 1983, 1995, 2003). Alternatively, complexity can be conceptualized as the number of dimensions along which an innovation can be evaluated by a potential receiver (Fidler and Johnson, 1984). An innovation that has a number of components to consider is one that involves more uncertainty for the potential adopter, because uncertainty is in part a function of the number of alternative ideas contained in an innovation. Reducing uncertainty is central to processes of innovation within organizations (Fidler and Johnson, 1984).

As Bohlen (1971, p. 807) has noted: 'Other factors equated, the more complex an idea is, the more slowly it tends to be adopted.' The greater the complexity related to using an innovation or in merely understanding it cognitively, the greater the resistance (Perry and Kraemer, 1978; Zaltman and Duncan, 1977). In the case of the CIS, an innovation that is perceived to be too complex to understand or implement may result in a state of information overload among organizational members.

Trialability

Trialability, or the degree to which an innovation may be experimented with on a limited basis, has generally been considered to be positively related to innovation adoption (Rogers, 1983, 1995, 2003). The knowledge delivery innovations under examination in this study were in the pilot stage. For this reason we would expect the attribute of trialability to be exceptionally relevant to innovation adoption in the CIS. One characteristic of information technology innovations, is they are difficult to trial, since they must have a critical mass of users.

Observability

Observability, or the degree to which the effects of an innovation are visible, is generally thought to have a positive impact on innovation adoption (Rogers, 1983, 1995, 2003): An organizational member who can see the impact that an intervention has on the target audience (for example a health information campaign that results in behavioural changes in a targeted population), is more likely to view the innovation in a favourable light. We anticipate that the health services projects will differ in levels of observability because they vary in terms of the number of sites in which they are currently being piloted. Health campaigns rarely produce a direct, observable link between an intervention and health behaviour change. It may be difficult for organizational members to see the impact that a programme has on a target population for two reasons: intervening variables may mediate or moderate the effect of an intervention, and the desired behaviour change may take place over an extended period of time. The latter condition may apply to the CIS, where it may simply be too soon for organizational members to make attributions about the extent to which an intervention has visible outcomes.

Adaptability

Adaptability can be conceptualized as the degree to which an innovation can be modified to fit local needs. This construct is especially relevant to the CIS because of its structure, which is centralized and formalized, yet geographically dispersed. The degree to which new innovations are perceived to be easily adapted to local needs is an indicator of how likely organizational members will be to adopt these strategies.

Riskiness

The degree to which organizational members perceive the new interventions to be risky ventures may have a significant impact on whether or not the innovations are accepted or rejected. The very novelty of the innovation entails more risk for the organization as a whole (Rogers and Adhikayra, 1979). In essence, the greater the uncertainty of outcome regarding an innovation, the greater the degree of perceived risk toward implementing the innovation (Fidler and Johnson, 1984). Specifically, the NCI and OCC have made a strategic choice in piloting three knowledge service delivery innovations, investing a great deal in the initiatives in the hope that they will prove to be effective means of delivering cancer information.

Acceptance

Social science research generally assumes that pre-existing attitudes are linked to behavioural outcomes. In the context of the CIS, an organization that is currently in the stage of piloting preventive health innovations, it is too soon to measure behavioural outcomes such as innovation adoption and implementation across the network. Therefore we choose to look at the level of acceptance of innovations revealed through organizational members' perceptions about the degree to which an innovation is essentially a good idea. A high level of innovation acceptance would indicate a higher probability that an intervention would be adopted and implemented. User perceptions of the success or failure of innovations often relate more to organizational outcomes to which they are linked, than to objective features of the innovations (Lewis, 1995).

6.3 THREE KNOWLEDGE SERVICE DELIVERY INNOVATIONS

The CISRC piloted three new intervention strategies to facilitate the dissemination of cancer information to the public. The first and third innovations were connected to the CIS 1-800-4-CANCER telephone service, utilizing the toll-free number as a nexus from which to disseminate cancer information to targeted populations. The second and third projects were tailored to the health information needs of traditionally underserved sectors of the American public. These projects have been described in much more detail in Chapter 4; here we will focus on their innovation attributes. (More detail on these results can be found in: Johnson, Chang, Ethington, Meyer, and LaFrance, 1994; Johnson, Chang, LaFrance, Meyer, Ethington, and Pobocik, 1996b; Johnson, LaFrance, Kiyomiya, and Ethington, 1997; Meyer et al., 1995; Meyer et al., 1997). It is important to remember that the CISRC innovations were dynamic and that the time at which respondents completed the data collection instruments occurred at different points in the progression of each project. Therefore a chronology of all the CISRC projects is provided on my website.

In general, Project 3 was seen as more compatible than Project 1, maintaining this rating across all three time periods (see Tables 6.1, 6.2 and 6.3). Project 2 was clearly seen as not compatible with CIS operations by

Time 3. People saw these projects as adaptable to the ongoing operations of the CIS, except for a drop in Project 2 at Time 3. Except for Project 2, respondents generally reported low perceptions of risk for the three projects. There was a slight dip for some indicants of relative advantage for Project 1 at Time 3. Clearly Project 2 had the lowest relative advantage, and sharply declining scores for this attribute. Project 3 had the highest scores that were also stable over the three time periods.

Table 6.1 Perceptions of attributes for CISRC Project 1

Items	Time 1 (n = 89)	Time 2 (n = 70)	Time 3 (n = 71)
Compatibility			
Is similar to the techniques we have used in the past.	7.2	6.7	4.8
Is compatible with our office's customary method of providing cancer information to the public.	5.4	6.5	6.0
Adaptability			
Can be adapted to fit local needs.	7.5	7.3	7.1
Can be modified for use in future campaigns.	7.6	8.1	8.3
Is something we can build on in the future.	7.7	8.4	7.6
Can be easily adapted to different situations that arise at our office.	6.1	6.8	6.9
Riskiness			
Presents risks to our office.	3.2	3.6	3.5
Has a number of uncertain outcomes.	6.4	5.3	4.9
Is a reliable way to communicate cancer information to a target audience.	7.2	7.7	7.8
Has unpredictable results.	4.5	4.7	4.4
Is a risky method for communicating cancer information to members of a target audience.	3.0	2.5	3.3

Items	Time 1 (n = 89)	Time 2 (n = 70)	Time 3 (n = 71)
Relative advantage			
Is more effective in communicating with targeted populations than our previous efforts.	5.5	6.7	6.4
Will have a greater impact on public's cancer awareness than previous national initiatives.	6.0	6.3	5.7
Will result in greater behavioral change for callers.	6.1	6.8	7.5
Is a better way to provide callers with cancer information.	6.7	6.3	5.5
Observability			
Will produce a visible change in our office's call busy rate.	5.9	6.6	7.7
Will produce a visible change in our call abandonment rate.	4.9	6.2	6.8
Complexity			
Is too complex.	2.6	5.6	5.2
Means that information specialists can't meet other job responsibilities as well as they used to.	3.7	4.2	5.1
Raises a number of issues for information specialists.	7.7	6.4	7.2

Items	Time 1 (n = 89)	Time 2 (n = 70)	Time 3 (n = 71)
Trialability			
Piloting this intervention strategy in a few offices ...			
Informs people in other offices of its strengths and weaknesses.	8.7	8.8	8.7
Informs people in other offices about its effectiveness before it is adopted by the entire network.	8.6	8.9	8.6
Enables people in other offices to see how well the strategy works in the target audience.	8.5	8.8	8.3
Helps people in other offices gain information about whether the project will work across the entire network.	8.1	8.7	8.3
Lets people in other offices learn about new procedures before the entire network to adopt them.	8.9	8.9	8.3
Acceptance			
Should be supported by people at all levels of the CIS.	8.8	8.2	8.2
Is a positive way to reach members of a target audience.	7.4	8.1	7.8
Is a policy option for reaching members of a target audience.	7.0	7.6	7.6
Is an acceptable method of outreach for the CIS.	7.4	7.6	6.4

Note: Respondents were asked to respond to each item, indicating how much they agreed or disagreed with each statement on a scale of 0 to 10 where 0 indicates 'total disagreement' and 10 indicates 'total agreement'.

Table 6.2 Perceptions of attributes for CISRC Project 2

Items	Time 1 (n = 89)	Time 2 (n = 70)	Time 3 (n = 71)
Compatibility			
Is similar to the techniques we have used in the past.	8.1	7.8	1.3
Is compatible with our office's customary method of providing cancer information to the public.	2.7	3.1	2.6
Adaptability			
Can be adapted to fit local needs.	8.1	6.9	4.7
Can be modified for use in future campaigns.	7.7	7.3	5.7
Is something we can build on in the future.	7.6	6.3	5.8
Can be easily adapted to different situations that arise at our office.	5.4	4.2	4.0
Riskiness			
Presents risks to our office.	5.2	6.8	4.2
Has a number of uncertain outcomes.	6.9	6.7	6.4
Is a reliable way to communicate cancer information to a target audience.	6.9	6.2	7.5
Has unpredictable results.	3.2	5.8	6.9
Is a risky method for communicating cancer information to members of a target audience.	4.5	4.1	5.9

Items	Time 1 (n = 89)	Time 2 (n = 70)	Time 3 (n = 71)
Relative advantage			
Is more effective in communicating with targeted populations than our previous efforts.	7.4	5.0	3.8
Will have a greater impact on public's cancer awareness than previous national initiatives.	6.8	5.9	3.7
Will result in greater behavioral change for callers.	6.1	6.4	4.6
Is a better way to provide callers with cancer information.	6.4	4.6	4.6
Observability			
Will produce a visible change in our office's call busy rate.	6.2	5.9	6.1
Will produce a visible change in our call abandonment rate.	4.5	5.8	5.5
Complexity			
Is too complex.	3.9	7.3	8.0
Means that information specialists can't meet other job responsibilities as well as they used to.	4.4	6.0	6.8
Raises a number of issues for information specialists.	8.7	8.5	9.1

Items	Time 1 (n = 89)	Time 2 (n = 70)	Time 3 (n = 71)
Trialability			
Piloting this intervention strategy in a few offices ...			
Informs people in other offices of its strengths and weaknesses.	8.7	8.7	8.5
Informs people in other offices about its effectiveness before it is adopted by the entire network.	8.6	9.0	8.5
Enables people in other offices to see how well the strategy works in the target audience.	8.5	8.9	7.8
Helps people in other offices gain information about whether the project will work across the entire network.	8.0	8.7	8.6
Lets people in other offices learn about new procedures before the entire network to adopt them.	8.8	8.9	7.7
Acceptance			
Should be supported by people at all levels of the CIS.	7.8	6.1	6.2
Is a positive way to reach members of a target audience.	7.8	6.7	5.7
Is a policy option for reaching members of a target audience.	6.7	5.7	5.3
Is an acceptable method of outreach for the CIS.	6.4	5.9	4.0

Note: Respondents were asked to respond to each item, indicating how much they agreed or disagreed with each statement on a scale of 0 to 10 where 0 indicates 'total disagreement' and 10 indicates 'total agreement'.

Table 6.3 Perceptions of attributes for CISRC Project 3

Items	Time 1 (n = 89)	Time 2 (n = 70)	Time 3 (n = 71)
Compatibility			
Is similar to the techniques we have used in the past.	6.5	5.6	6.0
Is compatible with our office's customary method of providing cancer information to the public.	6.7	7.2	7.2
Adaptability			
Can be adapted to fit local needs.	7.7	8.1	7.4
Can be modified for use in future campaigns.	7.9	8.3	8.5
Is something we can build on in the future.	7.7	8.3	7.9
Can be easily adapted to different situations that arise at our office.	6.1	6.4	6.3
Riskiness			
Presents risks to our office.	2.2	3.0	2.7
Has a number of uncertain outcomes.	6.0	5.8	5.2
Is a reliable way to communicate cancer information to a target audience.	7.7	8.2	8.5
Has unpredictable results.	4.3	4.4	4.2
Is a risky method for communicating cancer information to members of a target audience.	2.1	1.7	2.5

Note: Respondents were asked to respond to each item, indicating how much they agreed or disagreed with each statement on a scale of 0 to 10 where 0 indicates 'total disagreement' and 10 indicates 'total agreement'.

Items	Time 1 (n = 89)	Time 2 (n = 70)	Time 3 (n = 71)
Relative advantage			
Is more effective in communicating with targeted populations than our previous efforts.	7.4	6.9	7.4
Will have a greater impact on public's cancer awareness than previous national initiatives.	6.9	6.7	6.3
Will result in greater behavioral change for callers.	6.4	6.6	7.5
Is a better way to provide callers with cancer information.	7.3	6.9	6.5
Observability			
Will produce a visible change in our office's call busy rate.	6.0	6.4	6.2
Will produce a visible change in our call abandonment rate.	4.8	6.3	5.2
Complexity			
Is too complex.	3.4	5.3	5.4
Means that information specialists can't meet other job responsibilities as well as they used to.	3.5	3.5	4.4
Raises a number of issues for information specialists.	5.8	5.8	5.9

Items	Time 1 (n = 89)	Time 2 (n = 70)	Time 3 (n = 71)
Trialability			
Piloting this intervention strategy in a few offices ...			
Informs people in other offices of its strengths and weaknesses.	8.7	8.4	8.7
Informs people in other offices about its effectiveness before it is adopted by the entire network.	8.6	8.7	8.6
Enables people in other offices to see how well the strategy works in the target audience.	8.6	8.8	8.3
Helps people in other offices gain information about whether the project will work across the entire network.	8.1	8.5	8.4
Lets people in other offices learn about new procedures before the entire network to adopt them.	8.7	8.7	8.4
Acceptance			
Should be supported by people at all levels of the CIS.	8.5	8.3	8.6
Is a positive way to reach members of a target audience.	7.9	8.4	8.5
Is a policy option for reaching members of a target audience.	7.6	7.8	8.0
Is an acceptable method of outreach for the CIS.	7.9	8.1	7.1

Perhaps some of the drop in the acceptance of Project 1 at Time 3 was associated with the perceptions that it produced an observable change in busy signals and call abandonment rates. The other two projects had more moderate, stable reactions to observability over three points in time.

Project 3 was generally viewed as the least complex and had the highest stability of perceptions over three points in time. There were higher scores, which appeared to be increasing, for the complexity of Project 1. Clearly the increasing scores for the complexity of Project 2 contributed to its overall negative perception. Since Project 2 (Making Outcalls to Promote Mammography) involved many new component parts for the CIS ISs (that is placing calls and following a new protocol for making outcalls in addition to meeting other job responsibilities such as answering incoming calls), it was viewed to be significantly more complex than either Project 1 or Project 3. This might be especially problematic in the CIS given the already high, and ever-increasing, volume of calls placed to the telephone service.

Trialability had the most stable and the most consistently high evaluations of any of the attributes. Project 3 had the highest, most stable ratings of acceptance over the three projects, with Project 2 having the lowest and declining scores. However given some of the low scores for other attributes, the responses to the critical question 'Should be supported by people at all levels of the CIS' at consistently above 8 for Projects 1 and 3 and above 6 even for Project 2, suggested some other factors might be at play in determining respondent perceptions of acceptability.

The clearest outcome across the projects was the dramatic drop for Project 2 and the somewhat smaller drop for Project 1 in overall evaluations. It must be noted that it did not come as a surprise that respondents rated Project 2 (Making Outcalls to Promote Mammography) more highly in terms of complexity and risk: there were indications from the start that Project 2 might be controversial because of the relatively radical change that it entailed for members of the CIS. However its promise as a means of reaching priority audiences not typically reached by the CIS (Freimuth et al., 1987) made it worth the gamble. This realization was factored into the innovation adoption decision-making process by key players in the CIS. Project 1 switched focus early on from mammography screening, because of its rapid adoption by the public, to five-a-day fruit and vegetable consumption, which might have been partially responsible for its slightly declining ratings. Project 3 had more favourable evaluations for compatibility, relative advantage, complexity and acceptance over time. These scores indicated why it was the only CISRC project to be even partially incorporated into the ongoing operations of ROs (Marcus, 2004). Trialability was clearly the most highly rated attribute, with elements of riskiness, reflecting NCI and OCC buy-in, having the lowest scores. The acceptance findings across the projects, especially given the differential evaluations of the attributes, led to deeper explorations and richer insights into the various levels of innovation process in the CIS.

6.4 FOUR INFORMATION TECHNOLOGY INNOVATIONS

> Although it will require a significant commitment of funds by NCI, integration of nationally standardized state-of-the-art telecommunications and information-management technology not only will enhance CIS programme operations but also will increase the flow of information to the public; that flow of information is the primary purpose of the CIS. As the CIS programme prepares for the most significant structural change in its 15-year history, there should be no delay in the adaptation of technology that will allow the programme to reach its full potential. (Wooldridge et al., 1993, p. 176)

One way organizations cope with their changing environment is through information technology, which is of course intimately tied to KM. Developing improved information technology is often the first move of a firm into KM operations (Davenport and Prusak, 1998). Information technologies have been defined as those changes that introduce a tool, technique, physical equipment or system by which the employees or the units of an organization extend their capabilities (Schon, 1967). Information technology is at the root of many organizational changes as either a cause or an enabler (Hoffman, 1994). Many organizations have realized that there are real strategic advantages, especially in enhancing quality, efficiency and competitiveness, from adopting new information technologies (Porter and Millar, 1985).

However in spite of often rosy predictions, the impacts of information processing technologies on organizational productivity and profitability have been a matter of some controversy (Hoffman, 1994). While computerization of information should make it possible for organizations to deliver the right information at the right time to the right place, accomplishing this has proven to be much more difficult than it would appear to be on the surface (McGee and Prusak, 1993). It appears obvious that the impact of technologies would be dramatic, both structurally and spatially (Morgan, 1986), especially in relation to the enhanced ability to control and coordinate organizational processes. This has not been the case in actual practice, where many promising technologies are used to do the old jobs in old ways (Carter and Culnan, 1983). However there is a consensus that eventually, often after a considerable lag-time, new information technologies have an impact on organizational effectiveness (Huber and McDaniel, 1988).

While optimists wait for the next generation of computer software and hardware, realists are increasingly looking at the organization itself, especially its culture and structures, as the major impediment to improved information processing (McGee and Prusak, 1993). It has almost become a cliché that the reason information technologies and systems fail is that they do not consider the needs of users (for example Kuhlthau, 1991; Pinelli, 1991; Rouse and Rouse, 1984; Steinke, 1991; Varlejs, 1986), with estimates of failure rates of 30 per cent attributable to non-technical factors (More, 1990). In this research we will examine how classic factors related to the perceptions of innovation attributes related to four contrasting information processing technologies which were at various stages of implementation within the CIS.

Information Technology in the Cancer Information Service

The CIS's primary activities focus on providing information about cancer and cancer-related resources to cancer patients and their families, health professionals and the public. In some ways the CIS's operation is evocative of more generic call centre operations. The virtual explosion of technology in telecommunications and computerized information management has had widespread application to the CIS programme and call centres generally (Downing, 2004). As we have seen in Chapter 2, the adoption of information technologies is increasingly important for the long-term survival of government agencies. Several ROs had individually taken advantage of information technology in a variety of applications. The CIS as an organization however had lacked a national strategic plan and the necessary resources for coordinating a network-wide application of information technology at the beginning of the study contract period. The result of this lack of a national plan was the preservation of a paper-based system within the network, and a piecemeal approach to the application of information technology.

In 1993, computerization was identified as the top priority for the network. As a result, in 1994 a CAG formed within the CIS to develop a strategic approach to computerization. This advisory group, which had certain similarities to a CoP, developed a plan for technology development based on four programme areas: telephone service, outreach, communications, and office management. This sort of involvement of end-users in computer system development has been seen as playing a critical role in overcoming resistance and the sort of reinvention needed for successful implementation (Gardner and Shabot, 1994). To be successful it is also important that systems are seen by users as not only improving efficiency, but also increasing quality of outputs, as well as enhancing individual skill levels (Gardner and Shabot, 1994).

Telephone service

Since 1975 the OCC has increasingly standardized the information to be disseminated, to assure that all offices were providing the same information in the same manner to all callers. The standardization was necessary for quality assurance of the accuracy of the information disseminated to the caller. (For more detail on formalization in the CIS see Chapter 3.) The information and formats include PDQ, NCI brochures, fact sheets, standard textbooks, journal articles, subject matter files and other standard technical sources. Hard copy of PDQ information files alone numbered between 1500 and 2000 pages of print text, with the files updated on a monthly basis (Hibbard et al., 1995). The priority and most frequently used information such as PDQ and NCI brochures were required to be maintained at each telephone call station to provide timely response to each caller. In addition to these technical resources, each CIS office was required to maintain a directory of cancer-related resources within their service region. The result of these requirements was an overwhelming plethora of disparate information sources that were utilized on-line by the IS. Management of these resources was the focus of previous local efforts to computerize. These efforts included the development of an indexing system to assist the IS in locating the source of information, the development of a key-word indexing system to locate community resources, and the use of word-search-based software to facilitate storage and retrieval for a portion of the information.

In addition to the information resources that were maintained in each office, each call that came into the CIS network was documented by the IS. This documentation was done on a Call Record Form (CRF) that included information fields on the type of caller, subject of inquiry, cancer site, response to caller, call follow-up and demographic data. In addition to these data fields, a narrative of requests and responses was maintained for each call. Several offices historically had developed data collection programmes whose data tapes were then transmitted to NCI. Other offices however were sending their CRFs to OCC for data entry. This system was cumbersome, expensive and resulted in inaccessibility to the data for many offices.

The CAG identified the management of information resources and the automation of the CRF as two of the highest priority programme areas for application of information technology. The automation of these two areas was expected to increase productivity, increase staff efficiency and significantly reduce overall programme costs. It would also provide a database that could be both a research and a management tool.

While most of our research had focused on key decision-makers in the ROs, because of the importance of ISs' reactions for the implementation of the CISRC innovations, we gathered data separately at each of the data collection periods related to the implementation of IS-related computerization efforts. One potential consequence of a computerization effort was a blending of status differentials, although a recent study of health professionals found that computer conferencing actually solidified and sharpened them. There was a real need to study these issues over time in a variety of settings (Saunders et al., 1994). For the IS portion of the research we focused on three specific telephone service functions: record keeping (for example the CRF), information resources (for example resource retrieval) and mailings (for example automated publication ordering).

Outreach

The function of the Outreach Program in each of the ROs was to provide a link between the NCI and the health professionals who serve the priority audiences identified by the NCI. Outreach had always been a part of the CIS programme; however it was not until the 1990s that an organized approach to outreach had been identified and supported through the CIS contracts. This relatively new programme component required an ability to track contacts with intermediaries in much the same way that a corporate sales representative tracks client contacts. Records of previous contacts, including actions taken, materials ordered and services requested and supplied, were essential for future programme planning and work organization. In addition, lists of media representatives and other communications partners facilitated the rapid dissemination of OCC information to the RO. The collection and maintenance of this information was essential for future efforts in programme evaluation. The use of computer technology for the development of new educational materials, newsletters and regular correspondence had also been identified as a critical area for the outreach programme.

Internal communication

Given the geographic dispersion of the CIS, various communication integrating mechanisms have played a critical role in the effort of ensuring coordinated actions towards national goals (Morra, Van Nevel et al., 1993). There had been an evolution of communication techniques during the 20 years of the CIS. Communication began with a weekly package of information that included a numbered circular memo. Overnight courier services were used for time-sensitive materials. In 1984, electronic mail service facilitated rapid communication between the OCC and the ROs. More recently, in 1990 the FTS-2000 electronic mail service enabled all offices to communicate on a daily basis. This system had a drawback in that the message centre was located on one dedicated personal computer and timely reception of e-mail was dependent upon when the mail centre was checked (see Chapter 5). The demand for user-friendly, as well as timely, message transfer had prompted the initiation of Internet use in concert with local e-mail packages and development of procedures to apply this next step in communication enhancement. Internal communication planning also focused on newer computer-related tools such as bulletin boards, network directories and scheduling.

Office management

As in other organizations, the efficient management of budgets, contract administration, quality assurance, spreadsheets and other miscellaneous forms of office functions through standard software applications enhanced overall productivity and reduced costs through more efficient use of staff resources. The development of this area of computer enhancement was to be left to the individual RO and based on available institutional support services. The ability to share data, particularly in the area of budgets, needed coordination through a common communication channel. This aspect of programme development was facilitated through the CAG.

In sum, the CIS was implementing information technologies in its efforts to computerize the CIS in the areas of telephone service, outreach, communication and office management during the last two years of this project. Although some CIS offices retained paper-based systems across many areas of computerization, several offices were being innovative by using information management technology to develop more effective and efficient computer-based systems. As these four areas of information technologies were being developed and implemented in the CIS, the CAG began the process of integrating other technological advances into the cancer information resources network. The CAG produced the sort of user involvement critical to the successful implementation of technologies in organizations (Leonard-Barton and Sinha, 1993).

Innovation Attributes Results for Information Technology

Earlier I developed in detail definitions of the innovation attributes classically focused on in diffusion research. In this section I will focus primarily on how these attributes related to the computerization effort for the leadership of the CIS (see Table 6.4 and Table 6.5 for specific questions for telephone service and outreach respectively and Table 6.6 and 6.7 for the results for communication and office management). The specific questions reflected the most psychometrically appropriate items (more details on methods and the results can be found in: Johnson, Chang, Meyer, et al., 1995a; Johnson, Chang, LaFrance et al., 1995; Johnson, LaFrance, Chang et al., 1997; Johnson et al., 1998). We added computer knowledge as an attribute for these innovations, while maintaining similar specific questions to those asked for the knowledge delivery innovations.

In general there was a mixed picture for the specific indicators of compatibility with relatively low scores for similarities to past approaches at the CIS. However computerization for communication, which had the longest history of recent information technology in the CIS was seen as more similar to past techniques. Computerization for communication was also perceived as more compatible than computerization for outreach, telephone service and office management in our baseline study (Johnson, Meyer, Woodworth et al., 1996).

The results for adaptability were uniformly high across all items, time periods and innovation types. This construct was especially relevant to the CIS because of its unique nature as an organization that marries a centralized, formal structure with geographically dispersed ROs. The degree to which information technologies were perceived to be easily adapted to local needs is an indicator of how likely organizational members will be to adopt these strategies. Leonard-Barton and Sinha (1993), in their study of the dissemination of information technologies to operational subunits within an organization, a situation somewhat similar to the CIS, found that mutual adaptation, the degree to which users refine a system to fit their particular needs, was a key factor in successful technology transfer.

The pattern of results for relative advantage was somewhat similar to compatibility, with lower scores for the ultimate outcomes of CIS operations in cancer awareness and behavioural change, but high scores for its impact on internal efficiency (see Tables 6.4, 6.5, 6.6 and 6.7). Others have focused on perceived usefulness, a similar construct, and found that it was the most important factor over time in the intention to use a computer technology (Davis et al., 1989).

In the case of the CIS, the OCC had made a strategic choice in computerizing the CIS, investing a great deal in innovations they hoped would increase the efficiency with which the CIS delivered cancer information to the public. Because it was less central to the ongoing work of most individuals in the CIS, computerization related to office management was perceived as less risky at Time 1 (Johnson, Meyer, Woodworth et al., 1996). The results indicated that there were not high concerns for risk, but there was more uncertainty about outcomes and the predictability of results.

One of the reasons for the interest in this area was that some aspects of computerization have been tried with some success in a variety of ROs. Therefore, we would expect the attribute of trialability to be exceptionally relevant to innovation adoption in the CIS, and this was confirmed across all innovations and time periods.

Table 6.4 Computerization attributes for telephone service

Items	Time 1 (n = 82)	Time 2 (n = 86)	Time 3 (n = 71)
Compatibility			
Is similar to the techniques we have used in the past.	3.8	4.8	5.6
Will change the way that information is disseminated by the CIS.	8.2	7.8	8.0
Is compatible with our office's customary method of providing cancer information to the public.	7.4	8.1	7.8
Is like other initiatives we have implemented in the past.	3.8	4.8	4.3
Is different from previous national initiatives.	7.7	6.9	6.8
Adaptability			
Can be adapted to fit the needs of our office.	8.7	8.9	8.8
Can be modified for use in our office.	8.8	8.6	8.4
Can accommodate unique outreach efforts in our regional CIS office.	8.5	7.3	8.6
Can be easily adapted to different situations that arise at our office.	8.2	7.8	7.2
Relative advantage			
Will lead to more effective methods of communicating with callers than our previous efforts.	8.3	8.3	7.6
Will have a greater impact on caller's cancer awareness than previous national initiatives.	4.8	4.7	4.8
Will result in greater behavioral change for callers.	3.8	3.7	4.3
Is a more efficient means to reach callers than techniques we have used in the past.	7.1	6.5	6.5
Is a better way to provide callers with cancer information.	8.0	7.3	8.0

Items	Time 1 (n = 82)	Time 2 (n = 86)	Time 3 (n = 71)
Riskiness			
Presents risks to our office.	3.6	3.3	3.7
Has a number of uncertain outcomes.	4.9	4.7	4.9
Is a risky method for communicating cancer information to callers.	2.3	2.3	3.0
Is a reliable way to communicate cancer information to callers.	7.7	7.6	7.9
Has predictable results.	6.6	6.2	6.5
Trialability			
Piloting computerization in a few offices...			
Informs people in other offices about its strengths and weaknesses.	9.2	8.9	9.0
Informs people in other offices about its effectiveness before it is adopted by the entire network.	9.2	9.2	8.9
Enables people in other offices to see how well the strategy works with callers.	9.0	9.0	8.7
Provides a valuable learning experience for other CIS offices.	9.0	9.2	8.6
Helps people in other offices gain information about whether the project will work across the entire network.	8.9	9.1	8.9
Lets people in other offices learn about new procedures before the entire network is asked to adopt them.	9.2	9.2	9.1

Items	Time 1 (n = 82)	Time 2 (n = 86)	Time 3 (n = 71)
Computer Knowledge			
I am knowledgeable in this area of computers.	5.1	6.3	6.3
I have appropriate skills for this computer effort.	6.1	7.2	7.0
I have been adequately trained to handle computer tasks.	4.8	6.5	6.3
I like to use computers for my work in this area.	7.9	8.5	7.9
I am comfortable using computers in this area.	7.2	7.7	7.6
Observability			
Will produce a visible change in our office's call busy rate.	6.3	7.1	7.7
Will produce a visible change in our call abandonment rate.	6.5	6.9	7.4
Complexity			
Places a number of additional demands on me.	5.6	5.3	5.2
Is complex.	6.5	6.6	6.1
Means that I can't meet other job responsibilities as well as I used to.	1.8	2.2	2.8
Raises a number of issues for me.	6.1	5.4	5.2

Items	Time 1 (n = 82)	Time 2 (n = 86)	Time 3 (n = 71)
Acceptance			
Should be supported by people at all levels of the CIS.	9.4	9.3	9.5
Is a positive way to reach callers.	6.5	6.7	7.3
Is a sound approach for reaching callers.	7.3	7.0	7.5
Is an acceptable method of communication for the CIS.	7.9	7.4	7.8

Note: Respondents were asked to respond to each item, indicating how much they agreed or disagreed with each statement on a scale of 0 to 10 where 0 indicates 'total disagreement' and 10 indicates 'total agreement'.

Computer knowledge was also directly relevant to the study of information technologies. Computer literacy has been defined in a number of different ways, many of which are too technical to be helpful in organizational settings. Definitions range from an understanding of computer capabilities, applications and algorithms (Conference Board of the Mathematical Sciences, 1972) to an understanding of computer applications, computer systems, computer programming and an anxiety-free attitude toward computing (Simonson et al., 1987). Low levels of computer literacy in organizations have increased the salience of training efforts, especially since they may reduce the level of uncertainty and stress associated with major changes in organizational technology (Kacmar et al., 1997). Assessing computer knowledge can allow managers to assess the level of computer skills in an office to determine the kind of computer support necessary to facilitate implementation. Because of its greater familiarity, respondents reported significantly higher levels of computer knowledge for communication initially (Johnson et al., 1996) and throughout the project. Somewhat surprisingly, given the demographics of CIS personnel, respondents expressed relatively high levels of liking for computers and comfort in using them for these applications.

An organizational member who can see the impact that a new technology has on his or her office is more likely to view the innovation in a favourable light. As might be expected, given their focus, higher evaluations were reported for the telephone service operations.

Table 6.5 Computerization attributes for outreach

Items	Time 1 (n = 82)	Time 2 (n = 86)	Time 3 (n = 71)
Compatibility			
Is similar to the techniques we have used in the past.	2.8	4.3	4.8
Will change the way that information is disseminated by the CIS.	8.0	7.9	8.2
Is compatible with our office's customary method of providing cancer information to the public.	7.0	7.8	7.2
Is like other initiatives we have implemented in the past.	3.4	4.4	4.1
Is different from previous national initiatives.	7.7	7.1	7.0
Adaptability			
Can be adapted to fit the needs of our office.	8.6	8.8	8.8
Can be modified for use in our office.	8.8	8.2	8.6
Can accommodate unique outreach efforts in our regional CIS office.	8.5	7.8	8.7
Can be easily adapted to different situations that arise at our office.	8.2	8.0	7.5
Relative advantage			
Will lead to more effective methods of communicating with callers than our previous efforts.	8.3	7.6	8.0
Will have a greater impact on caller's cancer awareness than previous national initiatives.	5.0	4.9	5.1
Will result in greater behavioral change for callers.	4.5	4.3	4.8
Is a more efficient means to reach callers than techniques we have used in the past.	7.8	6.9	7.4
Is a better way to provide callers with cancer information.	8.0	7.3	8.2

Items	Time 1 (n = 82)	Time 2 (n = 86)	Time 3 (n = 71)
Riskiness			
Presents risks to our office.	3.3	3.2	3.7
Has a number of uncertain outcomes.	5.1	4.8	5.7
Is a risky method for communicating cancer information to callers.	2.6	2.2	3.1
Is a reliable way to communicate cancer information to callers.	7.1	7.7	7.9
Has predictable results.	6.2	6.1	6.1
Trialability			
Piloting computerization in a few offices...			
Informs people in other offices about its strengths and weaknesses.	9.1	9.0	9.2
Informs people in other offices about its effectiveness before it is adopted by the entire network.	9.2	9.2	9.2
Enables people in other offices to see how well the strategy works with callers.	8.9	8.9	8.9
Provides a valuable learning experience for other CIS offices.	9.1	9.1	8.8
Helps people in other offices gain information about whether the project will work across the entire network.	8.8	9.0	9.1
Lets people in other offices learn about new procedures before the entire network is asked to adopt them.	9.3	9.2	9.4

Items	Time 1 (n = 82)	Time 2 (n = 86)	Time 3 (n = 71)
Computer Knowledge			
I am knowledgeable in this area of computers.	4.7	5.8	6.6
I have appropriate skills for this computer effort.	5.8	6.9	7.2
I have been adequately trained to handle computer tasks.	5.0	6.0	6.5
I like to use computers for my work in this area.	7.8	8.5	8.8
I am comfortable using computers in this area.	7.2	7.3	7.7
Observability			
Will produce a visible change in our office's call busy rate.	5.7	4.3	5.2
Will produce a visible change in our call abandonment rate.	4.6	3.3	4.2
Complexity			
Places a number of additional demands on me.	6.0	5.3	6.0
Is complex.	6.7	6.7	6.7
Means that I can't meet other job responsibilities as well as I used to.	2.0	2.7	2.5
Raises a number of issues for me.	6.7	5.2	5.8
Acceptance			
Should be supported by people at all levels of the CIS.	9.2	9.4	9.4
Is a positive way to reach callers.	6.6	6.7	7.5
Is a sound approach for reaching callers.	8.0	6.7	7.6
Is an acceptable method of communication for the CIS.	7.8	8.1	8.3

Note: Respondents were asked to respond to each item, indicating how much they agreed or disagreed with each statement on a scale of 0 to 10 where 0 indicates 'total disagreement' and 10 indicates 'total agreement'.

Computerization for communication and office management, perhaps because of their less pervasive impact on the work of others, were perceived as less complex than computerization for outreach and telephone service initially (Johnson, Meyer, Woodworth et al., 1996) and throughout this time period. Overall the results indicated only moderate concern for the complexity of these innovations.

Perhaps because of the broad-based consensus-building effort, all elements of computerization had relatively high levels of acceptance in our initial data gathering (Johnson, Meyer, Woodworth et al., 1996) and throughout the project across all types of innovation. This was especially noteworthy given the preceding pattern of findings that detailed differential reactions to specific attributes and innovations for the knowledge service delivery innovations. Especially noteworthy was the reaction to the question 'Should be supported by people at all levels of the CIS', with scores in the mid-9s, by far the highest evaluation of any of the items studied.

In sum, there was a slight dip in many items at Time 2. There was no clear loser for any of these innovations, although respondents were clearly more familiar with the communication innovations. Acceptance was clearly the most highly rated item across the innovations.

Information specialists' perceptions of computerization.

We asked ISs their perception of the CIS's computerization effort at three time points (Johnson, Chang, Meyer et al., 1995; Johnson, Chang, LaFrance, Meyer and Ethington, 1996; Johnson, LaFrance, Chang et al., 1997). We distributed the survey to PDs in every RO and asked that they photocopy the number of surveys so that every IS in each RO completed the instrument. As with the innovation characteristics survey, we focused on seven specific attributes that have been shown to be theoretically as well as pragmatically related to perceptions of innovations. However we did not ask ISs questions that were primarily related to management prerogatives - riskiness and trialability. ISs were asked to apply items indicating these various attributes to the operations of the telephone service with which they were directly charged with implementing: record keeping, information resources, and mailings (see Table 6.8 and Table 6.9).

Table 6.6 Computerization attributes for communication

Items	Time 1 (n = 82)	Time 2 (n = 86)	Time 3 (n = 71)
Compatibility			
Is similar to the techniques we have used in the past.	6.5	6.6	6.8
Will change the way that information is disseminated by the CIS.	7.4	7.7	8.1
Is compatible with our office's customary method of providing cancer information to the public.	7.5	8.2	7.5
Is like other initiatives we have implemented in the past.	4.5	5.3	5.2
Is different from previous national initiatives.	6.6	6.0	5.9
Adaptability			
Can be adapted to fit the needs of our office.	8.8	9.0	9.0
Can be modified for use in our office.	8.9	8.6	8.8
Can accommodate unique outreach efforts in our regional CIS office.	7.9	7.7	8.9
Can be easily adapted to different situations that arise at our office.	8.6	8.3	8.0
Relative advantage			
Will lead to more effective methods of communicating with callers than our previous efforts.	8.1	8.2	8.3
Will have a greater impact on caller's cancer awareness than previous national initiatives.	4.8	5.8	5.6
Will result in greater behavioral change for callers.	4.4	3.7	5.1
Is a more efficient means to reach callers than techniques we have used in the past.	7.4	7.1	7.6
Is a better way to provide callers with cancer information.	8.0	7.4	7.6
Is a better way to provide callers with cancer information.	8.0	7.4	7.6

Items	Time 1 (n = 82)	Time 2 (n = 86)	Time 3 (n = 71)
Riskiness			
Presents risks to our office.	2.5	3.0	3.4
Has a number of uncertain outcomes.	3.9	4.2	4.9
Is a risky method for communicating cancer information to callers.	2.2	2.5	3.6
Is a reliable way to communicate cancer information to callers.	7.7	7.0	7.7
Has predictable results.	6.7	6.1	6.6
Trialability			
Piloting computerization in a few offices...			
Informs people in other offices about its strengths and weaknesses.	9.0	8.9	8.9
Informs people in other offices about its effectiveness before it is adopted by the entire network.	9.1	9.0	8.9
Enables people in other offices to see how well the strategy works with callers.	9.0	8.8	8.7
Provides a valuable learning experience for other CIS offices.	9.0	9.0	8.6
Helps people in other offices gain information about whether the project will work across the entire network.	8.7	8.9	8.8
Lets people in other offices learn about new procedures before the entire network is asked to adopt them.	9.2	9.1	9.2

Items	Time 1 (n = 82)	Time 2 (n = 86)	Time 3 (n = 71)
Computer Knowledge			
I am knowledgeable in this area of computers.	6.4	7.4	7.5
I have appropriate skills for this computer effort.	6.7	7.6	7.7
I have been adequately trained to handle computer tasks.	5.8	7.0	7.0
I like to use computers for my work in this area.	8.2	8.5	8.8
I am comfortable using computers in this area.	7.9	8.0	8.2
Observability			
Will produce a visible change in our office's call busy rate.	4.7	3.9	5.2
Will produce a visible change in our call abandonment rate.	4.0	3.5	4.6
Complexity			
Places a number of additional demands on me.	4.9	4.0	5.2
Is complex.	5.6	5.7	5.6
Means that I can't meet other job responsibilities as well as I used to.	1.4	2.3	2.7
Raises a number of issues for me.	5.8	4.9	5.3

Items	Time 1 (n = 82)	Time 2 (n = 86)	Time 3 (n = 71)
Acceptance			
should be supported by people at all levels of the CIS.	9.4	9.3	9.6
Is a positive way to reach callers.	7.4	6.1	7.7
Is a sound approach for reaching callers.	7.4	6.8	7.5
Is an acceptable method of communication for the CIS.	7.5	7.6	8.1

Note: Respondents were asked to respond to each item, indicating how much they agreed or disagreed with each statement on a scale of 0 to 10 where 0 indicates 'total disagreement' and 10 indicates 'total agreement'.

While respondents did not see these three innovations as very similar to past initiatives, especially so for mailings, they still saw them as compatible with the operations of their offices. Adaptability received the highest ratings of any attribute, with a slight dip for mailings at Time 3. ISs generally saw these innovations as moderately effective and efficient, but, save for resources, generally saw them as only tangentially related to the central mission of the CIS of responding to callers (for example scores uniformly below 3 for the question: 'Will result in greater behavioral change in callers'). ISs had moderately high responses to the possibility of these innovations impacting upon the policy issues of busy signals and call abandonment rate, with a slight dip at Time 2. They were slightly less optimistic than their managers on this critical observability issue. Complexity had some of the most favourable scores, in the sense that ISs did not see these innovations as terribly complex nor increasing their responsibilities.

Table 6.7 Computerization attributes for office management

Items	Time 1 (n = 82)	Time 2 (n = 86)	Time 3 (n = 71)
Compatibility			
Is similar to the techniques we have used in the past.	4.1	5.3	5.3
Will change the way that information is disseminated by the CIS.	7.7	7.1	7.7
Is compatible with our office's customary method of providing cancer information to the public.	7.6	7.4	7.5
Is like other initiatives we have implemented in the past.	3.7	4.9	4.4
Is different from previous national initiatives.	7.7	6.7	6.5
Adaptability			
Can be adapted to fit the needs of our office.	8.8	8.9	8.9
Can be modified for use in our office.	8.8	8.8	8.7
Can accommodate unique outreach efforts in our regional CIS office.	7.9	7.8	8.8
Can be easily adapted to different situations that arise at our office.	8.4	8.4	7.8
Relative advantage			
Will lead to more effective methods of communicating with callers than our previous efforts.	7.3	8.0	7.7
Will have a greater impact on caller's cancer awareness than previous national initiatives.	4.4	4.7	4.8
Will result in greater behavioral change for callers.	4.0	3.3	4.6
Is a more efficient means to reach callers than techniques we have used in the past.	6.5	6.0	7.4
Is a better way to provide callers with cancer information.	7.4	7.1	7.8

Items	Time 1 (n = 82)	Time 2 (n = 86)	Time 3 (n = 71)
Riskiness			
Presents risks to our office.	2.4	2.6	3.0
Has a number of uncertain outcomes.	4.0	4.3	4.8
Is a risky method for communicating cancer information to callers.	1.6	1.9	3.2
Is a reliable way to communicate cancer information to callers.	7.4	6.9	7.5
Has predictable results.	6.3	5.9	6.3
Trialability			
Piloting computerization in a few offices...			
Informs people in other offices about its strengths and weaknesses.	9.0	9.1	8.9
Informs people in other offices about its effectiveness before it is adopted by the entire network.	9.0	9.1	8.9
Enables people in other offices to see how well the strategy works with callers.	9.0	8.8	8.7
Provides a valuable learning experience for other CIS offices.	8.9	9.0	8.6
Helps people in other offices gain information about whether the project will work across the entire network.	8.7	8.9	8.9
Lets people in other offices learn about new procedures before the entire network is asked to adopt them.	9.2	9.2	9.2

Items	Time 1 (n = 82)	Time 2 (n = 86)	Time 3 (n = 71)
Computer knowledge			
I am knowledgeable in this area of computers.	5.5	6.2	6.5
I have appropriate skills for this computer effort.	5.9	6.8	6.8
I have been adequately trained to handle computer tasks.	5.2	6.0	6.0
I like to use computers for my work in this area.	7.7	8.3	8.4
I am comfortable using computers in this area.	7.5	7.8	7.4
Observability			
Will produce a visible change in our office's call busy rate.	4.7	4.8	6.2
Will produce a visible change in our call abandonment rate.	3.9	4.9	5.3
Complexity			
Places a number of additional demands on me.	5.2	4.6	4.6
Is complex.	6.2	6.1	5.6
Means that I can't meet other job responsibilities as well as I used to.	1.5	2.4	2.4
Raises a number of issues for me.	5.7	5.0	5.4

Items	Time 1 (n = 82)	Time 2 (n = 86)	Time 3 (n = 71)
Acceptance			
Should be supported by people at all levels of the CIS.	9.2	9.2	9.3
Is a positive way to reach callers.	6.1	5.4	7.2
Is a sound approach for reaching callers.	6.7	6.2	7.7
Is an acceptable method of communication for the CIS.	7.5	7.3	7.7

Note: Respondents were asked to respond to each item, indicating how much they agreed or disagreed with each statement on a scale of 0 to 10 where 0 indicates 'total disagreement' and 10 indicates 'total agreement'.

Interestingly, in the first wave of data, people with more than four years of tenure reported lower levels of computer knowledge than did people with less than one year. In computerization related to information resources, people with more than four years of tenure reported lower levels of computer knowledge than did people with three to four years. In terms of mailings, people with more than four years of tenure reported lower levels of computer knowledge than did people with one to two years. In general, respondents reported a high level of comfort and a positive reaction to computerization, although their self-reported knowledge was only moderate. Interestingly, old-timers, while initially resistant to change, with more success and reference points to improvement over past practice, were more positive about computerization as time went on. There were increases in self-reported knowledge between Times 1 and 2, with a slight falling off for mailings at Time 3.

Table 6.8 Information specialists' perceptions of computerization attributes for record keeping

Items	Time 1 (n = 173)	Time 2 (n = 170)	Time 3 (n = 136)
Computerization...			
Compatibility			
Is similar to the techniques we have used in the past.	3.6	5.2	5.1
Is compatible with our office's customary method of providing cancer information to the public.	7.3	8.4	8.3
Allows me to apply my existing skills.	7.7	8.3	8.1
Is like other initiatives we have implemented in the past.	3.7	4.5	4.6
Adaptability			
Can be adapted to fit the needs of our office.	9.1	9.1	8.8
Can be modified for use in our office.	8.8	8.8	8.6
Is something we can build on in the future.	9.0	9.5	8.8
Can be easily adapted to different situations that arise at our office.	7.7	7.7	7.4

Note: Respondents were asked to respond to each item, indicating how much they agreed or disagreed with each statement on a scale of 0 to 10 where 0 indicates 'total disagreement' and 10 indicates 'total agreement'.

Items	Time 1 (n = 173)	Time 2 (n = 170)	Time 3 (n = 136)
Relative advantage			
Will lead to more effective methods of communicating with callers than our previous efforts.	6.7	6.5	6.6
Will have a greater impact on caller's cancer awareness than previous national initiatives.	3.3	2.3	4.1
Will result in greater behavioral change for callers.	2.2	1.6	2.2
Is a more efficient means to reach callers than techniques we have used in the past.	6.1	6.0	6.3
Is a better way to provide callers with cancer information.	6.6	6.8	6.4
Observability			
Will produce a visible change in our office's call busy rate.	6.4	8.1	6.7
Will produce a visible change in our call abandonment rate.	5.7	7.0	6.5
Complexity			
Places a number of additional demands on me.	4.3	4.1	3.7
Is complex.	4.3	3.9	3.2
Means that I can't meet other job responsibilities as well as I used to.	2.1	2.5	3.2
Raises a number of issues for me.	4.9	3.3	3.4

Items	Time 1 (n = 173)	Time 2 (n = 170)	Time 3 (n = 136)
Computer Knowledge			
I am knowledgeable in this area of computers.	5.3	7.4	7.8
I have appropriate skills for this computer effort.	7.2	8.2	8.4
I have been adequately trained to handle computer tasks.	6.2	8.2	8.2
I like to use computers for my work in this area.	8.2	8.8	8.8
I am comfortable using computers in this area.	8.0	8.6	8.7
Acceptance			
Is a positive way to reach callers.	8.9	9.3	8.7
Is a sound approach for reaching callers.	6.0	5.9	5.8
Is an acceptable method of outreach for the CIS.	6.3	6.6	6.2
Should be supported by people at all levels of the CIS.	6.9	7.9	7.4

ISs had slightly less favourable responses than managers for acceptance, especially so for mailings, for the critical question 'Should be supported by people at all levels of the CIS'. Again, contrary to our expectations, acceptance did not differ across innovations. One possible explanation for this pattern was that there may be a normative pro-innovation bias shared by organizational members. In other words, respondents may generally agree that information technology is a good idea, in part because of the Denver consensus-building national conference which stressed the importance of computerization for the long-term survival of the CIS (Johnson, Chang, et al., 1995).

Table 6.9 Information specialists' perceptions of computerization attributes for information resources

Items	Time 1 (n = 173)	Time 2 (n = 170)	Time 3 (n = 136)
Computerization...			
Compatibility			
Is similar to the techniques we have used in the past.	4.4	5.9	4.7
Is compatible with our office's customary method of providing cancer information to the public.	7.4	8.6	8.0
Allows me to apply my existing skills.	8.1	8.5	8.2
Is like other initiatives we have implemented in the past.	3.8	4.9	4.8
Adaptability			
Can be adapted to fit the needs of our office.	9.1	8.9	8.7
Can be modified for use in our office.	8.8	8.7	8.6
Is something we can build on in the future.	9.0	9.4	8.9
Can be easily adapted to different situations that arise at our office.	7.8	7.8	7.5

Note: Respondents were asked to respond to each item, indicating how much they agreed or disagreed with each statement on a scale of 0 to 10 where 0 indicates 'total disagreement' and 10 indicates 'total agreement'.

Items	Time 1 (n = 173)	Time 2 (n = 170)	Time 3 (n = 136)
Relative advantage			
Will lead to more effective methods of communicating with callers than our previous efforts.	7.7	7.4	7.4
Will have a greater impact on aller's cancer awareness than previous national initiatives.	4.0	2.9	4.6
Will result in greater behavioral change for callers.	2.6	2.0	3.0
Is a more efficient means to reach callers than techniques we have used in the past.	7.0	6.3	6.7
Is a better way to provide callers with cancer information.	8.0	7.7	7.7
Observability			
Will produce a visible change in our office's call busy rate.	6.6	7.3	6.6
Will produce a visible change in our call abandonment rate.	6.0	6.2	6.3
Complexity			
Places a number of additional demands on me.	4.1	4.1	3.7
Is complex.	4.5	4.4	4.0
Means that I can't meet other job responsibilities as well as I used to.	2.0	2.2	3.2
Raises a number of issues for me.	4.8	4.0	3.9

Items	Time 1 (n = 173)	Time 2 (n = 170)	Time 3 (n = 136)
Computer knowledge			
I am knowledgeable in this area of computers.	6.7	7.4	7.3
I have appropriate skills for this computer effort.	7.6	8.2	8.1
I have been adequately trained to handle computer tasks.	6.7	8.0	7.7
I like to use computers for my work in this area.	8.4	8.7	8.3
I am comfortable using computers in this area.	8.1	8.5	8.1
Acceptance			
Is a positive way to reach callers.	9.0	9.1	8.7
Is a sound approach for reaching callers.	6.8	6.7	6.9
Is an acceptable method of outreach for the CIS.	7.3	6.7	7.0
Should be supported by people at all levels of the CIS.	7.3	8.1	7.7

This favourable attitude toward computerization was supported by respondents' open-ended comments at the end of the survey such as 'computerization is a must' and 'computerization is a great idea'. These types of responses indicated that CIS members, who deliver an information-based product to the public, recognized the potential for improved information processing that comes with computerization, and the policy significance of computerization in the federal government (McGinnis et al., 1995). As we discussed in Chapter 2, this reiterates the importance of the interaction of different levels.

Table 6.10 Information specialists' perceptions of computerization attributes for mailing

Items	Time 1 (n = 173)	Time 2 (n = 170)	Time 3 (n = 136)
Computerization...			
Compatibility			
Is similar to the techniques we have used in the past.	1.9	2.5	3.2
Is compatible with our office's customary method of providing cancer information to the public.	6.3	6.6	6.5
Allows me to apply my existing skills.	7.6	7.7	6.9
Is like other initiatives we have implemented in the past.	3.4	3.6	3.6
Adaptability			
Can be adapted to fit the needs of our office.	9.1	8.7	8.1
Can be modified for use in our office.	8.8	8.5	8.0
Is something we can build on in the future.	8.7	8.8	8.4
Can be easily adapted to different situations that arise at our office.	7.5	7.8	6.7

Note: Respondents were asked to respond to each item, indicating how much they agreed or disagreed with each statement on a scale of 0 to 10 where 0 indicates 'total disagreement' and 10 indicates 'total agreement'.

Items	Time 1 (n = 173)	Time 2 (n = 170)	Time 3 (n = 136)
Relative advantage			
Will lead to more effective methods of communicating with callers than our previous efforts.	6.7	6.4	5.5
Will have a greater impact on caller's cancer awareness than previous national initiatives.	3.4	2.5	3.7
Will result in greater behavioral change for callers.	2.7	1.9	1.0
Is a more efficient means to reach callers than techniques we have used in the past.	6.8	4.9	5.8
Is a better way to provide callers with cancer information.	7.4	6.2	6.0
Observability			
Will produce a visible change in our office's call busy rate.	6.6	6.5	5.6
Will produce a visible change in our call abandonment rate.	5.9	6.0	5.8
Complexity			
Places a number of additional demands on me.	3.4	3.6	2.3
Is complex.	4.1	4.4	3.1
Means that I can't meet other job responsibilities as well as I used to.	1.6	2.4	3.0
Raises a number of issues for me.	4.9	4.8	4.4

Items	Time 1 (n = 173)	Time 2 (n = 170)	Time 3 (n = 136)
Computer knowledge			
I am knowledgeable in this area of computers.	4.0	6.3	5.9
I have appropriate skills for this computer effort.	7.2	8.1	7.9
I have been adequately trained to handle computer tasks.	5.3	7.4	7.0
I like to use computers for my work in this area.	7.7	8.2	7.4
I am comfortable using computers in this area.	7.5	8.4	7.2
Acceptance			
Is a positive way to reach callers.	6.6	8.4	5.6
Is a sound approach for reaching callers.	6.7	5.5	5.9
Is an acceptable method of outreach for the CIS.	7.3	7.3	7.2
Should be supported by people at all levels of the CIS.	8.7	7.7	7.7

In general, ISs were less favourable to the computerization effort than their managers, but still reacted positively overall. This reflects the generally lower enthusiasm of ISs also reported by their PDs (Fleisher et al., 1998). There did not appear to be the slight dip in many items at Time 2 experienced by management. For ISs, it appeared there might be a tendency for them to be more favourable as time went on. Adaptability was clearly the most highly rated attribute, which bodes well for the eventual implementation of these innovations. There was no clear loser, like Project 2, for this cluster of innovations, but some greater problems for mailings.

6.5 LESSONS LEARNED

This study provided us with a unique opportunity to examine a new organizational form as it simultaneously implemented multiple innovations designed to meet strategic objectives and faced the challenge of how best to cultivate an innovative organizational climate. If one can sample different innovations, one can get a more realistic picture of an organization's level of innovativeness (Meyer et al., 1995).

With knowledge of innovation attributes, managers can develop appropriate communication strategies to facilitate the implementation of innovations. For example innovations that are seen as more risky may require higher volumes of persuasive communication in the implementation stage (Fidler and Johnson, 1984). As we will see later in this section, often these processes are volatile, with dramatic changes in the perceptions of innovation attributes associated with other processes. There were also unintended consequences, with ironically CAG PDs for example later complaining about the increased complexity of decision-making and information overload resulting from the information technology innovations, a fairly common outcome of such innovations (Bennett and Bennett, 2003). All organizations should consciously weigh the attributes examined here before implementing innovations. These results emphasized the importance of paying attention to differences in the attributes of innovations in empirical work (Damanpour, 1991; Dearing et al., 1994; Johnson, Donohue et al., 1995; Ashmos et al., 1990; Downs and Mohr, 1976).

Innovation Profile

The innovation profile (Dearing and Meyer, 1994), an instrument that calculates potential adopters' perceptions about an innovation by summing an innovator's score for each attribute and calculating the mean, is a promising predictive tool. Further, this research supported Dearing et al.'s (1994) finding that reliability (riskiness), applicability (adaptability) and effectiveness (one component of relative advantage) are central to innovation adoption processes.

Four decades ago, Katz stated that 'the capacity of interpersonal channels to provide social support and enhanced confidence in the outcomes of the innovation can be crucial in innovation implementation' (Katz, 1963). Pragmatically, in an organization where contrasting innovations are compared to one another, managers should carefully match their communication efforts to the nature of the innovations they are implementing (Johnson, Donohue et al., 1995). Perceptions of innovation characteristics may entail more or less challenging communication tasks (Fidler and Johnson, 1984), which in turn may make more or less salient the role of communication in innovation processes, suggesting a contingent impact of innovation characteristics.

For innovations with high levels of perceived relative advantage and acceptance, a mediated communication strategy is perhaps most appropriate. The use of mediated communication, such as company newsletters, videos, magazines and so on, may create an atmosphere of involvement and interest, producing a certain receptivity to organization-wide innovations (Johnson, Donohue et al., 1995). These channels are also more cost efficient than interpersonally driven participation or persuasion strategies (Fidler and Johnson, 1984; Nutt, 1986). Especially in situations where there is a highly motivated set of organizational members, the direct provision of information may be a highly effective strategy (Katz and Kahn, 1978). Alternatively, in the case of certain complex and risky information technologies, or situations with low levels of computer knowledge, direct interpersonal communication and additional training may be necessary ingredients for successful innovation implementation (Fidler and Johnson, 1984; Dearing et al., 1994).

A focus on innovation attributes allows us to explore the nuances of contrasting innovations within an organization. It is important to acknowledge differences, because generalizing from one innovation to innovativeness of the larger organization may be misleading. For managers of preventive health innovations, such a mistake could be costly in two ways. Firstly while innovations that are perceived to be high in risk may be warmly received in highly innovative organizations, they run the risk of being rejected in less innovative organizational climates. Secondly the failure of a risky innovation can have a dampening effect on the innovative climate of an organization, causing organizational members to view future innovations as having increasingly uncertain outcomes. In other words, managers need to be aware that contextual factors impact upon the ways in which innovation attributes affect innovation outcomes (Downs and Mohr, 1976; Bigoness and Perrault, 1981).

Managers who assess organizational members' perceptions of innovation attributes can employ this information as a diagnostic tool to evaluate the fit of an innovation with an organization, to anticipate problems arising as a result of innovation, and to modify innovations to reflect the changes that stakeholders deem necessary. These steps are ones which will enable managers to secure the successful implementation of an innovation within their organization. In addition, the process of asking organizational members about their perceptions of innovation creates a dialogue about innovation within the organization. This dialogue has the potential for generating creative solutions to problems and the organizational learning necessary to produce more effective interventions in the future. Additionally, these outcomes of innovation-related communication may increase the extent to which organizational members perceive that they work in an innovative climate.

Management's influence on innovation outcomes through communication may be especially salient to new organizational forms such as the CISRC, that provide a strategic alliance between researchers and practitioners within a geographically dispersed network. In this case, managers play a key role in building support for innovation by developing and maintaining an innovation-related communication structure across the network as we saw in the sociometric results in Chapter 5. In addition, managers of innovation in new organizational forms need to develop competent conflict resolution skills. Since researchers and practitioners represent distinct groups of stakeholders in the innovation process, they are likely to have differing interests in the innovation process (Weiss, 1983). For example practitioners may be primarily concerned with the consequences of innovation that impact upon their organization's functioning, while researchers may be chiefly interested in the theoretical implications or the generalizability of their findings. Skilful managers need to mediate conflicts that may arise as a result of competing interests between groups of stakeholders.

If organizational members do not perceive that their voices are heard in the dialogue about innovation, they may engage in dysfunctional outcomes such as withholding information on the innovation implementation process (Coch and French, 1948). While some might view the involvement of multiple stakeholders in evaluating innovations as potentially leading to unproductive conflict, bogging stakeholders down in time-consuming discussion and debates, it can also democratize access to innovation-related information (Weiss, 1983). Thus strategic innovation-related organizational communication can facilitate the process by which stakeholders in new organizational forms pool resources to generate, adopt or implement multiple innovations in the face of competitive pressures.

Finally, managers of new organizational forms must not only be concerned with the successful adoption and implementation of innovations to meet specific strategic objectives; they must also focus on the generation of innovations, the process by which organizational members become more innovative. The way in which managers respond to stakeholders' perceptions of innovation influences the organization's ability to generate future innovations. For example managers who demonstrate the importance of organizational members' perceptions of innovation by soliciting feedback and incorporating suggestions to reinvent innovations are also cultivating the climate of innovation within their organization. If organizational members feel that their voices are heard, then they will perceive that they have a higher level of participation in innovation processes. In contrast, organizational members who do not perceive that management listens to their ideas will experience lower levels of involvement in the innovation process. Since participation has been linked to innovativeness in general (Damanpour, 1991; Fidler and Johnson, 1984; Johnson, Donohue et al., 1995; Johnson, Meyer et al., 1997), managers who are responsive to stakeholders' participation in innovation processes have the potential to influence an organization's level of innovativeness, hence its ability to generate future innovations. In new organizational forms such as the CISRC, where innovation is often the *raison d'être,* understanding how to organize innovation at the meta level is critical.

Project 2 and the Strength of Weak Ties

> ... implementation effectiveness ... is a function of (a) the strength of an organization's climate for the implementation of that innovation and (b) the fit of the innovation to targeted users' values. (Klein and Sorra, 1996, p. 1055)

In many ways Project 2 was the most interesting, novel and fundamentally different of the interventions contained in the CISRC. Marcy Meyer (1996a), in her award-winning dissertation work, focused on weak ties, perceived organizational innovativeness and perceptions of innovation characteristics over four points in time to examine the underlying theoretic dynamics. Longitudinally, this research explored the degree to which organizational members form general perceptions about organizational innovativeness based on their experience with a specific innovation.

Range and prominence measures are indicators of informal communication network structure (Burt, 1991), specifically weak ties, which have important implications for innovation. Individuals who are exposed to information about innovation from a variety of sources are more likely to perceive that they work in an innovative environment, and use that information to make evaluations about the pros and cons of an innovation. Meyer's (1996a) study measured weak ties with the range measures of contacts and non-redundant contacts and the prominence measure of choice status using the STRUCTURE network analysis program (Burt, 1991). Since these indices are characteristics of an organizational member's number of diverse contacts, they are comparable to that individual's weak ties within the network (Granovetter, 1973). In the interest of parsimony and as a result of detailed psychometric work (Meyer, 1996b), the innovation attributes of relative advantage, observability, adaptability and acceptance tapped one manifest trait, pros, while complexity and risk comprised cons.

Based on the previous discussion, it seems likely that weak ties, perceived organizational innovativeness, and the pros and cons of innovation are intimately connected constructs. As we have seen, informal communication structure at one point in time should impact upon perceived organizational innovativeness and perceptions about the pros and cons of innovation at later points in time. An innovative climate should be a predictor of the degree to which organizational members will be supportive of a particular innovation. Likewise, organizational members should form general perceptions about the extent to which they work in an innovative climate through their experience with a specific innovation in the organizational context. In a detailed examination of various theoretical alternatives, Meyer and Johnson (1997) developed an optimal model of the interaction of these various factors. This research demonstrated that, over time, weak ties affected perceptions of innovation characteristics and perceived organizational innovativeness impacted upon perceptions of pros. These findings suggest that climate is a predictor of the degree to which organizational members will be supportive of particular innovations.

Although weak ties affected perceptions of innovation characteristics, predicted links were surprisingly weak; the most notable effects were produced by unexpected lag effects. This finding indicated that it takes time for organizational members to process novel ideas; similarly it has been observed that knowledge transfers are not instantaneous: it takes time for people to absorb information (Jensen and Meckling, 1995). Although individuals with high levels of weak ties may be exposed to information about innovation from a variety of sources, this type of communication does not have an immediate impact on the degree to which they perceive that they work in an innovative environment, nor does it noticeably impact upon the degree to which they are supportive of particular innovations in the short term. In the long run however, informal innovation-related communication can have more pronounced consequences for organizational members' evaluations of pros and cons.

The 'amplification effect' (Renn, 1991) suggests that weak ties should impact upon future perceptions of innovation by amplifying existing attitudes about their pros and cons. If people communicate with their weak ties about the favourable aspects of the innovation, then this could have a positive effect on attitudes about that innovation over time. If, on the other hand, organizational members communicate with their weak ties about the unfavourable aspects of the innovation, then this could have a negative effect on attitudes about innovation over time. In contrast to the amplification effect, the 'spiral of silence' phenomenon (Noelle-Neumann, 1974) suggests that attitudes about innovation may not necessarily get converted to talk among weak ties. Organizational members may share dissimilar views about innovation, but the person with relatively less knowledge about the topic may fail to express his or her opinions because he or she perceives that he or she lacks expertise or is unwilling to go against prevailing opinions. In this case, vocal views about innovation would eventually become paramount in the network.

Congruent with the 'amplification effect' (Renn, 1991), the data suggested that weak ties do indeed impact upon future perceptions of innovation, by amplifying existing attitudes. At least in this case, weak ties at Time 1 and Time 2 had relatively strong negative impacts on perceptions of the pros of innovation at Time 4. The time lag between weak ties at Time 1 and Time 2 and pros of innovation at Time 4 may be due in part to the sparseness of innovation-related communication in this organization. This finding suggested that perceptions of innovation were influenced by the social amplification effect in highly segmented networks, but to a lesser extent, and at a much slower rate than would be expected in dense networks. This finding suggested the importance of studying the strength of strong ties (Krackhardt, 1992) in securing support for innovations.

In addition, the lag effects mirror Weenig and Midden's (1991) unexpected finding that negative advice was obtained more frequently from weak than strong ties, and reiterates the importance of both positive and negative information from opinion leaders, with negative information often having more weight in adoption decisions (Leonard-Barton, 1985). It might be that organizational members were more likely to make negative evaluations of an innovation if they do not have a vested interest in it. Since perceived organizational innovativeness at Time 1 had a strong negative impact on pros at Time 4, organizational members may have been unsupportive of this particular innovation because they did not perceive it to be a good match with the current innovative climate of their organization. These unanticipated findings accent the importance of evaluating the fit of an innovation within an organization (Klein and Sorra, 1996).

Additionally, the unexpected finding that cons at Time 2 had a strong negative effect on weak ties at Time 3 points to a structurational account of innovation and communication (Lewis and Seibold, 1993). Apparently, perceptions of negative outcomes associated with innovation can put a damper on future levels of innovation-related innovation communication among organizational members. This finding puts a new twist on the old saying 'If you don't have anything nice to say, don't say anything at all'. Unfortunately this spiral of silence can have negative consequences for the course of particular innovations in organizations.

7. Innovation in knowledge management organizations: lessons learned

7.1 INTRODUCTION

The complexity of political, regulatory, and technological changes confronting most organizations has made organizational change and adaptation a central research issue ... (Greenwood and Hinings, 1996, p. 1022)

Innovations are met with a variety of reactions by potential adopters, from skepticism and derision to excitement and hope. All of us assess innovations on the basis of what we already know, already own, currently use, and currently have invested. (Dearing et al., 1994, p. 17)

As we have seen, the study of innovation related to KM in new organizational forms is one of great pragmatic importance for our society, especially so given the high failure rate of innovation implementation (Klein et al., 2001). Concrete cases, such as this one, contribute to a more certain view of KM which has sometimes seemed an amorphous concept (Stewart, 2001). Chapter 1 focused on the overall context of this four–year project, detailing the emergence of new organizational forms in the health services arena. In Chapter 2 I focused on the intersection of three levels – framing, climate and attributes – crucial to these processes and the important issue of the varying goals of researchers and practitioners. Chapter 3 developed a more complete picture of the history and formal structure of the CIS, including the importance of CoPs and conferences, as well as discussing the changing face of cancer–related information in our society. In Chapter 4 I specified the CIS's external relations and its approach to developing coalitions with partners, including the CISRC program project grant. I concluded this chapter with lessons learned for consortia and the human side of organizations. Chapter 5 described the array of informal communication channels used by CIS members to communicate about innovation, and presented the network analysis results for the project. It also discussed the relationships between formal and informal structures, the incredible diversity of communication channels that can be used in the contemporary organization, and the theoretically problematic finding of low levels of innovation communication. Chapter 6 reported the results of our research on the innovation processes related to KM within the CIS, providing an interesting contrast between the information technology and the CISRC knowledge delivery innovations. I focused at the end of this chapter on predictive tools that can be used to analyse innovations a priori, and the relatively understudied problems associated with negative communication and opinion leadership relating to Project 2.

This chapter focuses on the broader lessons learned from this four–year project. While there has been an increasing volume of conceptually oriented KM literature, this case answers a need for richer empirical studies (Landry and Amara, 2001). Here I discuss how the richly detailed case can be generalized to KM and innovation in other organizations. I then focus on the problematic area of RPR in consortia. I then bring these themes together to discuss what is success. Finally, the chapter ends with a Postscript on what has happened to the CIS since the completion of this study.

7.2 LESSONS FOR INNOVATION WITHIN KM ORGANIZATIONS

> Even though creators have definite ideas about how their innovations should be applied, it is what potential users do with innovations that matter most (and frequently what potential users 'do' with innovations is ignore them). (Dearing et al., 1994, p. 17)

A compelling feature of research on innovation is that it stands at the intersection of so many important theoretical and policy issues. This longitudinal research project in a new organizational form suggests that the classic diffusion of innovation paradigm does not work particularly well in this context. The fundamental issue for today's organization may not be any one innovation, but what that innovation teaches us about the underlying structures and processes that will produce subsequent innovations. The CISRC was the most visible element of a 'factory for innovations' approach within the CIS. This strategy created a meta–innovation that provided an overall structural framework for continuous learning, especially about innovation processes and how they should be changed to be more effective.

Future Directions for Innovation Research

> For some there is no release from the overwhelming weight of information, from the task of structuring and clarifying, from the requirement for inductive conceptualization. The result is death by data asphyxiation – the slow and inexorable sinking into the swimming pool that started so cool, clear, and inviting and now has become a clinging mass of maple syrup. (Pettigrew, 1990, p. 111)

> However, it was clear even at the beginning of the study that such abundant data could also smother me, obscuring the very process patterns I wished to discern. (Leonard–Barton, 1990, p. 49)

A central meta–level issue concerning innovation research, which is after all a quest for knowledge, is how to generate wisdom about generating wisdom. In some ways, especially for longitudinal research, we need a KM system for innovation research. Recently a literature has begun to emerge on the management of longitudinal research studies in organizations (Huber and Van de Ven, 1995) and communication (Watt and Van Lear, 1996; Poole et al., 2000). One of the central assertions of this literature, that a researcher should sample a wide variety of innovations with different attributes (Van de Ven and Poole, 1990), is a cornerstone of this study.

Aside from the call for more theory, there has been no clearer clarion call in communication and innovation research than the one for more over time research (for example Monge et al., 1984; Galaskiewicz, 1996; Kimberly, 1976; Klein et al., 2001; Monge, 1990). Arguments have suggested that longitudinal research will lead to more theoretical insights, as well as being more in tune with the fundamental assumptions (for example process) of current theories (for example Van de Ven and Poole, 1990).

While nearly everyone agrees that significant theoretical and empirical pay–offs would result from increased research studies conducted over time, there has been a lot of time for this to occur, with very few empirical demonstrations of this assumption. Instead the literature has been dominated by cross–sectional research designs (which, at least in terms of access, are often difficult enough to realize). But moving to longitudinal research vastly complicates the research enterprise, introducing a host of concerns that are often told in folktales, rather than in explicit formal treatment in the literature. In particular researchers are confronted with information overload in the face of often overwhelming data; they must manage relationships with respondents for the long term; and they must balance concerns of validity with the practical realities of longitudinal research (see Johnson, Bettinghaus et al., 1997). While in cross–sectional research there has been a trend to ever more complex models, the longitudinal researcher quickly realizes that they must simplify their conceptual approach to add a temporal dimension, focusing on central issues. They must recognize both the limits of their respondents to report very complicated information, as well as the limits of available analytic techniques to deal with complex models over time (Leonard–Barton, 1990).

Certainly this research stream points to a number of compelling over time findings: the strength of weak ties temporal lag and the associated flow of negative news through weak ties (Meyer, 1996a), the CIS's approach to convention planning continually improving an organizational process (Pobocik et al., 1996), and the evidence for competing models of the relationship between internal and external communication (Johnson and Chang, 2000) which suggested a lagged communication stars explanation, and so on. The unexpected lag effects for weak ties had two KM implications. Firstly it takes time for organizational members to process novel ideas, with certain similarities with the move from tacit to explicit knowledge; secondly informal innovation–related communication has pronounced long–term consequences for organizational members' evaluations of the pros and cons of innovation.

Who are the customers?

For different innovations at different levels, people in the CIS were simultaneously or sequentially customers, clients, opinion leaders and change agents. Under the assumption that individuals who hold positions as OCC staff, PIs, PDs, TSMs, OMs and PP personnel were the most influential players in the adoption and implementation of preventive health innovations in the CIS, we focused most of our research efforts on them. While the majority of CIS members were key stakeholders, innovation studies have traditionally focused on adopters or end–users, individuals who actually make adoption decisions. Earlier I stated that of all CIS members, OCC staff and PDs were most like adopters because they were most involved in centralized decision–making processes related to innovation implementation. In contrast, OMs were probably least like adopters because they were not very involved in implementing the three new intervention strategies studied here. Results indicated that there were significant differences in perceptions about Project 2 between PDs and individuals in all other functional groups. These findings suggest that innovation adopters and stakeholders form contrasting views about specific innovations based in part on their roles.

What kind of knowledge, in what form, did its external customers want was also a major problem for the CIS. The CIS was not only changing the types of knowledge it dealt with but also its ultimate customers – client and consumers vs. researchers – and its manner of distribution. Historically the

CIS had developed very effective means of service delivery to a wide array of external users by means of the telephone and mailings. Towards the end of our data collection these services were broadening to include outreach partners and Web–based delivery. The computerization effort was primarily aimed at personnel within the CIS and the personal transfer of knowledge that was often tacit.

The CISRC's research output was the most problematic – how does the CIS measure the results of these research projects? Clearly the PDs thought not enough effort was devoted to translating these results into practice within the CIS (Fleisher et al., 1998). Perhaps more importantly, how do we assess its impact as a communication laboratory: citations in the scientific literature (of which there were few for the CISRC publications), new theory, dissemination to other organizations? The answers to these questions are still being developed and pose important questions for policy–makers within NCI who are increasingly focused on how best to translate all of their research products into practice (NCI, 2003). All this is perhaps most poignantly summarized in the following quote from a report of a replication of Project 1:

> Although such research could make important contributions to the science of cancer prevention and control, sustaining interventions like the one tested here is of major concern. At the present time, there would seem to be few organizations prepared to adopt this type of intervention beyond the research setting. (Marcus et al., 2001, p. 213)

What is the stage?

In the early stages of innovation a maximum amount of diversity and freedom is needed; in the implementation stage greater certainty is required, at least in terms of formal authority and design (Galbraith, 1982; Rogers and Agarwala–Rogers, 1976). However the distinction between stages may not be clear–cut or linear. Neither is adoption a binary adopt–not adopt decision, but rather often really shades of grey, and contingent. Indeed partial adoption may be more the norm for innovations than wholesale, unequivocal transference of identical ideas.

According to Albrecht and Bach (1997), during the implementation stage the innovation may be initially tested on a small–scale, trial basis. This could be the 'little teeny trial' or pilot stage discussed in Chapter 2, which in organizations produces the important insight that the same innovation may be at different stages in differing units. In large, complex organizations the future is often already here in some divisions, and far in the distance in others. Some units are early adopters, and are well ahead on the implementation learning curve, by the time others choose to adopt. So stages for the same innovation may be multiple throughout the same organization.

Somewhat similarly, a multilevel innovation may be operating within different stages and time frames. The decision to adopt the innovation factory of the CISRC occurred prior to the adoption and implementation of specific innovations and provided the framework in which they became possible. So adoption (at least of the CISRC) had by and large been accomplished when this research started, although that was not clear to all parties, and while there was adoption of individual projects and computerization efforts, in a larger sense this was fine–tuning the products of a larger process.

How is it communicated?

One basic obstacle in striving for simplicity for the organizational communication researcher is the complexity and proliferation of communication channels in the contemporary organization. Even cross–sectionally, in a relatively rich resource environment, we found it was not possible to inventory the full range of communication in the CIS. We had to choose, based on the traditional diffusion literature, to focus in depth on one form of communication – interpersonal – while more selectively researching others. Unfortunately events such as the growth of electronically mediated communication overtook us, and we had to change our emphasis as the project unfolded. Over time research then is confronted with both meta–research questions such as 'How do we study what we are interested in?' as well as the classic questions of 'What is it that we should study?'

Somewhat ironically, given the proliferation of communication channels, there was a dearth of communication at a national level in the interpersonal modality. While this type of communication has been the classic focus of diffusion research (for example Rogers and Kincaid, 1981), it may not be the most important type for new organizational forms that are geographically dispersed. Barry Wellman (1995), in the context of his work focusing on the new media and the development of community, has made the observation that mediated communication, such as the telephone, served to perpetuate close relationships. However face–to–face contacts often were based on more 'accidental' factors (for example proximity, work relationships) and thus more subject to variations. Increasingly there are fragmented communication structures developing in organizations, with individuals divided by their modalities, as well as more substantive issues. So some people use e–mail, others fax, and still others telephone, all of which reduces the amount of communication in any one channel.

It was our general perception that the various CIS national meetings (see Chapter 3), especially those involving CoPs, were the critical communication and social influence events during the course of this project (also see Pettigrew, 1990). In effect, during meetings time was condensed, ideas were crystallized and larger events were set in motion (Morra, Van Nevel et al., 1993). The processes involved may be akin to the classic findings of Lawrence and Lorsch (1967a, b, c), with the more uncertain world of the contemporary organization requiring a move upward from interpersonal innovation communication to more group–level activities.

As we have seen, a whole host of factors cause the selection of an exponentially proliferating array of channels. The focus on channels is somewhat akin to classic demographic approaches to social research; it focuses on crude surface distinctions (for example e–mail versus voice mail) that mask more powerful underlying processes. A focus on selection, rather than on the effects of media, may be posing the wrong questions for research in this area (Walther, 1994). While some work has focused on interpretation and meaning, dealing with issues like the symbol–carrying capacity of various media, unfortunately underlying processes associated with context the content of messages and frameworks for understanding meaning are only tangentially addressed in this literature (Sitkin et al., 1992).

Historically we must also confront issues related to the growth and development of channels, which unexpectedly became an important issue as our project unfolded. While the Pony Express constituted a very interesting (some might even say romantic) conduit for messages in the nineteenth century American West, it was quickly supplanted by other channels that offered compelling competitive advantages. If channels are a tool, then it is easy to understand how they can be quickly discarded if another channel, more useful for accomplishing the underlying function comes along. However for some individuals, channels also become a 'signature skill', that reveals their unique talents and experience (Leonard, 1995). So channel specialization, not equivalence or substitutability, may be the critical issue (Reder and Conklin, 1987).

As we have suggested, channels may be only the tip of the iceberg. The question is not which channel we choose, but why. There may be an infinite combination of sources and channels that will provide us with an answer. So the real issue is what answers will satisfy our quest and how much time and effort we are willing to expend. The more important the problem, the greater the variety of sources and channels we will consult and the more exotic and different from our normal information field they will be. In the modern organization, at any one time period, an individual has incredible freedom of choice in the selection of communication channels, which unfortunately makes it more and more difficult to conduct organizational communication research.

How much communication is needed?

Following the classic diffusion of innovation literature, we focused on the network of interpersonal innovation–related communication in this research. However we found levels of communication that do not conform to either our normative or theoretic understandings of innovation processes. They do however conform to other empirical findings. We believe that this pattern suggests interesting new lines of inquiry for an area of research that sorely needs them (Drazin and Schoonhoven, 1996; Fiol, 1996).

In spite of decades of research on organizational communication, we have at best only a fuzzy notion of what 'dosage' is needed for particular effects. What volume of communication do we need to achieve particular purposes (Farace et al., 1978)? Ultimately, in spite of what are on the face of it very low levels of communication, as we will soon see, at least on some levels the CISRC was successful.

Managers' most important role in many innovation perspectives is as a stimulus or cue to action. They must define the most important issues that an organization needs to face (for example Rogers, 2003). As we have seen, this is precisely what OCC staff did during the Denver conference. They defined computerization as a critical organizational issue. However they left the actual implementation to a CoP representing all elements of the CIS in the form of the CAG. Generally managers should encourage employees to develop weak ties to encourage information sharing throughout the organization (Johnson, 1996); the structure of CAG promoted just this sort of sharing. As Duncan Watts (2003) has ably pointed out, to achieve certain contagion effects, volume may not be the issue; but who or what groups are 'infected' and 'percolating' the change, because of their centrality, may be more critical.

Summary

Most interestingly, paradox and moderation often govern innovation processes in organizations. Fundamentally, in organizations there is a tension between need to restrict innovation and to support it (Dougherty and Hardy, 1996; Johnson, 1993). The literature has focused too much on individual roles, rather than formal structures that sustain innovations (Dougherty and Hardy, 1996). A balance must be reached between efficiency, which results from highly constrained systems, and effectiveness. While it is important to reduce information load for example, it is also important to allow some leakage between units, so that new ideas and perspectives can be brought to problems (Peters and Waterman, 1982). Zaltman et al. (1973) have argued that low formalization, decentralization and high complexity lead to idea generation that reflects the market–driven forces necessary for informally generated innovations. Networks may be especially useful for more qualitative information exchanges based on expert knowledge or ideas; they also create incentives for learning and the dissemination of information that promotes the quick translation of ideas into action (Powell, 1990). One way of resolving this paradox is to focus on symbolically important projects that convince both internal and external groups of the organization's 'success' in working on innovations. Moderation, a balancing of forces, is also critical for slack resources, with both too little and too much contributing to higher odds of innovation failure (Nohria and Gulati, 1996).

As we have seen, innovation is a dynamic process, with often subtle and unexpected relationships between variables. It may be time for a new paradigm, one with a more critical edge, for innovation research: not only is the existing literature pro–innovation, it is also pro–communication. The most important issue may be the interaction of multiple contextual levels (for example ROs, the OCC), each with different interpretations, each with different cost–benefit equations, for a particular innovation (Meyer and Goes, 1988). This approach also offers some hope of bridging micro and macro levels of organizational behaviour related to innovations (Lewis and Seibold, 1996).

7.3 LESSONS LEARNED FOR CONSORTIA

The transfer of knowledge from researchers to potential users is impeded, however, by the social separation of researchers from users. The two belong to different communities with few shared activities or sentiments and little social interaction ... (Beyer and Trice, 1994, p. 675)

The development of consortia can be couched as a structural hole problem (Johnson, 2004). It has been empirically examined in a number of economic contexts including initial public offering markets, the market for employee talent, residential real estate markets, purchases of agricultural technology and so on (Pollock et al., 2004). The possibility of bridging the RPR structural hole has been a recurring theme of leaders of academic disciplines (Applegate, 2001, 2002; Cullen et al., 2001; Van de Ven, 2000, 2002). It has also been noted that even for applied sub–fields such as health communication, our greatest research shortcoming is our lack of relevance to practitioners (Babrow and Mattson, 2003; Dorsey, 2003; Thompson, 2003).

Initially, CIS practitioners saw many advantages, often noted in the literature, to participating in the CISRC. Firstly ultimately their primary goal was the improved practice that could be gained by accessing intellectual resources to solve problems (Cullen et al., 1999), primarily in this case expanding the reach of the CIS to include a more diverse set of users. Secondly they could also gain a buffer to ultimate accountability by using researchers as stalking horses who floated trial balloons for their problem solutions, gaining the considerable benefit of having someone else to blame for changes or failures, thus spreading their risks (Cullen et al., 1999). This reasoning was particularly important for Project 2, the most radical departure from CIS practice (Fleisher et al., 1998). Thirdly practitioners could enhance their professional status by appealing to professional standards (Cullen et al., 1999), especially in the university and medical settings of CIS ROs, where research carries much weight in the status game. Fourthly especially when students or more junior faculty members are involved, practitioners can feel good about making a pro–social contribution to someone's education or career development. The TEAM project was the focus of several students' MA and preliminary PhD work, as well as two doctoral dissertations (Johnson, LaFrance, Chang, Pobocik et al., 1997).

The parties have substantial potential common benefits from a successful RPR, including securing both physical and material resources and intellectual stimulation (Cullen et al., 1999; March, 2000). It was also obvious that policy–makers saw substantial benefits to be had from interactions between the various parties in the research enterprise, with increasing calls from the NCI (NCI, 2003) and the Fund for the Improvement of Postsecondary Education (2003) among others, for holistic examinations of research problems through the development of synergistic relationships among often fractured disciplines (Wandersman et al., 1997). Many have suggested that a richer intellectual synergy can develop from combining theory and practice (Walton, 1985), resulting in greater understanding and a more comprehensive view of phenomena of interest. Such consortia can also make implementation of solutions more likely (Beyer and Trice, 1994) and increase the policy significance of research resulting in greater societal–level benefits. With such compelling advantages, one is left to ask: 'Why don't more consortia develop?' The answers to this question lie in a closer examination of SHBs.

The RPR can easily be cast as a structural hole problem given the separate communities represented by these two groups (Cullen et al., 2001), with little communication occurring naturally (Amabile et al., 2001), but with considerable potential system benefits that could accrue from brokered linkages between them. Brokers who translate, coordinate and align perspectives are needed, but these SHBs also need to be able to address often conflicting interests (Kuhn, 2002). The marketable commodity in this research environment is not individual scientific expertise, but the scientific capital one can bring to the table through the network of relationships they have with others. The substantial differences in the motives and perceptual frameworks stemming from the different cultures in which they are embedded (Rynes et al., 2001), highlight the importance of SHBs in the emergence, maintenance and dissolution of RPRs, such as the CISRC. As Burt (2000) has established, sometimes SHBs are needed in situations when two parties are aware of each other, and may even have modest communication activity, but are so focused on their own projects they cannot establish meaningful relationships. The SHB acting as a *tertius*, or the third who benefits, strategically moves accurate, ambiguous, or distorted information to achieve control benefits (Burt, 2000).

Failure to meet the earlier promise of relationships may result in a move to institutionalize trust through formalizing relationships (for example written contracts with performance obligations) (Johnson, 2004), something clearly revealed in the PD's 'lessons learned' monograph (Fleisher et al., 1998). In the end, the parties need each other's specialized contributions (for example access to a research site, research expertise) to gain the benefits of an overarching system (for example a granting agency to which they must attend) (Cullen et al., 1999; Walton, 1985; Amabile et al., 2001; Mohrman et al., 2001).

While both parties have things to gain from an RPR, they often have even more to lose, which can lead to difficulties in maintaining relationships and even their eventual dissolution. One of the paramount values of any science is the objectivity of the researcher and the preservation of their ability to maintain their independence and integrity. Often practitioners, by questioning some assumptions, threaten researchers' autonomy in ways that call into question these fundamental principals. Practitioners seldom have any great concern for the integrity of the research process, especially relating to traditional scientific verities associated with rigorous research and internal validity (Killman et al., 1993). They will change interventions if they sense they are not working to the benefit of their project, since this is after all what they do daily in their operations. 'Because sponsors' needs come first, program improvement second, and evaluator's needs are only a third priority, in many evaluation studies you'll have little control over the evaluation itself and none, typically, over the object of evaluation' (Dearing, 2000, p. 8). Practitioners also may not respect researchers' needs for confidentiality of privileged scientific information, thus interfering with patent, publication, and other intellectual property rights (Keen and Stocklmayer, 1999). All of these elements point to the critical need for the mediation of an SHB for the continued development of the RPR.

Relationships with practitioners can also be very threatening to researchers' self–concepts, something to which an SHB must attend. Firstly as Goodall (1989) has articulated, researchers are often manipulated by skilled practitioners so that these practitioners can achieve their own ends. Secondly critique from practitioners often centres around two opposing themes of common sense or naivety: either 'you're not telling us anything we do not already know' or your ideas are so 'pie in the sky' or abstract, that they could never work. Since these judgements are often based on professional experience and anecdote, they are not easily refutable. They also may be quite telling, since we seek to often describe the world as it is, we lag behind real world events and often merely describe the experience of a skilled practitioner. So practitioners often feel researchers are out of touch with real world practices (Rynes et al., 2001; Ford et al., 2003), a critical shortcoming in this fast–moving world. Similarly, in our quest for methodological rigour, we often ignore variables, especially political and legal ones, that any practitioner must consider before implementing a new practice. Paradoxically the more sophisticated our methods and theories, the less useful they appear to practitioners (Rynes et al., 2001).

One interesting feature of RPRs is that it is quite possible for one party to achieve his or her goals while the overall system fails. So an innovation might be adopted that benefits practitioners, but the research is so commonplace, or flawed because of lack of rigour, that it is not diffused through the academic literature. A true partnership with practitioners is very time consuming, and the resulting rewards are typically slight since it is seldom valued institutionally (Keen and Stocklmayer, 1999).

More disturbingly, often a failed project results in interesting research. Herein lies a clear challenge for researchers. Often we learn as much or more from failed efforts we are involved in as from successful ones. So our own individual goals are likely to be achieved regardless of the outcomes of the overall project. And we can often take comfort in the fact that we preserved the canons of our profession. Unfortunately citation analyses also indicate that relationships in which researchers define the problems and pursue their own questions are most likely to be successful in academic terms (Rynes et al., 2001). So in some ways you have the paradox of success: the more successful one entity in a system is in attaining its more limited individual goals, the more unlikely it is that the overall system will attain its wider objective (Senge, 1990). Similarly it has been found that centrality in advice networks, a fundamental property of SHBs, is positively associated with individual performance but negatively related to group performance (Sparrowe et al., 2001).

A key finding of the classic differentiation and integration literature is that the costs of integration can be quite high and only really need to be borne in certain organizational environments (Lawrence and Lorsch, 1967a, b, c). The personal investments of SHBs are significant. It is little wonder that so few people emerge in such roles. A focus on maintenance and dissolution also suggests that the need to recoup these costs can result in dysfunctions at the overall system level (Johnson, 2004). Central to these dysfunctions is the need of the SHB to insure ties with the parties are non–redundant, or structurally autonomous in Burt's (1992, 2000) language (Finlay and Coverdill, 2000).

Do differences between researcher and practitioners really make a difference (Beyer and Trice, 1994)? While there should be tension in these relationships, if the overall system is to function successfully, as in a dialogic view, it is important to maintain and if anything sharpen these differences, while downplaying threats, if the overall system is to work. Ultimately achieving balance in all things is the central issue faced by an SHB.

As we have seen, being an SHB requires unique combinations of interests and skills. Ron Burt (1992, 2000) has provided us with a compelling framework for understanding why individuals would want to assume these demanding roles. But we still have much to learn about how they interact with the parties they bridge in the operation of consortia. Can we rely on individual action to fill these gaping holes, resulting from differentiation into specialized roles of social structures? Unfortunately the traditional answer has been no. Few individuals appear to have the vision and the will to take advantage of these opportunities (Reynolds and Johnson, 1982), something borne out in the sociometric findings reported in Chapter 5.

All of this suggests that collaborations in consortia may be more idiosyncratic and ephemeral than we first thought, because they are so uniquely tied to the interests of one individual, at least at the outset. I have focused on the initial act of creation of a consortia, the ultimate structural act of creativity found when bridging structural holes, but for continued benefits, the more mundane work of formalizing these relationships must also occur, something that the network literature seldom addresses. How this transition is made, is the critical issue for long–term system benefits accruing from RPRs. These larger system benefits are indeed compelling: greater likelihood of implementation of innovative ideas; greater understanding and more comprehensive view of the system of interest resulting from a richer intellectual synergy that can develop from research informed by practice (Walton, 1985); and ultimately, a lower failure rate for consortia.

7.4 WHAT IS SUCCESS?

The Cooperative Research Centre approach to research management in Australia has shown that the boundary between users and providers of knowledge is a complex one, and the relationship does not work well if dominated by either party … The CRC structure encourages sustained dialogue between users and producers of knowledge … (Cullen et al., 1999, p. 136)

... the CISRC is well on its way to establishing the CIS as a viable laboratory for cancer control research in this country. (Marcus, Morra et al., 1998, p. S14)

Embedded in the latter quote is one of the central problems in consortia, the primacy of the goals of one of the parties and the ignoring, by implication, of the primary goal of the others. Naturally the major goal of the practitioners was improved practice, but as we have seen, the exact mechanism for accomplishing this had yet to be specified and work towards implementation of research results had not even begun at the end of the first four–year cycle of the CISRC (Marcus, 1998a).

I have used symbolic interactionism as a conceptual framework for analysing these critical problems in consortia (Johnson, 2002). To summarize, the relationship between researchers and practitioners in the CISRC was characterized by only periodic co–presence, somewhat limited reciprocal attention, a primitive level of mutual responsiveness, surface attempts at creating functional identities, and an increasing felt need to formalize the shared focus. However there was an overriding social objective, the continued survival of the CIS, that eventually compelled the practitioners to articulate how their original goals were not being met, and thus started a dialogue on how their grievances could be addressed, in a way emulating Giddens's (1979) classic observations on the production and reproduction of social life.

As discussed by Deetz (2000), the fundamental goal of a dialogic approach is to reclaim conflict in the organization, recognizing the natural tension between parties in organizations and examining how they maintain relationships in the face of their inherent conflicts. Thus a leader's conflict management style is critical to successful collaboration (Amabile et al., 2001). The point here is not that conflicts can be managed, minimized and overcome, but that some relationships have inherent tensions that actually might result in the growth of the two parties and more effective collaborations. So researchers and practitioners can continually learn from each other, but they must realize that it is not to their benefit for one to ever totally subsume the other, that creative tensions enhance both the quality and rate of knowledge production (Rynes et al., 2001). Successful cooperative relationships must recognize the creative struggle that is an inherent part of living. As Sennet (1998) has observed, that conflict can lead to stronger relations than a focus on casual, facile teamwork. This separation of members of the CISRC may lead to the dynamic tension needed for truly innovative approaches, since it is not subject to the same forces that lead to homogenous approaches in industries that are too tightly clustered together (Pouder and St John, 1996).

Those most likely to succeed are those who can immerse themselves in multiple frameworks (Johnson, 1997b), while still clearly maintaining their own identity. The ultimate goal of parties in these relationships must be sustaining dialogic conflict, while both parties are accomplishing some larger subordinate goal such as the advancement of both management knowledge and practice (March, 2000). Not only can managers utilize information about stakeholders' perceptions of innovation to facilitate the adoption and implementation of innovations in the interest of meeting specific strategic objectives; the ways in which managers respond to stakeholders' attitudes towards innovation may influence the organization's ability to generate future innovations. Managers who are sensitive to the needs of all parties in an innovation process, in the contemporary pluralistic organization, have the potential to sustain and to build an organization's innovation environment. Thus they also need to pay attention to middle management's organic, bridging role and their concerns with costs and benefits, as well as efficiency.

Differentiation is necessary for the synergy essential to the creation of ideas, partly through the creation of requisite variety (Van de Ven, 1986; Hage, 1999). The diverse nature of this information is often crucial to the development of unique ideas and approaches that are holistic and concerned with the overall organization and new directions for it. But it also makes it difficult to insure the consensus necessary for their implementation. Van de Ven (1986) has described this as a part–whole problem, with the tendency to focus on what is good for the individual entity rather than the organization as a whole.

A central tenet of systems theory is that one of the ways they fail is for one entity or component to be too successful. As a result other units are starved for resources and cannot function, resulting in the downfall of the overall organism (Senge, 1990). In human systems, there is also a psychological component to this; envy over additional resources and recognition can lead to various acts of jealousy and pique that become dysfunctional for the overall operation of the system (Rosovsky, 1990). All of this can be heightened by feelings that one's own goals are hampered, even if indirectly and unconsciously by the actions of another party.

The CISRC was created to frame the CIS as a viable state–of–the–science communication laboratory for the NCI. 'One of the major management challenges at the regional level was to transmit to the staff the excitement and value of conducting research in a mainly service program' (Fleisher et al., 1998, p. S88). By many common definitions of success in KM, the CISRC was successful – it grew the resources available to the CISRC, and it resulted in a growth in knowledge and the development of an infrastructure for sustaining it (Davenport and Prusak, 1998).

Organizational members are increasingly cynical about the motivations underlying major change efforts (Reichers et al., 1997), partly because they do not understand the underlying assumptions of framing. This in turn highlights the difference between routine, grudging compliance with innovation efforts, as opposed to internalization of them due to their fit with individual normative commitments (Klein and Sorra, 1996) and their inherent attributes. The CIS, a service–oriented organization, was also being asked to pilot interventions to establish effective protocols. The balance of these two duties, service versus research, was not easily achieved. As evidence, Fleisher et al. (1998) reported that only half of the ISs, those who actually provide information to callers, reported that they felt research should be a part of the CIS programme.

Framing ideas in terms of overcoming resistance to change, probably the most popular approach in the literature traditionally, may be exactly the wrong approach for proactive organizations (Armenikas et al., 1993) like the CIS. Rather, a more promising approach seems to be to identify sustaining mechanisms, for example, broad–based support of organizational members, that will pull people toward an attractive future (Drucker, 1995; Klein and Sorra, 1996; Ross, 1974). A focus on what an organization should be doing in the future, rather than the more ego–threatening 'what we have done in the past' (Downs, 1967), contributes to the development of more positive climates. So does promoting a feeling of problem solving – encouraging feelings of experimentation and inquiry, all characteristics of the computerization project. The right framing of a project can contribute to the success of even very risky innovations.

Mohr (1969) has suggested that the primary motivation for public health organizations to innovate was the quest for prestige (see also Becker, 1970) rather than issues of internal effectiveness and efficiency. Similarly Brenner and Logan (1980) argued, based on their analysis of the diffusion of medical information systems, that outside innovation factors were much more important in the diffusion of innovation process than is represented in the prevailing view in the literature. While the classic Rogers (1983, 1995, 2003) attributes of innovation may be important in persuading individuals to implement innovations adopted by others, in the larger organizational context these are clearly secondary factors, more associated with 'fine–tuning' an innovation. As the CIS case makes clear, framing and the innovation environment may play more critical roles.

Predictive tools

Attributes of innovations are often the most immediate, objective indicators of success. As we have seen in Chapter 6, the innovation profile may be a useful analytic tool in evaluating the likelihood of success of any one particular innovation. An interesting research project by Boer and During (2001) suggests some interesting biases in company's a priori perceptions of attributes. Relative advantage, particularly in terms of profitability, was often substantially overestimated. Complexity, particularly in terms of reinvention issues, was often underestimated. This feeds into, or maybe is a result of, the pro–innovation bias noted earlier and creates a volatile mix that may in part explain the high rate of innovation failure. For a variety of reasons, people may often be overly optimistic concerning an innovation's likely success, downplaying barriers in the process. It is well known, partly because of the persuasive processes involved, that often initial project proposals are overly optimistic to insure the attainment of resource commitments (Dornblaser et al., 2000).

The success of an innovation implementation effort is often difficult to determine since it can mean differing things, at differing levels, to different constituencies (Connolly et al., 1980). It is especially hard to predict a priori which efforts will be successful (Watts, 2003). I have developed an approach to evaluating the likelihood of success of an innovation by combining the levels outlined in Chapter 2 (Johnson, 2000, 2001). By evaluating the nominal conditions (for example pros and cons) of innovation attributes, internal innovation environment and framing to external stakeholders, I have classified eight possible conditions of success.

Both sets of innovations we examined in Chapter 6 responded to issues critical to key stakeholders. However CIS members were predisposed to accept computerization innovations because of differences in the framing of arguments. The CISRC innovations were clearly seen by leaders of the CIS as a way of satisfying key decision–makers within the NCI by demonstrating that the CIS could also contribute to its research mission, but as we have seen, there was considerable debate within the CIS as to the centrality of research in relation to its traditional vision and mission statements (Fleisher et al., 1998; Marcus, Morra et al., 1998). The knowledge delivery innovations also benefited from additional resources provided to them by both PDs and the OCC as unanticipated difficulties arose, then envisioned at the outset (Fleisher et al., 1998). However the computerization effort responded to an even more influential set of stakeholders in the executive and congressional branches of the federal government. It also had the additional benefit of satisfying the needs of key 'customers' and interest and advocacy groups important to the CIS. The 'pull' of these influential stakeholders pointed to attractive outcomes from implementing these information technology innovations (for example more resources, satisfied consumers) (Mitchell et al., 1997). It also was the case that several ROs, some of whom are in university settings, at their own initiative had instituted partial trials of various elements of computerization. There was a classic bottom–up 'push' to various elements of the computerization effort and clear peer influence from CoPs that directed training and implementation efforts associated with it, reflecting the literature on informal innovation processes in organizations (Johnson,

1993). Thus the computerization project, by combining positive ratings on all three levels, can unequivocally be labelled a success.

On the other hand, the knowledge delivery innovations represented '*squeezed successes*'. A highly efficacious innovation, that was valued by organizational stakeholders, overcame a flawed innovation environment, in this case the internal participation mechanisms. While both sets of projects had active champions within the CIS, the computerization support was clearly more widespread across all status levels. In this sense the knowledge delivery innovations can be viewed as squeezed successes, which were pursued largely for their symbolic value.

Both sets of innovation had key indicators that demonstrated that they did indeed 'work'; however the success measures for the CISRC innovations were at the level of classic communication campaigns (for example changes in attitudes among clients of the CIS), while those of computerization were at the level of improvements in internal systems performance. Perhaps the ultimate indicator of the success of the computerization effort was in the conversion of 'old–timers' who moved from the least to the most receptive to it as the project unfolded and they could see for themselves that it resulted in improved practice. Ultimately none of the service delivery innovations was adopted as piloted on a system–wide basis (Marcus, 1998b), although some pre–existing components of Project 3 were reinvented, even though trials indicated a generally high level of pros on specific attributes (Boyd et al., 1998; Crane et al., 1998; Marcus, Heimendinger et al., 1998).

In sum, as we have seen, successful innovations represent a convergence of forces. The CIS's computerization effort had a pull from the top and a push from the bottom, coupled with an innovative approach to the internal innovation environment (Johnson, Meyer, Woodworth et al., 1998). Historically there had been a number of individuals pushing for this computerization effort, but literally nothing could be done until key stakeholders legitimized it.   This happened very dramatically, when it became apparent that the CIS's very survival was threatened if it did not join the information technology bandwagon.

Failure

> Victory has a hundred fathers, but defeat is an orphan (Ciano, September 9, 1942, also attributed to John F. Kennedy in April 1961 after the Bay of Pigs).

One has to wonder why some innovations are even attempted, when it becomes apparent there is no positive weighting on any of the levels. Perhaps this is attributable to rationality after the fact. Failure causes us to see the inherent qualities of the innovation more clearly, and what looked like a probable success, is viewed differently in the light of experience.

Failures can be quickly disowned, so nobody is left to defend the original idea, leaving us all to scratch our heads as to, What were we thinking? Why did we do this?

As Kanter (1983) has established, there is considerable reluctance in most organizations to label an innovation a failure because of the taboo of mentioning it, the threatening nature of failure for future risky ventures, the multiple goals of many projects that prevent them from being cast as outright failures, and the strategies by which clever innovators convert 'failures' into minor successes (Kanter, 1983). Indeed managers use multiple, diverse and idiosyncratic performance criteria for differing innovations even in the same organizational context, with the criteria used by resource controllers the most critical (Dornblaser et al., 2000). It is also difficult to measure the totality of an innovation's impact, in part because the new represents such a departure from the old that they cannot be meaningfully compared. (How do you compare mail merge on a word processor to a typewriter?)

However failure can have a critical role in learning and building knowledge in organizations (Leonard, 1988); no science can advance without recognizing it (failed hypotheses) and moving to alternative explanations. While there are deeply personal reasons for spinning failure, organizational learning, and eventually prosperity, are associated with how organizations cope with it.

A fundamental problem associated with the different factors is that each entails considerably different ways of viewing, interpreting and discussing innovations. As the parties involved in the innovation become associated with the different factors, their possibilities of engaging in a dialogue on the same ground diminish. If one of the three factors predominates, without addressing issues inherent in the other two, then major distortions may occur in the innovation process. For example workers have a tendency to view innovations in terms of their operational attributes, valuing their impacts on their routine work and the resulting enhancements in their effectiveness and sense of self–actualization. On the other hand, upper management may value an innovation for its ability to address directly the needs of major external stakeholders. They seek innovations that provide an image of a cutting–edge and prestigious organization. The classic diffusion of innovation paradigm assumes the purpose of innovation is the adoption of a more effective practice that will improve institutional efficiency; but often the primary purpose of participating in innovation is symbolic – a demonstration that you are forward–looking and modern, willing to jump on whatever bandwagon may be rolling by (Abrahamson, 1991; Abrahamson and Rosenkopf, 1993; Eisenberg et al., 1998). This results in the paradox of widespread adoption, but less effective implementation, perhaps associated with symbolic appropriation processes.

Adding to this often volatile mix is the tension between the need to restrict innovation and to support it. So accomplishing the work in an era of declining resources often means that only a limited range of innovations can be selected for attention, with perhaps the clearest criterion being appeasement of key external stakeholders. Thus opportunity costs and the feeling of loss, especially among workers, are quite real.

Often the institutional forces that determine organizational survival necessitate the pursuit of secondary goals, which are articulated by the 'gods outside' who must be appeased with sacrifices, as the only means of accomplishing certain ends. So government organizations may adopt new information technologies because they are seen by their key stakeholders (for example politicians) as the best means of accomplishing their primary goals. Indeed the criteria used for innovations in public and private sectors differ substantially, with an all–or–nothing, bottom–line approach in the latter, and a more incremental view taken in the former (Dornblaser et al., 2000).

This can be offset however, as in the case of computerization efforts within the CIS, when a large number of internal members accept the outside pull and use it as a way of changing legitimizing practices within their own organization. One of the interesting features of computerization efforts is their interpretation in multiple symbolic ways by different groups. Advocates of computerization in the CIS, following basic communication practice, sought to understand the interpretive frames of top management and pitched their ideas in terms of the issues inherent in a framing perspective (Johnson, Meyer, Woodworth et al., 1998). Effective organizations are often those that can balance multiple, often conflicting criteria for effectiveness (Dornblaser et al., 2000).

One of the key factors in understanding how innovations unfold is the differential ability of the parties to operate within a variety of levels. Only a few individuals appear to have the facility for dealing in multiple levels. In general, upper–level administrators have a deeper appreciation for differing perspectives. They use their understanding to implement organizational change processes, develop visions of the organization, and manipulate policy debates (Johnson, 1998). As Schon and Rein (1994) have argued, social designing relies on recognizing problems, providing feedback, reinventing and recognizing the intentions of the other party, all of which require at least a minimal level of communication. In the end, there must be a convergence of meaning about what is to be done (Donnelon et al., 1986), even if there are different interpretations of the reasons for action.

While reliable communication may at times deepen disputes when parties truly understand the disparity of their positions, it is still a critical condition for further inquiry that may be the only hope of adjustments leading to the convergence of factors needed for successful implementation. Too often managers do not listen to 'back talk', assuming that individuals are wilfully denying their arguments (they just do not understand) (Schon and Rein, 1994). Thus a failure to engage each other in dialogue may be the ultimate denial of the pluralistic world of the modern organization that is often splintered into different functional groupings and 'occupational communities' (Johnson, 1993). Each group has its own view of what is of value in KM. However understanding the interplay of these factors can result in more effective individual and institutional change strategies (Eisenberg et al., 1998). In turn this understanding can considerably increase the currently low odds of successful implementation of information technologies.

In a risk–averse organization, it might be better to frame innovations in terms of potential gains or the real risks of not changing (Fairhurst and Sarr, 1996). According to Frost and Egri, 'innovation is, at its core, a political and social process of change' (1991, p. 229). If as Van de Ven (1986) argues, the extent to which new ideas are 'managed into good currency' is a key measure of innovation outcomes, then organizational stakeholders' perceptions about the advantages and disadvantages associated with innovations may be an indicator of the extent to which managers are apt at manipulating innovation–related communication. Organizational innovation orchestrators manipulate information, control resources, set agendas, acquire power bases and frame decision premises to promote the political capital that they have invested in a given innovation (Frost and Egri, 1991).

KM has often been tagged with the label of the latest fad to hit organizations. The bandwagon effects often associated with it reveal both a deeply felt need and a cultural appreciation for what it offers. Similarly Kanter (1988) discussed the subjective nature of perceptions of innovation outcomes by exploring the phenomenon of pro–innovation bias (Rogers, 1983). She made the point that most research about organizational innovation is characterized by an implicit assumption that innovation is a good thing. According to Van de Ven, 'innovation is often viewed as a good thing because the new idea must be useful – profitable, constructive, or solve a problem. New ideas that are not perceived as useful are not normally called innovations: they are usually called mistakes' (1986, p. 592).

Kanter (1988a) concluded that the organizational context has a major impact on the conceptualization of innovation. According to Kanter's content analysis of participant dialogue, the difficulty inherent in identifying the failure to innovate can be attributed to one or more of the following reasons: the taboo nature of mentioning failure; the threatening nature of failure that discourages risky ventures; the multiple goals of many projects that prevent them almost by definition from being an outright failure; and the strategies by which clever innovators convert potential 'failures' into minor successes. In the case of the CISRC, perhaps innovation orchestrators' failure to acknowledge the discrepancy among idea champions' and orchestrators' perceptions of Project 2 indicated that the consortium leadership was reluctant to identify an innovation as problematic. Ultimately however, when would–be idea champions call an innovation a mistake, orchestrators need to listen (Meyer and Johnson, 1998). Feedback can be utilized by managers to modify innovations mid–stream or reconsider their communication strategies for promoting innovation.

In sum, the particular innovations we focused on had a range of success, some being fully assimilated into CIS processes, others providing interesting research in the academic literature. In some ways in an innovation factory, a state–of–the–science communication laboratory like the CISRC, the success of any one innovation and its various attributes is not the real story. The renewal of the CISRC and the continued operations of the CIS were the real indicators of the ultimate success of this enterprise.

7.5   LESSONS FOR KM

An interesting organizing scheme for determining where the CIS stood at the end of this process as a learning organization posed to perform a full range of KM activities is that provided by Garvin (1993) which suggests such organizations will be skilled in five main activities:

1. Systematic problem solving – The CIS through its various councils and ad hoc task forces developed CoPs and, most elaborately, the CISRC, which had a number of routinized approaches to tackling major political and practice problems. In fact the CIS and the CISRC both appeared to develop a fairly robust system for directly confronting issues in a proactive way.

2. Experimentation with new approaches – As we have seen, the CIS had a positive climate for innovations and developed a number of structures that promoted experimentation. The number of differing innovations at differing levels point to a willingness to experiment that one would have to consider unusual for a government organization, although often the impetus for change were the entrepreneurial contractors at ROs.

3. Learning from their own experience and past history – The published literature on the CIS by PDs reflects an appreciation for its history (for example Morra, Van Nevel et al., 1993), and even more importantly a willingness to develop lessons that would result in improved practice (Fleisher et al., 1998). The CIS is relatively unusual among organizations in focusing and attending to developing strategies for dealing with issues (Argyris, 1991; Wright and Taylor, 2003). The CIS did systematically review

successful and unsuccessful projects and disseminated their experience throughout the organization (Tidd, 2000).

4. Learning from experiences and best practices of others – Here the CIS receives more mixed marks. As we saw in Chapter 4, it developed primarily a one–way approach for developing coalitions with community partners. Especially in regards to scientific conclusions (for example the appropriate ages for mammography screening), the NCI would often disregard the input of organizations like the ACS, in a classic 'not invented here' approach to many issues that would at times splinter its support in the community. However in some ways the CISRC was designed to bring in ideas developed by others (for example tailored messaging for evaluation in its second iteration) that was somewhat akin to the classic merger and acquisitions strategies often found in the private sector.

5. Transferring knowledge quickly and efficiently throughout the organization – There were often complaints that the results of the CISRC projects were not adequately communicated to CIS members. Even the systematic series of technical reports developed by the TEAM was criticized because no one sat down with practitioners and explained their relevance to day–to–day operations. Within the government, there were not similar programmes within the NCI that could benefit from this information, and other NIH and NLM programmes tended to develop in their own way. There was however some modelling of the CIS in the development of other cancer–related programmes in differing countries. With the exception of one CISRC–sponsored supplement to *Preventive Medicine*, very little information concerning the knowledge service delivery and computerization innovations was distributed to the larger research community, at least by the limited number of later citations of articles in the supplement in the relevant academic literature.

7.6 POSTSCRIPT

There seems to be an assumption that innovation leads to organizational adaptation (Drazin and Schoonhoven, 1996). In a fundamental sense, the forgoing did result in the continued survival of the CIS, but in recent years its research mission has been formalized and it is often mentioned in the same breath as its information service, which now includes telephone, e–mail, and Web services, as well as outreach partnership functions (Johnson, in press). Other aspects of the CIS have changed significantly – so much so that in another two years the structure of the CIS might be unrecognizable to the organizational members who we worked with at the outset.

The CIS is now one section of the Health Communication and Informatics Research Branch (HCIRB) of the Behavioral Research Programme (BRP) of the Division of Cancer Control and Population Services (DCCPS). The DCCPS is a major research division of the NCI that also has research programmes focusing on Epidemiology and Genetics, Applied Research, and Surveillance Research. Where to put the CIS in the NCI's structure has been a continuing problem, with prior intervals of it being housed in research divisions leading to the conclusion that it did not fit well (Morra, Van Nevel et al., 1993). The BRP contains additional branches relating to Applied Cancer Screening, Basic BioBehavioral Research, Health Promotion, and Tobacco Control. (For more information see http://dccps.nci.nih.gov). The 'HCIRB seeks to advance communication and information science across the cancer continuum–prevention, detection, treatment, control, survivorship, and end of life' (http://dccps.nci.nih.gov/hcirb). While this change in organizational home further solidified the research focus of the CIS, it has also meant that it was removed from the richly integrated KM functions of the OCC described in Chapter 3.

Ironically the CISRC which focused on tailored messaging in its second round (Marcus, 1998a), and was originally funded by the successor unit of DCCPS, not the OCC, in part has been replaced with the Centers for Excellence in Cancer Communications Research which focuses on a variety of communication approaches (NCI, 2003), but still with a latent function of automating information delivery. No substantial publication output has resulted from the second round of CISRC projects and there has been no formal approval for a third round of funding (Marcus, 2004).

The CIS responds to nearly 400 000 calls annually and many more requests for assistance on its LiveHelp website feature (http://cis.nci.nih.gov/about/underserved.html). *In toto,* in 2002 the CIS handled over 1.4 million requests for service (NCI, 2003). The computerization effort has been followed by even more advanced efforts to enhance information technology and service delivery. Ironically these changes have enabled a major change in the RO structure of the CIS; the current contract renewal calls for four super–regions, a substantial reduction from the 19 we investigated. The submission and competition for these regions has overtly revealed the 'co–opetition forces' (Brandenburger and Nalebuff, 1996) that may in part have underlain the minimal raw volumes of communication, which decreased as we approached contract renewal, and the fractured sociometric network described in Chapter 5. In the current contract renewal process very little attention has been paid to the potential loss of tacit knowledge possessed by PDs and TSMs that had made the CIS so effective over the years. This downsizing will also drastically impact the diversity of its CoPs.

It has often been observed that permanent changes in organization structure and power relations may be necessary to sustain innovations (Dougherty and Hardy, 1996). It also may be no coincidence that the one person who filled multiple roles in the CISRC – PI of an RO, investigator in two of the research projects, boundary spanner to the NCI, who later headed the National Cancer Advisory Board and the DCCPS – left the NCI at the same time these major changes were occurring. While the CISRC had originally been a means to an end for most organizational members, its successors became the ultimate ends.

Bibliography

Abrahamson, E. (1991), 'Managerial fads and fashions: The diffusion and rejection of innovations', *Academy of Management Review*, **16**, 586-612.

Abrahamson, E. and L. Rosenkopf (1993), 'Institutional and competitive bandwagons: using mathematical modeling as a tool to explore innovation diffusion', *Academy of Management Review*, **18**, 487-517.

Abrams, L.C., R. Cross, E. Lesser, and D.Z. Levin (2003), 'Nurturing interpersonal trust in knowledge sharing networks', *Academy of Mnagement Executive*, **17**, 64-77.

Adams, J.S. (1976), 'The structure and dynamics of behavior in organizational boundary roles', in M.D. Dunnette (ed.), *Handbook of Industrial and Organizational Psychology*, Chicago, IL: Rand McNally, pp. 1175-99.

Adelman, M.B., M.R. Parks and T.L. Albrecht (1987), 'Beyond close relationships: support in weak ties', in T.L. Albrecht and M. B. Adelman (eds), *Communicating Social Support*, Newbury Park, CA: Sage, pp. 126-47.

Aiken, M. and J. Hage (1971), 'The organic model and innovation', *Sociology*, **5**, 63-82.

Albrecht, T.L. (1979), 'The role of communication in perceptions of organizational climate', in D. Nimmo (ed.), *Communication Yearbook 3*, New Brunswick, NJ: Transaction Books, pp. 343-57.

Albrecht, T.L. and M.B. Adelman (1987), 'Dilemmas of supportive communication', in T.L. Albrecht and M.B. Adelman (eds), *Communicating Social Support*, Newbury Park, CA: Sage, pp. 240-54.

Albrecht, T.L. and B.W. Bach (1997), *Communication in complex organizations: A relational approach*, Fort Worth, TX: Harcourt,

Brace Jovanovich.

Albrecht, T.L. and B. Hall (1989), 'Relational and content differences between elites and outsiders in innovation networks', paper presented to the Annual Meetings of the International Communication Association Convention, San Francisco, CA.

Albrecht, T.L. and V.A. Ropp (1984), 'Communicating about innovation in networks of three US organizations', *Journal of Communication*, **34**, 78-91.

Aldrich, H. and D. Herker (1977), 'Boundary spanning roles and organizational structure', *Academy of Management Review*, **2**, 217-30.

Allen, M.W. (1989), *Factors Influencing the Power of a Linking Role: An Investigation Into Interorganizational Boundary Spanning*, unpublished doctoral dissertation, Baton Rouge, LA: Louisiana State University.

Allen, T.J. (1966), 'Performance of information channels in the transfer of technology', *Industrial Management Review*, **8**, 87-98.

Allen, T.J. (1977), *Managing the Flow of Technology: Technology Transfer and the Dissemination of Technological Information within the R&D Organization*, Cambridge, MA: MIT Press.

Altman, D.G. (1985), 'Utilization of a telephone cancer information program by symptomatic people', *Journal of Community Health*, **10**, 156-71.

Amabile, T.M., C. Patterson, J. Mueller, T. Wojcik, P.W. Odomirok, M.M. Marsh and S.J. Kramer (2001), 'Academic-practitioner collaboration in management research: a case of cross-profession collaboration', *Academy of Management Journal*, **44**, 418-31.

American Cancer Society (1995), *Medical Affairs Newsletter*, Atlanta, GA: American Cancer Society.

Amidon, D.M. and P. Mahdjoubi (2003), 'An atlas for knowledge innovation: Migration from business planning to innovation strategy', in C.W. Holsapple (ed.), *Handbook for Knowledge Management: Knowledge Directions*, New York: Springer Verlag, pp. 331-51.

Ancona, D.G. and D.F. Caldwell (1992), 'Bridging the boundary: external activity and performance in organizational teams', *Administrative Science Quarterly*, **37**, 634-65.

Anderson, D.M., K. Duffy, C.D. Hallett and A.C. Marcus (1992), 'Cancer prevention counseling on telephone helplines', *Public Health Reports*, **107**, 278-82.

Anderson, D.M., H.I. Meissner and B. Portnoy (1989), 'Media use and the health information acquisition process: how callers learned about the NCI's Cancer Information Service', *Health Education Research*, **4**, 419-27.

Applegate, J.L. (2001), 'Engaged graduate education: skating to where the puck will be', *Spectra*, **37**, 1-5.

Applegate, J.L. (2002), 'Skating to where the puck will be: engaged research as a funding strategy for the communication discipline', *Journal of Applied Communication Research*, **30**, 402-10.

Argyris, C. (1991), 'Teaching smart people how to learn', *Harvard Business Review*, 81-108.

Arkin, E.B., R.M. Romano, J.P. Van Nevel and J.W. McKenna (1993), 'Effect of the mass media in promoting calls to the Cancer Information Service', *Journal of the National Cancer Institute*, **14**, 35-44.

Armenikas, A.A., S.G. Harris and K.W. Mossholder (1993), 'Creating readiness for organizational change', *Human Relations*, **46**, 681-703.

Arnold, M.F. and D.L. Hink (1968), 'Agency problems in planning for community health needs', *Medical Care*, **6**, 454-66.

Ashmos, D.P., R.R. McDaniel, Jr and D. Duchon (1990), 'Differences in perceptions of strategic decision-making processes: the case of physicians and administrators', *Journal of Applied Behavioral Science*, **26**, 201-18.

Astley, W.G. and E.J. Zajac (1991), 'Intraorganizational power and organizational design: reconciling rational and coalitional models of organization', *Organization Science*, **2**, 399-411.

Atkin, C. (1973), 'Instrumental utilities and information seeking', in P. Clarke (ed.), *New Models For Mass Communication Research*, Beverly Hills, CA: Sage, pp. 205-42.

At-Twaijri, M.I.A. and J.R. Montanari (1987), 'The impact of context and choice on the boundary-spanning process: an empirical extension', *Human Relations*, **40**, 783-98.

Augier, M. (2004), 'James March on education, leadership, and Don Quixote: introduction and overview', *Academy of Management Learning and Education*, **3**, 169-77.

Axelrod, D. (1992), 'Getting everyone involved: How one organization involved its employees, supervisors, and managers in redesigning the organization', *Journal of Applied Behavioral Science*, **28**, 499-509.

Axley, S.R. (1984), 'Managerial and organizational communication in terms of the conduit metaphor', *Academy of Management Review*, **9**, 428-37.

Babrow, A.S. (1992), 'Communication and problematic integration: understanding diverging probability and value, ambiguity, ambivalence and impossibility', *Communication Theory*, **2**, 95-130.

Babrow, A.S. (2001), 'Guest editor's introduction to the special issue on uncertainty, evaluation, and communication', *Journal of Communication*, **51**, 453-5.

Babrow, A.S. and M. Mattson (2003), 'Theorizing about health communication', in T.L. Thompson, A.M. Dorsey, K.I. Miller and R. Parrott (eds), *Handbook of Health Communication*, Mahwah, NJ:

Lawrence Erlbaum Associates, pp. 35-61.

Bach, B. (1989), 'The effect of multiplex relationships upon innovation adoption: a reconsideration of Rogers' model', *Communication Monographs*, **56**, 133-50.

Bailey, D. and S. Dupré (1992). 'The future search conference as a vehicle for educational change: a shared vision for Will Rogers middle school, Sacramento, California, *Journal of Applied Behavioral Science*, **28**, 510-19.

Baker, W.E. (1992), 'Network organization in theory and practice', in N. Nohria and R.G. Eccles (eds), *Networks and Organizations: Structure, Form, and Action*, Boston, MA: Harvard Business School Press, pp. 397-429.

Baldridge, J.V. and R.A. Burnham (1975), 'Organizational innovation: individual, organizational, and environmental impacts', *Administrative Science Quarterly*, **20**, 165-76.

Ballard, D. (1996), 'Capacity-building approach to breast cancer awareness and screening', presentation to the Michigan Department of Community Health, Lansing, MI, November.

Barabasi, A.L. (2003), *Linked: How Everything is Connected to Everything Else and What it Means for Business, Science, and Everyday Life*, New York: Plume.

Barnes, J.A. (1972), *Social Networks*, Reading, MA: Addison-Wesley.

Baron, R.M. and D.A. Kenny (1986), 'The moderator-mediator variable distinction in social psychological research: conceptual, strategic, and statistical considerations', *Journal of Personality and Social Psychology*, **51**, 1173-82.

Becker, M.H. (1970), 'Factors affecting diffusion of innovations among health professionals', *American Journal of Public Health*, **60**, 294-304.

Becker, M.H. and I.H. Rosenstock (1989), 'Health promotion, disease prevention, and program retention', in H.E. Freeman and S. Levine (eds), *Handbook of Medical Sociology*, Englewood Cliffs, NJ: Prentice-Hall, pp. 284-305.

Beetham, D. (1987), *Bureaucracy*, Milton Keynes: Open University Press.

Beninger, J.R. (1990), 'Conceptualizing information technology as organization, and vice versa', in J. Fulk and C. Steinfield (eds), *Organizations and Communication Technology*, Newbury Park, CA: Sage, pp. 29-45.

Bennet, D. and A. Bennet (2003), 'The rise of the knowledge organization,' in C. Holsapple (ed.), *Handbook on Knowledge Management 1: Knowledge Matters*, New York, NY: Springer-Verlag, pp. 5-20.

Bennis, W.G. (1965), 'Theory and method in applying behavioral science to planned organizational change', *Applied Behavioral Science*, **1**, 337-60.

Benoit, G. (2002), 'Data mining', *Annual Review of Information Science and Technology*, **36**, 265-310.

Berelson, B. and G.A. Steiner (1964), *Human Behavior: An Inventory of Scientific Findings*, New York: Harcourt, Brace & World.

Berger, C.R. and S.H. Chaffee (eds) (1987), *Handbook of Communication Science*, Newbury Park, CA: Sage.

Berlo, D.K. (1960), *The Process of Communication: An Introduction to Theory and Practice*, New York: Holt, Rinehart & Winston.

Berscheid, E. (1966), 'Opinion change and communicator-communicatee similarity and dissimilarity', *Journal of Personality and Social Psychology*, **4**, 670-80.

Beth Israel Hospital (1992), *Your Rights as a Patient*, Boston, MA: Beth Israel Hospital.

Beyer, J.M. and H.M. Trice (1994), 'Current and prospective roles for linking organizational researchers and users', in R.H. Kilmann, K.W. Thomas, D.P. Slevein, R. Nath and S.L. Jerell (eds), *Producing Useful Knowledge for Organizations*, San Francisco, CA: Jossey-Bass, pp. 675-702.

Biggart, N.W. and R. Delbridge (2004), 'Systems of exchange', *Academy of Management Review*, **29**, 28-49.

Bigoness, W.J. and W.D. Perrault (1981), 'A conceptual paradigm and approach for the study of innovators', *Academy of Management Journal*, **24**, 68-82.

Boahene, M. and G. Ditsa (2003), 'Conceptual confusions in knowledge management and knowledge management systems: clarifications for better KMS development', in E. Coakes (ed.), *Knowledge Management: Current Issues and Challenges*, London: IRM Press, pp. 12-24.

Boer, H. and W.E. During (2001), 'Innovation, what innovation? A comparison between product, process and organizational innovation', *International Journal of Technology Management*, **22**, 83-107.

Bohlen, J.M. (1971), 'Research needed on adoption models', in W. Schramm and D.F. Roberts (eds), *The Process and Effects of Mass Communication*, Urbana, IL: University of Illinois Press, pp. 798-815.

Bolman, L.G. and T.E. Deal (1991), *Reframing Organizations: Artistry, Choice, and Leadership*, San Francisco, CA: Jossey-Bass.

Borgatti, S.P., M.G. Everett and L.C. Freeman (2002), *UCINET for Windows: Software for Social Network Analysis*, Harvard, MA: Analytic Technologies.

Borys, B. and D.B. Jemison (1989), 'Hybrid arrangements as strategic alliances: theoretical issues in organizational combinations', *Academy of Management Review*, **14**, 234-49.

Boyd, N.R., C. Sutton, C.T. Orleans, M.W. McClatchey, R. Bingler, L. Fleisher, D. Heller, S. Baum, C. Graves and J.A. Ward (1998), 'Quit today! A targeted communications campaign to increase use of the cancer information service by African-American smokers', *Preventive Medicine*, **27**, S50-S61.

Bradach, J.L. and R.G. Eccles (1989), 'Price, authority, and trust: from ideal types to plural forms', *Annual Review of Sociology*, **15**, 97-118.

Brandenburger, A.M. and B.J. Nalebuff (1996), *Co-Opetition: A Revolutionary Mindset that Combines Competition and Cooperation*, New York: Doubleday.

Brass, D.J. (1981), 'Structural relationships, job characteristics, and worker satisfaction and performance', *Administrative Science Quarterly*, **26**, 331-48.

Brenner, D.J. and R. Logan (1980), 'Some considerations in the diffusion of medical technologies: medical information systems', in D. Nimmo (ed.), *Communication Yearbook 4*, New Brunswick, NJ: Transaction Books, pp. 609-24.

Brief, A.P. and R.J. Aldag (1976), 'Correlates of role indices', *Journal of Applied Psychology*, **61**, 468-72.

Brimm, I.M (1988), 'Risky business: why sponsoring innovations may be hazardous to career health', *Organizational Dynamics*, **16**, 28-41.

Brink, S. (1995), 'The American way of dying', *US News and World Report*, 4 December, 70-75.

Brittain, J.M. (1985), 'Introduction', in J.M. Brittain (ed.), *Consensus and Penalties for Ignorance in the Medical Sciences: Implications for Information Transfer*, London: British Library Board, pp. 5-10.

Broadway, M.D. and S.B. Christensen (1993), 'Medical and health information needs in a small community', *Public Libraries*, September/October, 253-6.

Broder, S. (1993), 'Foreward', *Journal of the National Cancer Institute*, Monograph 14, vii.

Browning, L.D., J.M. Beyer and J.C. Shetler (1995), 'Building cooperation in a competitive industry: SEMATECH and the semiconductor industry', *Academy of Management Journal*, **38**, 112-51.

Buchanan, M. (2002), *Nexus: Small Worlds and the Groundbreaking Theory of Networks*, New York: W.W. Norton.

Burk, J. (1994), 'Training MNC employees as culturally sensitive boundary spanners', *Public Relations Quarterly*, **39**, 40-44.

Burt, R.S. (1980), 'Innovation as a structural interest: rethinking the impact of network position on innovation adoption', *Social Networks*, **2**, 327-55.

Burt, R. S. (1982), *Toward a Structural Theory of Action: Network Models of Social Structure, Perception, and Action*. New York: Academic Press.

Burt, R.S. (1983), 'Cohesion versus structural equivalence as a basis for network subgroups', in R.S. Burt and M.J. Minor (eds), *Applied Network Analysis,* Beverly Hills: Sage, pp. 262-82.

Burt, R.S. (1987), 'Social contagion and innovation: cohesion versus structural equivalence', *Applied Journal of Psychology,* **92,** 1287-335.

Burt, R.S. (1991), *Structure Reference Manual Version 4.2,* New York: Center for the Social Sciences, Columbia University.

Burt, R.S. (1992), *Structural Holes: The Social Structure of Competition,* Cambridge, MA: Harvard University Press.

Burt, R.S. (2000), 'The network structure of social capital', *Research in Organization Behavior,* **22,** 345-423.

Burt, R.S. (2003), *Social capital and good ideas,* presentation to the Gatton College of Business and Economics, University of Kentucky, Lexington, KY, 3 April.

Burt, R.S. and P. Doreian (1982), 'Testing a structural model of perception: conformity and deviance with respect to journal norms in elite sociological methodology', *Quality and Quantity,* **16,** 109-50.

Burt, R.S. and T. Uchiyama (1989), 'The conditional significance of communication for interpersonal influence', in M. Kochen (ed.), *The Small World,* Norwood, NJ: Ablex.

Burton-Jones, A. (1999), *Knowledge Capitalism: Business, Work, and Learning in the New Economy,* New York: Oxford University Press.

Caplan, N. (1979), 'The two-communities theory of knowledge utilization', *American Behavioral Scientist,* **22,** 459-70.

Carlson, J.R. and R.W. Zmud (1999), 'Channel expansion theory and the experiential nature of media richness perception', *Academy of Management Journal,* **42,** 153-71.

Carothers, J.E. and L.J. Inslee (1974), 'Level of empathic understanding offered by volunteer telephone services', *Journal of Counseling Psychology,* **21,** 274-6.

Carroll, G.R. and A.C. Teo (1996), 'On the social networks of managers', *Academy of Management Journal,* **39,** 421-40.

Carter, N.M. and J.B. Culnan (1983), *The Computerization of Newspaper Organizations: The Impact of Technology on Organizational Structuring,* Lanham, MD: University Press of America.

Case, D., J.D. Johnson, J.E. Andrews, S. Allard and K.M. Kelly (2004), 'From two-step flow to the Internet: the changing array of sources for genetics information seeking', *Journal of the American Society for Information Science and Technology,* **55,** 660-69.

Case, D.O., J.E. Andrews, J.D. Johnson and S.L. Allard (in press). 'Avoiding versus seeking: the relationship of information seeking to avoidance, blunting, coping, dissonance and related concepts', *Journal of Medical Libraries Association.*

Center for Information Technology Enterprise (2002), *Kentucky Prepares for a Networked World*, Bowling Green, KY: Center for Information Technology Enterprise.

Chang, H.-J. (1996), *Contrasting Three Alternative Explanations of Internal and External Boundary Spanning Activities*, unpublished doctoral dissertation, E. Lansing, MI: Department of Communication, Michigan State University.

Chang, H.-J. and J.D. Johnson (1997),   'Communication networks as predictors of social information processing', paper presented to the Midwest Academy of Management, Ann Arbor, MI   (published in electronic proceedings).

Chang, H.-J. and J.D. Johnson (2001), 'Communication networks as predictors of organizational members' media choices', *Western Journal of Communication*, **65**, 349-69.

Chang, H.-J., J.D. Johnson, D. Cox and T. Kiyomiya (1997), 'The communication environment of the CISRC: external communication and boundary spanning', paper presented to the International Communication Annual Convention, Montreal, Canada.

Chen, C. and P. Hernon (1982), *Information Seeking: Assessing and Anticipating User Needs*, New York: Neal-Schuman Publishers.

Child, J. and R.G. McGrath (2001), 'Organizations unfettered: organizational form in an information-intensive economy', *Academy of Management Journal*, **44**, 1135-48.

Choo, W.C. (1998), *The Knowing Organization: How Organizations Use Information to Construct Meaning, Create Knowledge, and Make Decisions*, New York: Oxford University Press.

Church, P.H. and J.D. Spiceland (1987), 'Enhancing business forecasting with input from boundary spanners', *Journal of Business Forecasting*, **6**, 2-6.

Ciano, G. (1942), Quote from *Diario 1939-43*. [CD-ROM]   Microsoft Bookshelf 1994-Quotations. Redwood, WA: Microsoft.

Clark, F. (1992), 'The need for a national information infrastructure', *Journal of Biomedical Communication*, **19**, 8-9.

Coase, R.H. (1937), 'The nature of the firm', *Economica*, **IV**, 386-405.

Coch, L. and J.R. French (1948), 'Overcoming resistance to change', *Human Relations*, **11**, 512-32.

Coleman, J. (1988), 'Social capital in the creation of human capital', *American Journal of Sociology*, **94**, S95-S120.

Conference Board of the Mathematical Sciences (1972), *Recommendations Regarding Computers in High School Education*, Washington, DC: Conference Board of the Mathematical Sciences.

Connolly, T., E.J. Conlon and S.J. Deutsch (1980), 'Organizational effectiveness: a multiple constituency approach', *Academy of Management Review*, **5**, 211-7.

Conrath, D.W. (1973), 'Communication environment and its relationship to organizational structure', *Management Science*, 20, 586-603.

Contractor, N.S. and P.R. Monge (2002), 'Managing knowledge networks', *Management Communication Quarterly*, 16, 249-58.

Contractor, N.S., D.R. Seibold and M.A. Heller (1996), 'Interactional influence in the structuring of media use in groups: influence in members' perceptions of group decision support systems use', *Human Communication Research*, 22, 451-81.

Couch, C.J. (1987), *Researching Social Processes in the Laboratory*, Greenwich, CT: JAI Press.

Crane, L.A., T.A. Leakey, G. Ehrsam, B.K. Rimer and R.B. Warnecke (2000), 'Effectiveness and cost-effectiveness of multiple outcalls to promote mammography among low-income women', *Cancer Epidemiology, Biomarkers and Prevention*, 9, 923-31.

Crane, L.A., T.A. Leakey, M.A. Woodworth, B.K. Rimer, R.B. Warnecke, D. Heller and V.S. George (1998), 'Cancer Information Service-initiated outcalls to promote screening mammography among low-income and minority women: design and feasibility testing', *Preventive Medicine*, 27, S29-S38.

Crawford, C.M. (1996), *Managed Care and the NII: A Public/Private Perspective*, Bethesda, MD: Department of Health and Human Services.

Cronin, B. and E. Davenport (1993), 'Social intelligence', in M.E. Williams (ed.), *Annual Review of Information Science and Technology, Volume 28*, Medford, NJ: Learned Information, pp. 3-44.

Cross, R., N. Nohria and A. Parker (2004), 'Six myths about informal networks and how to overcome them', in E. Lesser and L. Prusak (eds), *Creating Value with Knowledge: Insights from the IBM Institute for Business Value*, New York: Oxford University Press, pp. 47-60.

Cross, R., A. Parker and L. Sasson (eds) (2003), *Networks in the Knowledge Economy*, NY: Oxford University Press.

Cullen, P., P. Cottingham, J. Doolan, B. Edgar, C. Ellis, M. Fisher, D. Flett, D. Johnson, L. Sealie, S. Stoklmayer, F. Vanclay and J. Whittington (2001), *Knowledge Seeking Strategies of Natural Resource Professionals*, Cooperative Research Centre for Freshwater Ecology: Technical Report 2/2001.

Cullen, P.W., R.J. Norris, V.H. Resh, T.B. Reynoldson, D.M. Rosenberg and M.T. Barbour (1999), 'Collaboration in scientific research: a critical need for freshwater ecology', *Freshwater Biology*, 42, 131-42.

Culnan, M.J. and M.L. Markus (1987), 'Information Technologies', in F.M. Jablin, L.L. Putnam, K.H. Roberts and L.W. Porter (eds), *Handbook of Organizational Communication: An Interdisciplinary Perspective*,

Beverly Hills, CA: Sage, pp. 420-43.

Czepiel, J.A. (1975), 'Patterns of interorganizational communications and the diffusion of a major techological innovation in a competitive industrial community', *Academy of Management Journal*, **18**, 6-24.

Daft, R.L. (1978), 'A dual-core model of organizational innovation', *Academy of Management Journal*, **21**, 193-210.

Daft, R.L. and G.P. Huber (1987),'How organizations learn: a communication framework', in N.D. Tomoso and S.B. Bacharach (eds) *Research in Organizational Behavior*, Greenwich, CT: JAI Press, pp. 1-36.

Daft, R.L. and R.H. Lengel (1986), 'Organizational information requirements: media richness and structural design', *Management Science*, **32**, 554-71.

Daft, R.L. and N.B. Macintosh (1981), 'A tentative exploration into the amount and equivocality of information processing in organizational work units', *Administrative Science Quarterly*, **26**, 207-24.

Damanpour, F. (1991), 'Organizational innovation: A meta-analysis of effects of determinants and moderators', *Academy of Management Journal*, **34**, 555-90.

Darnell, D.K. (1972), 'Information theory: an approach to human communication', in R.W. Budd and B.D. Ruben (eds) *Approaches to Human Communication*, New York: Spartan Books, pp. 156-69.

Darrow, S.L., J.B. Speyer, A.C. Marcus, J.T. Maat and D. Krome (1998), 'Coping with cancer: the impact of the cancer information service on patients and significant others', *Journal of Health Communication*, **3**, 86-97.

Davenport, T.H. and L. Prusak (1998), *Working Knowledge: How Organizations Manage What They Know*, Boston, MA: Harvard Business School Press.

Davis, F.D., R.P. Bagozzi and P.R. Warshaw (1989), 'User acceptance of computer technology: a comparison of two theoretical models', *Management Science*, **35**, 982-1003.

Davis, S.E. and L. Fleisher (1998), 'Treatment and clinical trials decision making: the impact of the Cancer Information Service, Part 5', *Journal of Health Communication*, **3**, 71-86.

Deal, T.E. and A.A. Kennedy (1982), *Corporate Cultures: The Rites and Rituals of Corporate Life,* Reading, MA: Addison-Wesley.

Dearing, J. (2000), 'Dilemmas of evaluation research', *ICA News*, May, pp. 5, 7.

Dearing, J.W. and G. Meyer (1994), 'An exploratory tool for predicting adoption decisions', *Science Communication*, **16**, 43-57.

Dearing, J.W., G. Meyer and J. Kazmierczak (1994), 'Portraying the new: communication between university innovators and potential users', *Science Communication*, **16**, 11-42.

DeBresson, C. and F. Amesse (1991), 'Networks of innovators: a review and introduction to the issue', *Research Policy*, **20**, 363-79.

Deetz, S. (2000), 'Conceptual Foundations', in F.M. Jablin and L.L. Putnam (eds), *The New Handbook of Organizational Communication: Advances in Theory, Research, and Methods*, Thousand Oaks, CA: Sage, pp. 3-46.

De la Mothe, J. (2001), 'Knowledge, Learning and Innovation Policy', in J. de la Mothe and D. Foray (eds), *Knowledge Management in the Innovation Process*, Boston, MA: Kluwer Academic Publishers, pp. 205-13.

Dervin, B. (1980), 'Communication gaps and inequities: moving toward a reconceptualization', in B. Dervin and M.J. Voight (eds), *Progress in Communication Sciences, Volume II*, Norwood, NJ: ABLEX, pp. 74-112.

Dervin, B. (1989), 'Users as research inventions: how research categories perpetuate inequities', *Journal of Communication*, **39**, 216-32.

Dervin, B. (1998), 'Sense-making theory and practice: an overview of user interests in knowledge seeking and use', *Journal of Knowledge Management*, **2**, 36-46.

Diamond, G.A., B.H. Pollock and J.W. Work (1994), 'Clinical decisions and computers', in M.M. Shabot and R.M. Gardner (eds), *Decision Support Systems in Critical Care*, New York: Springer-Verlag, pp. 188-211.

Dierkes, M. (2001), 'Visions, technology, and organizational knowledge: an analysis of the interplay between enabling factors and triggers of knowledge generation', in J. de la Mothe and D. Foray (eds), *Knowledge Management in the Innovation Process*, Boston, MA: Kluwer Academic Publishers, pp. 9-42.

Doctor, R.D. (1992), 'Social equity and information technologies: moving toward information democracy', in M.E. Williams (ed.), *Annual Review of Information Science and Technology*, Medford, NJ: Learned Information, pp. 44-96.

Dollinger, M.J. (1984), 'Environmental boundary spanning and information process effects on organizational performance', *Academy of Management Journal*, **27**, 351-68.

Donnellon, A., B. Gray and M.G. Bougon (1986), 'Communication, meaning, and organized action', *Administrative Science Quarterly*, **31**, 43-55.

Dornblaser, B.M., T. Lin and A.H. Van de Ven (2000), 'Innovation outcomes, learning, and action loops', in A.H. Van de Ven, H.L. Angle, and M.S. Poole (eds), *Research on the Management of Innovation: The Minnesota Studies*, New York: Oxford University Press, pp. 193-217.

Dorsey, A.M. (2003), 'Lessons and challenges from the field', in T.L. Thompson, A.M. Dorsey, K.I. Miller and R. Parrott (eds), *Handbook of Health Communication*, Mahwah, NJ: Lawrence

Erlbaum, pp. 607-8.

Dougherty, D. and C. Hardy (1996), 'Sustained product innovation in large, mature organizations: Overcoming innovation-to-organization problems', *Academy of Management Journal*, **39**, 1120-53.

Dow, G.K. (1988), 'Configurational and coactivational views of organizational structure', *Academy of Management Review*, **13**, 53-64.

Downing, J.R. (2004), '"It's easier to ask someone I know": Call center technicians' adoption of knowledge management tools', *Journal of Business Communication*, **41**, 166-91.

Downs, A. (1967), *Inside Bureaucracy*, Boston, MA: Little, Brown.

Downs, C.W. and A.D. Adrian (2004), *Assessing Organizational Communication: Strategic Communication Audit*, New York: Guilford Press.

Downs, G.W., Jr and L.B. Mohr (1976), 'Conceptual issues in the study of innovation', *Administrative Science Quarterly*, **21**, 700-14.

Drazin, R., M.A. Glynn and R.K. Kazanjian (1999), 'Multilevel theorizing about creativity in organizations: a sensemaking perspective', *Academy of Management Review*, **24**, 286-307.

Drazin, R. and C.B. Schoonhoven (1996), 'Community, population, and organization effects on innovation: a multilevel perspective', *Academy of Management Journal*, **39**, 1065-83.

Drucker, P.F. (1995), 'Really reinventing government', *Atlantic Monthly*, February, 49-61.

Durlak, J.T. (1987), 'A typology of interactive media', in M.L. McLaughlin (ed.), *Communication Yearbook 10*, Beverly Hills, CA: Sage, pp. 743-57.

Dutton, J.E., S.J. Ashford, R.M. O'Neill and K.A. Lawrence (2001), 'Moves that matter: issue selling and organizational change', *Academy of Management Journal*, **44**, 716-36.

Dutton, W.H., J. Fulk and C. Steinfield (1982), 'Utilization of video conferencing', *Telecommunications Policy*, September, 164-78.

Ebadi, Y.M. and J.M. Utterback (1984), 'The effects of communication and technical innovation', *Management Science*, **30**, 572-85.

Eccles, R. and H. White (1988), 'Price and authority in inter-profit center transactions', *American Journal of Sociology, Supplement*, **94**, S17-S51.

Eisenberg, E.M. (1990), 'Jamming: transcendence through organizing', *Communication Research*, **17**, 139-64.

Eisenberg, E.M., R.V. Farace, P.R. Monge, E.P. Bettinghaus, R. Kurchner-Hawkins, K.I. Miller and L. Rothman (1985), 'Communication linkages in interorganizational systems: review and synthesis', in B. Dervin and M. Voight (eds), *Progress in Communication Sciences Vol. 6*, New York: Ablex, pp. 231-61.

Eisenberg, E.M., A. Murphy and L. Andrews (1998), 'Openness and decision making in the search for a university provost', *Communication Monographs*, **65**, 1-23.

Emery, F. and E. Trist (1965), 'The causal texture of organizational environment', *Human Relations*, **18**, 21-32.

Entman, R.M. and S.S. Wildman (1992), 'Reconciling economic and non-economic perspectives on media policy: transcending the "marketplace of ideas"', *Journal of Communication*, **42**, 5-19.

Etzioni, A. (1964), *Modern Organizations*, Englewood Cliffs, NJ: Prentice-Hall.

Evans, S.H. and P. Clarke (1983), 'When cancer patients fail to get well: flaws in health communication', in R.N. Bostrom (eds), *Communication Yearbook 7*, Beverly Hills, CA: Sage, pp. 225-48.

Fairhurst, G.T. and R.A. Sarr (1996), *The Art of Framing: Managing the Language of Leadership*, San Francisco, CA: Jossey-Bass.

Farace, R.V. and J.D. Johnson (1974), 'Comparative analysis of human communication networks in selected formal organizations', paper presented to the International Communication Association Annual Convention, New Orleans, LA.

Farace, R.V. and T. Mabee (1980), 'Communication network analysis methods', in P.R. Monge and J.N. Cappella (eds), *Multivariate Techniques in Human Communication Research*, New York: Academic Press, pp. 365-91.

Farace, R.V., P.R. Monge, E.P. Bettinghaus, E.M. Eisenberg, L. White, R. Kurchner-Hawkins and K.I. Williams (1982), *Communication and Coordination Among Health Care Organizations: Experiences from the Metropolitan Detroit Cancer Control Program*, E. Lansing, MI: Department of Communication, Michigan State University.

Farace, R.V., P.R. Monge and H. Russell (1977), *Communicating and Organizing*, Reading, MA: Addison-Wesley.

Farace, R.V., J.A. Taylor and J.P. Stewart (1978), 'Criteria for evaluation of organizational communication effectiveness: review and synthesis', in D. Nimmo (eds), *Communication Yearbook 2*, New Brunswick, NJ: Transaction Books, pp. 271-92.

Fidler, L.A. and J.D. Johnson (1984), 'Communication and innovation implementation', *Academy of Management Review*, **9**, 704-11.

Fine, G.A. (1993), 'The sad demise, mysterious disappearance, and glorious triumph of symbolic interactionism', *Annual Review of Sociology*, **19**, 61-87.

Finlay, W. and J.E. Coverdill (2000), 'Risk, opportunism, and structural holes: How headhunters manage clients and earn fees', *Work and Occupation*, **27**, 377-405.

Fiol, C.M. (1996), 'Squeezing harder doesn't always work: continuing the search for consistency in innovation research', *Academy of*

Management Journal, **21**, 1012-21.

Fisher, C.D. and R. Gitelson (1983), 'A meta-analysis of the correlates of role conflict and ambiguity', *Journal of Applied Psychology*, **68**, 320-33.

Fleisher, L., M. Woodworth, M. Morra, S. Baum, S. Darrow, S. Davis, R. Slevin-Perocchia, W. Stengle and J.A. Ward (1998), 'Balancing research and service: the experience of the Cancer Information Service', *Preventive Medicine*, **27**, S84-S92.

Florida, R. and W.M. Cohen (1999), 'Engine or infrastructure? The university role in economic development', in L.M. Branscomb, F. Kodoma and R. Florida (eds), *Industrializing Knowledge: University-Industry Linkages in Japan and the United States*, Cambridge, MA: MIT Press, pp. 589-610.

Foray, D. (2001), 'Continuities and ruptures in knowledge management practices', in J. de la Mothe and D. Foray (eds), *Knowledge Management in the Innovation Process*, Boston, MA: Kluwer Academic Publishers, pp. 43-52.

Ford, D.P. (2003), 'Trust and knowledge management: the seeds of success', in C.W. Holsapple (ed.), *Handbook on Knowledge Management 1*, New York: Springer-Verlag., pp. 553-75.

Ford, E.W., J.W. Duncan, A.G. Bedeian, P.M. Ginter, M.D. Rousculp and A.M. Adams (2003), 'Mitigating risks, visible hands, inevitable disasters, and soft variables', *Academy of Management Executive*, **17**, 46-60.

Fortner, R.S. (1995), 'Excommunication in the information society', *Critical Studies in Mass Communication*, **12**, 133-54.

Fouche, B. (1999), 'Knowledge networks: emerging knowledge work infrastructures to support innovation and knowledge management', *ICSTI Forum*, **32**,

Frances, J., R. Levacic, J. Mitchell and G. Thompson (1991), 'Introduction', in G. Thompson, J. Frances, R. Levacic and J. Mitchell (eds), *Markets, Hierarchies and Networks: The Coordination of Social Life*, Newbury Park, CA: Sage, pp. 1-19.

Freeman, L.C. (1977), 'A set of measures of centrality based on betweenness', *Sociometry*, **40**, 35-41.

Freimuth, V.S. (1987), 'The diffusion of supportive information', in T.L. Albrecht and M.B. Adelman (eds), *Communicating Social Support* Newbury Park, CA: Sage, pp. 212-37.

Freimuth, V.S. (1990), 'The chronically uninformed: closing the knowledge gap in health', in E.B. Ray and L. Donohew (eds), *Communication and Health: Systems and Applications*, Hillsdale, NJ: Lawrence Erlbaum Associates, pp. 171-86.

Freimuth, V.S., T. Edgar and M.A. Fitzpatrick (1993), 'Introduction: the role of communication in health promotion', *Communication Research*, **20**, 509-16.

Freimuth, V.S., J.A. Stein and T.J. Kean (1989), *Searching for Health Information: The Cancer Information Service Model,* Philadelphia, PA: University of Pennsylvania Press.

French, J.R.P., Jr and B. Raven (1959), 'The bases of social power', in D. Cartwright (ed.), *Studies in Social Power*, Ann Arbor, MI: Institute for Social Research, 150-67.

Friedkin, N. (1980), 'A test of structural features of Granovetter's strength of weak ties theory', *Social Networks*, **2**, 411-22.

Friedkin, N.E. (1982), 'Information flow through strong and weak ties in intraorganizational social networks', *Social Networks*, **3**, 273-85.

Friedkin, N.E. (1984), 'Structural cohesion and equivalence: Explanation of social homogeneity', *Sociological Methods and Research*, **12**, 235-61.

Friedman, R.A. and J. Podolny (1992), 'Differentiation of boundary spanning roles: labor negotiations and implications for role conflict', *Administrative Science Quarterly*, **37**, 28-47.

Frost, P.J. and C.P. Egri (1991), 'The political process of innovation', *Research in Organizational Behavior*, **13**, 229-95.

Fry, L.W. and D.A. Smith (1987), 'Congruence, contingency, and theory building', *Academy of Management Review*, **12**, 117-32.

Fulk, J. and B. Boyd (1991), 'Emerging theories of communication in organizations', *Journal of Management*, **17**, 407-46.

Fulk, J., C.W. Steinfield, J. Schmitz and J.G. Power (1987), 'A social information processing model of media use in organizations', *Communication Research*, **14**, 529-52.

Fund for the Improvement of Postsecondary Education (2003), *Innovation and Impact: The Comprehensive Program FY 2004*, Washington, DC: US Department of Education.

Galaskiewicz, J. (1996), 'The "New Network Analysis" and its application to organizational theory and behavior', in D. Iacobucci (ed.), *Networks in Marketing*, Thousand Oaks, CA: Sage, pp. 19-31.

Galbraith, J.R. (1973), *Designing Complex Organizations*, Reading, MA: Addison-Wesley.

Galbraith, J.R. (1982), 'Designing the innovating organization', *Organizational Dynamics*, **10**, 5-25.

Galbraith J.R. (1984), 'Designing the innovating organization', in D. Kolb, I. Rubin and J. McIntyre (eds), *Organizational Psychology: Readings on Human Behavior in Organizations*, Englewood Cliffs, NJ: Prentice-Hall.

Galbraith, J.R. (1995), *Designing Organizations: An Executive Briefing on Strategy, Structure, and Process*, San Francisco, CA: Jossey-Bass.

Gales, L., P. Porter and D. Mansour-Cole (1992), 'Innovation project technology, information processing and performance: a test of the Daft and Lengel conceptualization', *Journal of Engineering and*

Technology Management, **9**, 303-38.

Gardner, R.M. and M.M. Shabot (1994), 'The future of computerized decision support in critical care', in M.M. Shabot and R.M. Gardner (eds), *Decision Support Systems in Critical Care*,   New   York: Springer-Verlag, pp. 396-409.

Gargiulo, M. and M. Benassi (2000), 'Trapped in your own net? Network cohesion, structural holes, and the adaptation of social capital', *Organization Science*, **11**, 183-96.

Garton, L. and B. Wellman (1995), 'Social impacts of electronic mail in organizations: a review of the research literature', in B. Burleson (ed.), *Communication Yearbook 18*, Thousand Oaks, CA: Sage, pp. 434-53.

Garvin, D.A. (1993), 'Building a learning organization', *Harvard Business Review*, **71**, 78-92.

Ghosal, S. and C.A. Bartlett (1987), *Innovation Processes in Multinational Corporations*, Cambridge, MA: Harvard Business School Press.

Gibb, J.R. (1974), 'Dynamics of leadership and communication', in W.R. Lassey and R.R. Fernandez (eds), *Leadership and Social Change*, La Jolla, CA: University Associates, pp. 107-21.

Gibson, D.V. and E.M. Rogers (1994), *R&D Collaboration on Trial*, Cambridge, MA: Harvard Business School Press.

Giddens, A. (1979), *Central Problems in Social Theory*, Berkeley, CA: University of California Press.

Gingerich, W.J., R.J. Gurney and T.S. Wirtz (1988), 'How helpful are helplines? A survey of callers', *Journal of Contemporary Social Work*, **69**, 634-9.

Goes, J.B. and S.H. Park (1997), 'Interorganizational links and innovation: the case of hospital services', *Academy of Management Journal*, **40**, 673-96.

Goldenson, R.M. (1984), *Longman Dictionary of Psychology and Psychiatry*, New York, NY: Longman.

Goldhaber, G.M., M.P. Yates, T.D. Porter and R. Lesniak (1978), 'Organizational communication: 1978', *Human Communication Research*, **5**, 76-96.

Goldhar, J.D., L.K. Bragaw and J.J. Schwartz (1976), 'Information flows, management styles, and technological innovation', *IEEE Transactions on Engineering Management*, **23**, 51-62.

Goodman, R.M., M.A. Speers, K. McLeroy, S. Fawcett, M. Kegler, E. Parker, S.R. Smith, T.D. Sterling and N. Wallerstein (1998), 'Identifying and defining the dimensions of community capacity to provide a basis for measurement', *Health Education and Behavior*, **25**, 258-78.

Gotcher, J.M. and R. Edwards (1990), 'Coping strategies of cancer patients: actual communication and imagined interactions', *Health*

Communication, **2**, 255-66.

Granovetter, M.S. (1973), 'The strength of weak ties', *American Journal of Sociology,* **78**, 1360-80.

Granovetter, M. (1982), 'The strength of weak ties: a network theory revisited', in P.V. Marsden and N. Lin (eds), *Social Structure in Network Analysis,* Beverly Hills, CA: Sage, pp. 105-30.

Greene, C.N. (1978), 'Identification modes of professionals: relationships with formalization, role strain, and alienation', *Academy of Management Journal,* **21**, 486-92.

Greer, A.L. (1994), 'You can always tell a Doctor ...', in L. Sechrest, T.E. Backer, E.M. Rogers, T.F. Campbell and M.L. Grady (eds), *Effective Dissemination of Clinical and Health Information,* Rockville, MD: Agency for Health Care Policy Research, AHCPR Pub. No. 95-0015.

Grover, V., S.-R. Jeong, W.J. Kettinger and C.C. Lee (1993), 'The chief information officer: a study of managerial roles', *Journal of Management Information Systems,* **10**, 107-30.

Gudykunst, W.B. and Y.Y. Kim (1984), *Communicating with Strangers,* Reading, MA: Addison-Wesley.

Gulati, R. (1995), 'Social structure and alliance formation patterns: a longitudinal analysis', *Administrative Science Quarterly,* **40**, 619-52.

Hage, J. (1999), 'Organizational innovation and organizational change', *Annual Review of Sociology,* **25**, 597-622.

Hage, J. and M. Aiken (1970), *Social Change in Complex Organizations,* New York, NY: Random House.

Hakansson, H. and D.D. Sharma (1996), 'Strategic alliances in a network perspective', in D. Iacobucci (ed.), *Networks in Marketing,* Thousand Oaks, CA: Sage, pp. 108-24.

Hargadon, A. and R.I. Sutton (2000), 'Building an innovation factory', *Harvard Business Review,* May-June, 157-66.

Harter, L.M. and K.J. Krone (2001), 'The boundary-spanning role of a cooperative support organization: managing the paradox ostability and change in non-traditional organizations', *Journal of Applied Communication Research,* **29**, 248-77.

Hartman, R.L. and J.D. Johnson (1989), 'Social contagion and multiplexity: communication networks as predictors of commitment and role ambiguity', *Human Communication Research,* **15**, 523-48.

Hartman, R.L. and J.D. Johnson (1990), 'Formal and informal group communication structures: an examination of their relationship to role ambiguity', *Social Networks,* **12**, 127-51.

Haynes, R.B., N. Wilczynski, K.A. McKibbon, C.J. Walker and J.C. Sinclair (1994), 'Developing optimal search strategies for detecting clinically sound studies in MEDLINE', *Journal of the American Medical Informatics Association,* **1**, 447-58.

Health and Human Services (2002), press release: 'HHS affirms value of mammography for detecting cancer', 21 February.

Hibbard, J.H. (2003), 'Engaging health care consumers to improve the quality of care', *Medical Care*, **41**, I-61-I-70.

Hibbard, J.H. and E. Peters (2003), "Supporting informed consumer health care decisions: Data presentation approaches that facilitate the use of information in choice, *Annual Review of Public Health*, **24**, 413-33.

Hibbard, J.H. and E.C. Weeks (1987), 'Consumerism in health care', *Medical Care*, **25**, 1019-32.

Hibbard, S.M., N.B. Martin and A.L. Thurn (1995), 'NCI's cancer information systems-bringing medical knowledge to clinicians', *Oncology*, **9**, 302-96.

Hiemstra, G. (1982), 'Teleconferencing, concern for face, and organizational culture', in M. Burgoon (ed.), *Communication Yearbook 6*, Beverly Hills, CA: Sage, pp. 874-904.

Hiltz, S. and E. Kerr (1980), *On-Line Scientific Communities*, Norwood, NJ: Ablex.

Hoffman, E. and P.M. Roman (1984), 'Information diffusion in the implementation of innovation processes', *Communication Research*, **11**, 117-40.

Hoffman, G.M. (1994), *The Technology Payoff: How to Profit with Empowered Workers in Information Age*, New York: Irwin.

Hoke, F. (1995), 'News', *Scientist*, **9**, 3 April, 1, 6-7.

Hollander, H. (1990), 'A social exchange approach to voluntary cooperation', *American Economic Review*, **80**, 1157-67.

Holsapple, C.W. (2003), 'Knowledge and its attributes', in C.W. Holsapple (ed.), *Handbook on Knowledge Management 1: Knowledge Matters*, New York: Springer-Verlag, pp. 165-88.

Holsapple, C.W. and K.D. Joshi (2003), 'A knowledge management ontology', in C.W. Holsapple (ed.), *Handbook on Knowledge Management 1: Knowledge matters*, New York: Springer-Verlag, pp. 89-123.

Huber, G.P. and R.R. McDaniel, Jr (1988), 'Exploiting information technologies to design more effective organizations', in M. Jarke (ed.), *Managers, Micros and Mainframes*, New York, NY: John Wiley, pp. 221-36.

Huber, G.P. and A.H. Van de Ven (eds) (1995), *Longitudinal Field Research Methods: Studying Process of Organizational Change*, Thousand Oaks, CA: Sage.

Hurt, H.T., K. Joseph and C.D. Cook (1977), 'Scales for the measurement of innovativeness', *Human Communication Research*, **4**, 58-65.

Hurt, H.T. and C.W. Teigen (1977), 'The development of a measure of perceived innovativeness', in B.D. Ruben (ed.), *Communication*

Yearbook 1, New Brunswick, NJ: Transaction Books, pp. 377-85.

Huysman, M. and P. van Baalen (2002), 'Editorial', *Trends in Communication*, **8**, 3-5.

Indik, B.P. (1965), 'Organization size and member participation: some empirical tests of alternative explanations', *Human Relations*, **18**, 339-50.

Ireland, R.D., P.M. Van Auken and P.V. Lewis (1978), 'An investigation of the relationship between organizational climate and communication climate', *Journal of Business Communication*, **16**, 3-10.

Iverson, J.O. and R.D. McPhee (2002), 'Knowledge management in communities of practice: being true to the communicative character of knowledge', *Management Communication Quarterly*, **16**, 259-66.

Jablin, F.M. (1979), 'Superior-subordinate communication: the state of the art', *Psychological Bulletin*, **86**, 1201-22.

Jablin, F.M. (1980), 'Organizational communication theory and research: an overview of communication climate and network research', in D. Nimmo (ed.), *Communication Yearbook 4*, New Brunswick, NJ: Transaction Books, pp. 327-47.

Jablin, F.M. (1987), 'Formal organization structure', in F.M. Jablin, L.L. Putnam, K.H. Roberts and L.W. Porter (eds), *Handbook of Organizational Communication: An Interdisciplinary Perspective*, Newbury Park, CA: Sage, pp. 389-419.

Jablin, F.M., L.L. Putnam, K.H. Roberts and L.W. Porter (eds) (1987), *Handbook of Organizational Communication: An Interdisciplinary Perspective*, Newbury Park, CA: Sage.

Jackson, S.E. and R.S. Schuler (1985), 'A meta-analysis and conceptual critique of research on role ambiguity and role conflict in work settings', *Organizational Behavior and Human Decision Processes*, **36**, 16-78.

Jacoby, J. and W.D. Hoyer (1987), *The Comprehension and Miscomprehension of Print Communications: An Investigation of Mass Media Magazines*, Hillsdale, NJ: Lawrence Earlbaum Associates.

Jemison, D.B. (1984), 'The importance of boundary spanning roles in strategic decision-making', *Journal of Management Studies*, **21**, 131-52.

Jensen, M.C. and W.H. Meckling (1995), 'Specific and general knowledge, and organizational structure', *Journal of Applied Corporate Finance*, **8**, 4-18.

Johnson, J.D. (1990), 'Effects of communicative factors on participation in innovations', *Journal of Business Communication*, **27**, 7-23.

Johnson, J. D. (1993), *Organizational Communication Structure*, Norwood, NJ: Ablex.

Johnson, J.D. (1997a), *Cancer-Related Information Seeking*, Cresskill, NJ:

Hampton Press.

Johnson, J.D. (1997b), 'A frameworks for interaction (FINT) scale: extensions and refinement in an industrial setting', *Communication Studies*, **48**, 127-41.

Johnson, J.D. (1997c), 'Review of the books *The Art of Framing: Managing The Language of Leadership* and *Frame Reflection: Toward the Resolution of Intractable Policy Controversies'*, *Quarterly Journal of Speech*, **83**, 397-8.

Johnson, J.D. (1998), 'Frameworks for interaction and disbandments: a case study', *Journal of Educational Thought*, **32**, 5-20.

Johnson, J.D. (2000), 'Levels of success in implementing information technologies', *Innovative Higher Education*, **25**, 59-76.

Johnson, J.D. (2001), 'Success in innovation implementation', *Journal of Communication Management*, **5**, 341-59.

Johnson, J.D. (2002), 'Researcher-practitioner relationships in consortia: the Cancer Information Services Research Consortium', *AIC Journal of Business*, **14**, 34-56.

Johnson, J.D. (2003), 'Oh, those blinking lights: factors determining the success of consortia', unpublished paper, College of Communications and Information Studies, University of Kentucky, Lexington, KY.

Johnson, J.D. (2004). 'The emergence, maintenance, and dissolution of structural hole brokerage within consortia', *Communication Theory*, **14**, 212-36.

Johnson, J.D. (2005), 'A sociometric analysis of influence relations within a community of practice', unpublished paper, College of Communications and Information Studies, University of Kentucky, Lexington, KY.

Johnson, J.D. (in press), 'Organizing for knowledge management: the Cancer Information Service as an exemplar', in R.J. Bali (ed.), *Clinical Knowledge Management: Opportunities and Challenges,* Hershey, PA: Idea Group.

Johnson, J.D., J.A. Andrews, D.O. Case and S.L. Allard (in press), 'Genomics-The perfect information seeking research problem', *Journal of Health Communication*

Johnson, J.D., J. Berkowitz, C. Ethington and M. Meyer (1994a), *General Appendices to the Network Analysis Technical Reports*, E. Lansing, MI: Department of Communication, Michigan State University.

Johnson, J.D., J. Berkowitz, C. Ethington and M. Meyer (1994b), *Technical report #1: Analysis of the CIS/Program Project Network for the Period October 1993 to March 1994*, E. Lansing, MI: Department of Communication, Michigan State University.

Johnson, J.D., E. Bettinghaus, M. Woodworth, L. Fleisher, J.A. Ward and M. Meyer (1997), 'Lessons learned: implications for theory and the practice of research on communication networks', paper presented to the International Communication Association Annual Convention, Montreal, Canada.

Johnson, J.D. and H.-J. Chang (1999), 'An over-time comparison of three explanations of internal and external innovation communication in a new organizational form', paper presented to the International Sunbelt Social Network Conference, Charleston, SC.

Johnson, J.D. and H.-J. Chang (2000), 'Internal and external communication, boundary spanning, innovation adoption: an over-time comparison of three explanations of internal and external innovation communication in new organization form', *Journal of Business Communication*, **37**, 238-63.

Johnson, J.D., H.-J. Chang, J. Berkowitz, C. Ethington, M. Meyer and S.H. Johnson (1995), *Network Analysis Report #1: Network Analysis for the Period October 1993 to March 1994*, East Lansing, MI: Department of Communication, Michigan State University.

Johnson, J.D., H.-J. Chang, C. Ethington, B. LaFrance and M. Meyer (1996), *Network Analysis Report #6: Network Analysis for the Period February 1996 to May 1996*, East Lansing, MI: Department of Communication, Michigan State University.

Johnson, J.D., H.-J. Chang, C. Ethington, M. Meyer and B. LaFrance (1995), *Network Analysis Report #2: Network Analysis for the Period April 1994 to September 1994*, East Lansing, MI: Department of Communication, Michigan State University.

Johnson, J.D., H.-J. Chang, C. Ethington, B. LaFrance, M. Meyer and S. Pobocik (1996), *Technical Report #5: Analysis of the CISRC Project Network for the Period July 1995 to November 1995*, East Lansing, MI: Department of Communication, Michigan State University.

Johnson, J.D., H.-J. Chang, C. Ethington. M. Meyer and B.H. La France, (1994), *Technical report #2: Analysis of the CIS/Program Project Network for the period April 1994 to September 1994*, E. Lansing, MI: Department of Communication, Michigan State University.

Johnson, J.D., H.-J. Chang, T. Kiyomiya, C. Ethington and B. LaFrance (1997), *Network Analysis Report #7: Network Analysis for the Period June 1996 to August 1996*, East Lansing, MI: Department of Communication, Michigan State University.

Johnson, J.D., H.-J. Chang, B.H. LaFrance and M. Meyer (1995), *Network Analysis Report #3: Network Analysis for the period November 1994 to February 1995*, East Lansing, MI: Department of Communication, Michigan State University.

Johnson, J.D., H.-J. Chang, B.H. LaFrance, M. Meyer, C. Ethington and S. Pobocik (1996a), *Network Analysis Technical Report #4: Analysis of the CIS/Program Project Network for the period March 1995 to*

June 1995, E. Lansing, MI: Department of Communication, Michigan State University.

Johnson, J.D., H.-J. Chang, B. LaFrance, M. Meyer, C. Ethington and S. Pobocik (1996b), *Technical Report #6: Analysis of the CISRC Project Network for the Period November 1995 to May 1996*, East Lansing, MI: Department of Communication, Michigan State University.

Johnson, J.D., H.-J. Chang, B. LaFrance, M. Meyer, S. Pobocik and C. Ethington (1996), *Network Analysis Report #5: Network Analysis for the Period July 1995 to November 1995*, East Lansing, MI: Department of Communication, Michigan State University.

Johnson, J.D., H.-J. Chang, B. LaFrance, S. Pobocik and M. Meyer (1995a), *Technical Report #3: Analysis of the CIS/Program Project Network for the Period November 1994 to February 1995*. East Lansing, MI: Department of Communication, Michigan State University.

Johnson, J.D., H.-J. Chang, M. Meyer, S. Pobocik and B. LaFrance (1995a), *Technical Report #4: Analysis of the CIS/Program Project Network for the Period March 1995 to June 1995 and the Denver Conference*, East Lansing, MI: Department of Communication, Michigan State University.

Johnson, J.D., H.-J. Chang, M. Meyer, S. Pobocik and B. LaFrance (1995b), *Technical Report #4: Analysis of the CISRC Network for the Period March 1995 to June 1995 and the Denver Conference*, E. Lansing, MI: Department of Communication, Michigan State University.

Johnson, J.D., H.-J. Chang, S. Pobocik, M. Meyer, C. Ethington, D. Ruesch and J. Wooldridge (1995), 'Functional work groups and evaluations of communication channels: comparisons of six competing theoretical perspectives', paper presented at the meeting of the Speech Communication Association, San Antonio, TX.

Johnson, J.D., H.-J. Chang, S. Pobocik, M. Meyer, C. Ethington, D. Ruesch and J. Wooldridge (2000), 'Functional work groups and evaluations of communication channels: comparisons of six competing theoretical perspectives', *Journal of Computer Mediated Communication*,6,http://www.ascusc.org/jcmc/vol6/issue1/johnson.html.

Johnson, J.D., H.-J. Chang, S. Pobocik, M. Meyer, C. Ethington, D. Ruesch, J. Wooldridge and J. Murphy (1995), 'Functional work groups and evaluation of communication channels: comparisons of six competing theoretical perspectives', paper presented to the Organizational Communication Division at the Speech Communication Association Annual Convention, San Antonio, TX.

Johnson, J.D., W.A. Donohue, C.K. Atkin and S.H. Johnson (1994), 'Differences between formal and informal communication channels', *Journal of Business Communication*, 31, 111-22.

Johnson, J.D., W.A. Donohue, C.K. Atkin and S.H. Johnson   (1995a),   'A comprehensive model of information seeking: tests focusing on a technical organization', *Science Communication*, **16**, 274-303.

Johnson, J.D., W.A. Donohue, C.K. Atkin and S.H. Johnson (1995b), 'Differences between organizational and communication factors relating to contrasting innovations', *Journal of Business Communication*, **32**, 65-80.

Johnson, J.D., W.A. Donohue, C.K. Atkin and S.H. Johnson (2001), 'Communication, involvement, and perceived innovativeness: tests of a model with two contrasting innovations', *Groups and Organization Management*, **26**, 24-52.

Johnson, J.D., C. Ethington, S. Darrow and P. Lang (1997), 'The Cancer Information Service in context', paper presented to the International Communication Association annual convention, Montreal.

Johnson, J.D., C. Ethington, M. Meyer and B.H. LaFrance (1996), 'The development of the task interdependence scale: a tale of three studies', paper presented at the Speech Communication Association Convention, San Diego, CA.

Johnson, J.D., T. Kiyomiya, C. Ethington and B. LaFrance (1997), *Network Analysis Report #8:   Network Analysis for the Period September 1996 to March 1997*, East Lansing, MI: Department of Communication, Michigan State University.

Johnson, J.D., B. LaFrance, H.-J. Chang, T. Kiyomiya and C. Ethington (1997), *Technical Report #7:   Analysis of the CISRC Program Project for the Period June 1996 to September 1996,* East Lansing, MI: Department of Communication, Michigan State University.

Johnson, J.D., B. LaFrance, H.-J. Chang, S. Pobocik, C. Ethington and M. Meyer (1997), *Final Report for the CISRC Network Analysis Project: Period October 1993 to March 1997*, East Lansing, MI: Department of Communication, Michigan State University.

Johnson, J.D., B. LaFrance, T. Kiyomiya and C. Ethington (1997), *Technical Report #8:   Analysis of the CISRC Program Project for the period September 1996 to March 1997*, East Lansing, MI: Department of Communication, Michigan State University.

Johnson, J.D., B.H. LaFrance, M. Meyer, J.B. Speyer and D. Cox (1996), 'The impact of formalization, role conflict, role ambiguity, and communication quality on perceived organizational   innovativeness in the Cancer Information Service', paper presented   at the Speech Communication Association Convention, San Diego, CA.

Johnson, J.D., B.H. LaFrance, M. Meyer, J.B. Speyer and D. Cox (1998), 'The impact of formalization, role conflict, role ambiguity, and communication quality on perceived organizational   innovativeness in the Cancer Information Service', *Evaluation and the Health Professions*, **21**, 27-51.

Johnson, J.D. and H. Meischke (1993a), 'Cancer-related channel selection: An extension for a sample of women who have had a mammogram', *Women and Health*, **20**, 31-44.

Johnson, J.D. and H. Meischke (1993b), 'A comprehensive model of cancer-related information seeking applied to magazines', *Human Communication Research*, **19**, 343-67.

Johnson, J.D. and M. Meyer (1995), *Technical Report for the Office of Admissions & Scholarships Network Analysis Project*, East Lansing, MI: Department of Communication, Michigan State University.

Johnson, J.D., M. Meyer, J. Berkowitz and C. Ethington (1995), 'Tests of a model of perceived organizational innovativeness in a contractual network of health service organizations', paper presented at the International Communication Association conference, Albuquerque, NM.

Johnson, J.D., M. Meyer, J. Berkowitz, C. Ethington and V. Miller (1997), 'Testing two contrasting models of innovativeness in a contractual network', *Human Communication Research*, **24**, 320-48.

Johnson, J.D., M. Meyer, J. Berkowitz, C. Ethington, V. Miller, W. Stengle and D. Steverson (1996), 'The role of a conference in integrating a contractual network of health services organizations', *Journal of Business Communication*, **33**, 231-56.

Johnson, J.D., M. Meyer, J. Berkowitz, C. Ethington, W. Stengle and D. Steverson (1995), 'The role of a conference in integrating a contractual network of health service organizations', paper presented at the Speech Communication Association, San Antonio, TX.

Johnson, J.D., M. Meyer, H.-J. Chang, C. Ethington, S. Pobocik and B. LaFrance (1995). *Technical Report #2: Analysis of the CIS/Program Project Network for the Period April 1994 to September 1994*, East Lansing, MI: Department of Communication, Michigan State University.

Johnson, J.D., M. Meyer, M. Woodworth, C. Ethington and W. Stengle (1998), 'Information technologies within the Cancer Information Service: factors related to innovation adoption', *Preventive Medicine*, **27**, S71-S83.

Johnson, J.D., M. Meyer, M. Woodworth, C.T. Ethington, W. Stengle and D. Reusch (1996), 'Perceptions of innovation characteristics: a study of four contrasting technological innovations', paper presented at the International Communication Association Convention, Chicago, IL.

Kacmer, K.M., P.M. Wright and G.C. McMahan (1997), 'The effect of individual differences on technical training', *Journal of Managerial Issues*, **9**, 104-20.

Kadushin, C. (2004), 'Too much investment in social capital?', *Social Networks*, **26**, 75-90.

Kahn, R.L., D.M. Wolfe, R.P. Quinn, J.D. Snoek and R. Rosenthal (1964),

Organizational Stress: Studies in Role Conflict and Ambiguity, New York: Wiley.

Kaluzny, A.D., L.M. Lacey, R. Warnecke, D.M. Hynes, J. Morrissey, L. Ford and E. Sondik (1993), 'Predicting the performance of a strategic alliance: an analysis of the community clinical oncology program', *Health Services Research*, **28**, 159-82.

Kaluzny, A.D. and R.B. Warnecke (1996), *Managing a Health Care Alliance: Improving Community Cancer Care*, San Francisco, CA: Jossey-Bass.

Kanter, R.M. (1983), *The Change Masters: Innovation and Entrepreneurship in the American Corporation*, New York, NY: Simon & Schuster.

Kanter, R.M. (1988a), 'Three tiers for innovation research', *Communication Research*, **15**, 509-23.

Kanter, R.M. (1988b), 'When a thousand flowers bloom: structural, collective, and social conditions for innovation in organizations', *Research in Organizational Behavior*, **10**, 169-211.

Katz, D. and R.L. Kahn (1978), *The Social Psychology of Organizations*, New York: John Wiley.

Katz, E. (1957), 'The two-step flow of communication: an up-to-date report on an hypothesis', *Public Opinion Quarterly*, **21**, 61-78.

Katz, E. (1963), 'The characteristics of innovations and the concept of compatibility', paper presented at the Rehovoth Conference on Comprehensive Planning of Agriculture in Developing Countries, Rehovoth, Israel, August.

Katz, E. and P.F. Lazersfeld (1955), *Personal Influence: The Part Played by People in the Flow of Mass Communications*, New York: Free Press.

Katz, R. and T.J. Allen (1982), 'Investigating the Not Invented Here (NIH) syndrome: a look at the performance, tenure, and communication patterns of 50 R&D project groups', *R&D Management*, **12**, 7-19.

Katz, R. and M. Tushman (1979), 'Communication patterns, project performance, and task characteristics: an empirical evaluation and integration in an R&D setting', *Organizational Behavior and Human Performance*, **23**, 139-62.

Katz, R. and M.L. Tushman (1981), 'An investigation into the managerial roles and career paths of gatekeepers and project supervisors in a major R&D facility', *R & D Management*, **11**, 103-10.

Kayworth, T. and D. Leidner (2003), 'Organizational culture as a knowledge resource', in C.W. Holsapple (ed.), *Handbook on Knowledge Management 1: Knowledge Matters*, New York: Springer-Verlag, pp. 235-52.

Keen, M. and S. Stocklmayer (1999), 'Science communication: the evolving role of rural industry research and development corporations', *Australian Journal of Environmental Management*, **6**, 196-206.

Keen, P.G.W. (1990), 'Telecommunications and organizational choice', in J.

Fulk and C. Steinfield (eds), *Organizations and Communication Technology*, Newbury Park, CA: Sage, pp. 295-312.

Keller, R.T., A.D. Szillagyi and W.E. Holland (1976), 'Boundary spanning activity and employee reactions: an empirical study', *Human Relations*, **29**, 699-710.

Kelman, H.C.   (1961), 'Processes of opinion change', *Public Opinion Quarterly*, **25**, 57-78.

Kessler, L., C. Fintor, C. Muha, L.M. Wun, D. Annett and K.D. Mazan (1993), 'The Cancer Information Service Telephone Evaluation and Reporting System (CISTERS): a new tool for assessing quality assurance', *Journal of the National Cancer Institute Monographs*, **14**, 61-6.

Kilmann, R.H., D.P. Slevin and K.W. Thomas (1983), 'The problem of producing useful knowledge', in R.H. Kilmann, K.W. Thomas, D.P. Slevin, R. Nath and S.L. Jerrell (eds), *Producing Useful Knowledge for Organizations*, San Francisco, CA: Jossey-Bass, pp. 1-21.

Kim, L. (1980), 'Organizational innovation and structure', *Journal of Business Research*, **2**, 225-45.

Kimberly, J.R. (1976), 'Issues in the design of longitudinal organizational research', *Sociological Methods and Research*, **4**, 321-47.

Kimberly, J.R. and M.J. Evanisko (1981), 'Organizational innovation: the influence of individual, organizational, and contextual factors on hospital adoption of technological and administrative innovations', *Academy of Management Journal*, **24**, 689-713.

Klauss, R. and B.M. Bass (1982), *Interpersonal Communication in Organizations*, New York: Academic Press.

Klein, K.J, A.B. Conn and J.S. Sorra (2001), 'Implementing computerized technology: an organizational analysis', *Journal of Applied Psychology*, **86**, 811-24.

Klein, K.J. and J.S. Sorra (1996), 'The challenge of innovation implementation', *Academy of Management Review*, **21**, 1055-80.

Klein, K.J., H. Tosi and A.A. Cannella, Jr (1999), 'Multilevel theory building: benefits, barriers, and new developments', *Academy of Management Review*, **24**, 243-8.

Koop, C.E. (1995), 'Editorial: a personal role in health care reform', *American Journal of Public Health*, **85**, 759-60.

Kotter, J.P. (1979), 'Managing external dependence', *Academy of Management Review*, **4**, 87-92.

Krackhardt, D. (1990), 'Assessing the political landscape: structure, cognition, and power in organizations', *Administrative Science Quarterly*, **35**, 342-69.

Krackhardt, D. (1992), 'The strength of strong ties: the importance of philos in organizations', in N. Nohria (ed.), *Networks and Organizations: Structure, Form, and Action*, Boston, MA: Harvard Business

Review, pp. 216-39.

Krackhardt, D. (1994), 'Constraints on the interactive organization as an ideal type', in C. Heckscher and A. Donnelon (eds), *The Post-Bureaucratic Organization: New Perspectives on Organizational Change*, Thousand Oaks, CA: Sage, pp. 211-22.

Kreps, G.L., S.M. Hibbard and V.T. DeVita (1988), 'The role of the physician data query on-line cancer system in health information dissemination', in B.D. Ruben (ed.), *Information and Behavior, Volume 2*, New Brunswick, NJ: Transaction Books, pp. 1, 6-7.

Kuhlthau, C.C. (1991), 'Inside the search process: information seeking from the user's perspective', *Journal of the American Society for Information Science*, **12**, 361-71.

Kuhn, T. (2002), 'Negotiating boundaries between scholars and practitioners: knowledge, networks, and communities of practice', *Management Communication Quarterly*, **16**, 106-12.

Kumar, N., L.W. Stern and J.C. Anderson (1993), 'Conducting interorganizational research using key informants', *Academy of Management Journal*, **36**, 1633-51.

LaFrance, B.H., J.D. Johnson, C.E. Ethington, and M.M. Meyer (1997), 'Studying the Cancer Information Service over time', paper presented at the International Communication Association annual convention.

Landry, R. and N. Amara (2001), 'Creativity, innovation, and business practices in the matter of knowledge management', in J. de la Mothe and D. Foray (eds), *Knowledge Management in the Innovation Process*, Boston, MA: Kluwer Academic Publishers, pp. 55-79.

Larson, E.V. and I.T. Brakmakulam (2002), *Building a New Foundation for Innovation: Results of a Workshop for the National Science Foundation*, Santa Monica, CA: RAND.

Lawrence, P.R. and J.W. Lorsch (1967a), 'Differentiation and integration complex organizations', *Administrative Science Quarterly*, **12**, 1-47.

Lawrence, P.R. and J.W. Lorsch (1967b), 'New management job: the integrator', *Harvard Business Review*, November– December, 143-51.

Lawrence, P.R. and J.W. Lorsch (1967c), *Organizational and Environment: Differentiation and Integration*, Boston, MA: Harvard Graduate School of Business Administration.

Lawson, R.B. and C.L. Ventriss (1992), 'Organizational change: the role of organizational culture and organizational learning', *Psychological Record*, **42**, 205-19.

Lazega, E. and M. van Duijn (1997), 'Position in formal structure, personal characteristics and choice of advisors in a law firm: a logistic regression model for dyadic network data', *Social Networks*, **19**, 375-97.

Leavitt, H.J. (1951). 'Some effects of certain communication patterns on group performance', *Journal of Abnormal and Social Psychology*, **46**, 38-50

Leifer, R. and A. Delbecq (1978), 'Organizational/environmental interchange: a model of boundary spanning activity', *Academy of Management Review*, **20**, 40-50.

Lengel, R.H. and R.L. Daft (1988), 'The selection of communication media as an executive skill', *Academy of Management Executive*, **2**, 225-32.

Lenz, E.R. (1984), 'Information seeking: a component of client decisions and health behavior', *Advance in Nursing Science*, **6**, 59-72.

Leonard, D. (1995), *Wellsprings of Knowledge: Building and Sustaining the Source of Innovation*, Boston, MA: Harvard Business School Press.

Leonard-Barton, D. (1985), 'Experts as negative opinion leaders in the diffusion of a technological innovation', *Journal of Consumer Research*, **11**, 914-26.

Leonard-Barton, D. (1988), 'Implementation as mutual adaptation of technology and organization', *Research Policy*, **17**, 251-67.

Leonard-Barton, D. (1990), 'A dual-methodology for case studies', *Organizational Science*, **1**, 248-66.

Leonard-Barton, D. and I. Deschamps (1988), 'Managerial influence in the implementation of new technology', *Management Science*, **34**, 1252-65.

Leonard-Barton, D. and D.K. Sinha (1993), 'Developer-user interaction and user satisfaction in internal technology transfer', *Academy of Management Journal*, **36**, 1125-39.

Lerman, C., B. Rimer and P.F. Engstrom (1989), 'Reducing avoidable cancer mortality through prevention and early detection regimens, *Cancer Research*, **49**, 4955-62.

Lesser, E. and L. Prusak (2004), *Creating Value with Knowledge: Insights from the IBM Institute for Business Value*, New York: Oxford University Press.

Leutwyler, K. (1995), 'The price of prevention', *Scientific American*, April, 124-9.

Levin, D.Z., R. Cross, L.C. Abrams and E.L. Lesser (2004), 'Trust and knowledge sharing: a critical combination', in E. Lesser and L. Prusak (eds), *Creating Value with Knowledge: Insights from the IBM Institute for Business Value*, New York: Oxford University Press, pp. 36-43.

Lewis, L.K. (1995), 'Determinants of users' liking for innovations: the effects of perceptions of the context of change and concerns for performance, uncertainty, and normative influence', paper presented to the Speech Communication Association Annual Convention, San Antonio, TX.

Lewis, L.K., B.K. Richardson, and S. Hamel (2003), 'When the "stakes" are communicative: the lamb's and the lion's share during nonprofit planned change', *Human Communication Research*, **29**, 400-30.

Lewis, L.K. and D.R. Seibold (1993), 'Innovation modification during interorganizational adoption', *Academy of Management Review*, **18**, 322-54.

Lewis, L.K. and D.R. Seibold (1996), 'Communication during intraorganizational innovation adoption: predicting users' behavioral coping responses to innovations in organizations', *Communication Monographs*, **63**, 131-57.

Liebowitz, J. (2000), *Building Organizational Intelligence: A Knowledge Management Primer*, New York: CRC Press.

Lievrouw, L.A. (1994), 'Information resources and democracy: Understanding the paradox', *Journal of the American Society for Information Science*, **45**, 350-7.

Likert, R. (1967), *The Human Organization: Its Management and Value.* Hightstown, NJ: McGraw-Hill.

Lindberg, D.A.B., E.R. Siegel, B.A. Rapp, K.T. Wallingford and S.R. Wilson (1993), 'Use of MEDLINE by physicians for clinical problem solving', *Journal of the American Medical Association*, **269**, 3124-9.

Littlejohn, S.W. (1992), *Theories of Human Communication, 4th edn.*, Belmont, CA: Wadsworth.

Loehrer, P.J., H.A. Greger, M. Weinberger, B. Musick, M. Miller, C. Nichols, J. Bryan, D. Higgs and D. Brock (1991), 'Knowledge and beliefs about cancer in a socioeconomically disadvantaged population', *Cancer*, **68**, 1665-71.

Lozada, H.R. and R.J. Calantone (1996), 'Scanning behavior and the process of organizational innovation', *Journal of Managerial Issues*, **8**, 310-25.

Luke, R.D., J.W. Begun and D.D. Pointer (1989), 'Quasi-firms: strategic interorganizational forms in the health care industry', *Academy of Management Review*, **14**, 9-19.

Lyman, P. and H.R. Varian (2003), 'How much information?', available at http://www.sims.berkeley.edu/how-much-info-2003.

Lysonski, S.J. and E.M. Johnson (1983), 'The sales manager as a boundary spanner: a role theory analysis', *Journal of Personal Selling and Sales Management*, **3**, 8-21.

MacDougall, J. and J.M. Brittain (1994), 'Health informatics', *Annual Review of Information Science and Technology*, **29**, 183-217.

MacMorrow, N. (2001), 'Knowledge management: an introduction', *Annual Review of Information Science and Technology*, **35**, 381-422.

Maes, P. (1995), 'Intelligent software', *Scientific American*, September, 84-6.

Maibach, E.W., S.W. Davis, J.T. Maat and N. Rivera (1998), 'Promoting cancer prevention and screening: the impact of the Cancer

Information Service, Part 7', *Journal of Health Communication*, **3**, 97-8.

Manev, I.M. and W.B. Stevenson (1996) 'Balancing ties: internal and external contacts in the organization's extended network of communication', paper presented at annual meetings of the Academy of Management, Cincinnati, OH.

March, J.G. (1988), 'Introduction: a chronicle of speculations about decision-making in organizations', in J.G. March (ed.), *Decisions and Organizations*, New York: Basil Blackwell, 1-21.

March, J.G. (1994), *A Primer on Decision Making: How Decisions Happen*, New York: Free Press.

March, J.G. (2000), 'Citigroup's John Reed and Stanford's James March on management research and practice', *Academy of Management Executive*, **14**, 52-64.

March, J.G. and H.A. Simon (1958), *Organizations*, New York: John Wiley.

Marcus, A.A. and M.J. Weber (1989), 'Externally-induced innovation', in A.H. Van de Ven, H.L. Angle, and M.S. Poole (eds), *Research on the Management of Innovation*, New York: Oxford University Press, pp. 537-59.

Marcus, A.C. (1998a), 'The Cancer Information Service Research Consortium: a brief retrospective and preview of the future', *Preventive Medicine*, **27**, S93-S100.

Marcus, A.C. (1998b), 'Introduction: the Cancer Information Service Research Consortium', *Preventive Medicine,* **27**, S1-S2.

Marcus, A.C. (2004), 'The Cancer Information Service Research Consortium: successful research partnerships across the nation', presentation to the Kentucky Conference on Health Communication, Lexington, KY.

Marcus, A.C., R. Bastani, K. Reardon, S. Karlins, I. Prabhu Das, M.P. Van Herle, M.W. McClatchey and L.A. Crane (1993), 'Proactive screening mammography counseling within the Cancer Information Service: results from a randomized trial', *Journal of the National Cancer Institute*, **14**, 119-30.

Marcus, A.C., K.M. Garrett, A. Kulchak-Rahm, D. Barnes, W. Dortch and S. Juno (2002), 'Telephone counseling in psychosocial oncology: a report from the Cancer Information and Counseling Line', *Patient Education and Counseling,* **46**, 267-75.

Marcus, A.C., J. Heimendinger, P. Wolfe, D. Fairclough, B.K. Rimer, M. Morra, R. Warnecke, J.H. Himes, S.L. Darrow, S.W. Davis, K. Julesberg, R. Slevin-Perrochia, M. Steelman and J. Wooldridge (2001), 'A randomized trial of a brief intervention to increase fruit and vegetable intake: a replication study among callers to the CIS', *Preventive Medicine,* **33**, 204-16.

Marcus, A.C., J. Heimendinger, P. Wolfe, B.K. Rimer, M.E. Morra, D. Cox,

P.J. Lang, W. Stengle, M.P. Van Herle, D. Wagner, D. Fairclough and L. Hamilton (1998), 'Increasing fruit and vegetable consumption among callers to the CIS: results from a randomized trial', *Preventive Medicine*, **27**, S16-S28.

Marcus, A.C., M.E. Morra, E. Bettinghaus, L.A. Crane, G. Cutter, S. Davis, B.K. Rimer, C. Thomsen and R.B. Warnecke (1998), 'The Cancer Information Service Research Consortium: an emerging laboratory for cancer control research', *Preventive Medicine*, **27**, 3-15.

Marcus, A.C., M.A. Woodworth and C.J. Strickland (1993), 'The Cancer Information Service as a laboratory for research: the first 15 years', *Journal of the National Cancer Institute, Monograph 14*, 67-79.

Markus, M.L. (1994), 'Electronic mail as the medium of managerial choice', *Organization Science*, **5**, 502-27.

Marschak, J. (1968), 'Economics of inquiring, communicating, deciding', *American Economic Review*, **58**, 1-18.

Marsden, P.V., C.R. Cook and D. Knoke (1994), 'Measuring organizational structures and environments', *American Behavioral Scientist*, **37**, 891-911.

McBride, C.M. and B.K. Rimer (1999), 'Using the telephone to improve health behavior and health service delivery', *Patient Education and Counseling*, **37**, 3-18.

McCrosky, J.C., V.P. Richmond and J.A. Daly (1975), 'The development of a measure of perceived homophily in interpersonal communication', *Human Communication Research*, **1**, 323-32.

McGee, J.V. and L. Prusak (1993), *Managing Information Strategically*, New York: John Wiley.

McGinnis, J.M., M.J. Deering and K. Patrick (1995), 'Public health information and the new media: a view from the public health service', in L.M. Harris (ed.), *Health and the New Media: Technologies Transforming Personal and Public Health*, Mahwah, NJ: Lawrence Earlbaum, pp. 127-41.

McGuinness, T. (1991), 'Markets and managerial hierarchies', In G. Thompson, J. Frances, R. Levacic, and J. Mitchell (eds), *Markets, Hierarchies, and Networks: The Coordination of Social Life*, Newbury Park, CA: Sage, pp. 66-81.

McGuire, W.J. (1989), 'Theoretical foundations of campaigns', in R.E. Rice and C.K. Atkin (eds), *Public Communication Campaigns*, Newbury Park, CA: Sage, pp. 43-65.

McIntosh, J. (1974), 'Processes of communication, information seeking and control associated with cancer: a selective review of the literature', *Social Science and Medicine*, **8**, 167-87.

McKinney, M.M., J.M. Barnsley and A.D. Kaluzny (1992), 'Organizing for cancer control: the diffusion of a dynamic innovation in a community cancer network', *International Journal of Technology*

Assessment in Health Care, **8**, 268-88.

McKinney, M.M., J.P. Morrissey and A.D. Kaluzny (1996), 'Clinical networks as alliance structures', in A.D. Kaluzny and R.B. Warnecke (eds), *Managing a Health Care Alliance: Improving Community Cancer Care*, San Francisco, CA: Jossey-Bass, pp. 31-55.

McKinnon, S. (1995), 'Health homework', *Lansing State Journal*, 19 October, 8D.

McKinnon, S.M. and W.J. Bruns, Jr (1992), *The Information Mosaic*, Boston, MA: Harvard Business School Press.

McPhee. R.D. (1989), 'Organizational communication: A structurational exemplar', in B. Dervin, L. Grossberg, B. O'Keefe, and E. Wartella (eds), *Rethinking Communication: Volume 2: Paradigm Exemplars*, Newbury Park, CA: Sage, pp. 199-212.

McPhee, R.D. and M.S. Poole (2001), 'Organizational structures and configurations', In F.M. Jablin and L.L. Putnam (eds), *The New Handbook of Organizational Communication: Advances in Theory, Research, and Methods*, Thousand Oaks, CA: Sage, pp. 503-44.

Mead, G.H. (1934), *Mind, Self, and Society*, Chicago, IL: University of Chicago Press.

Menard, S. (1991), *Longitudinal Research*, Thousand Oaks, CA.: Sage.

Menon, A. and P.R. Varadarajan (1992), 'A model of marketing knowledge use within firms', *Journal of Marketing*, **56**, 53-71.

Mettlin, C., E. Mirand, R. Sciandra and D. Walsh (1980), 'Public use of Cancer Information Service', *Public Education about Cancer*, UICC Technical Report Series, 55.

Mettlin, C. and C.R. Smart (1994), 'Breast cancer detection guidelines for women aged 40 to 49 years: rationale for the American Cancer Society reaffirmation of recommendations', *CA- A Cancer Journal for Clinicians*, **44**, 248-55.

Meyer, A.D. and J.B. Goes (1988), 'Organizational assimilation of innovations: a multilevel contextual analysis', *Academy of Management Journal*, **31**, 897-923.

Meyer, M. (1996a), 'The effects of weak ties on perceived organizational innovativeness and innovation characteristics', unpublished doctoral dissertation, E. Lansing, MI: Dept. of Communication, Michigan State University.

Meyer, M. (1996b), 'Reconceptualizing innovation characteristics: a confirmatory factor analysis of the pros and cons of three contrasting preventive health innovations', paper presented to the Central States Speech Association Convention, St. Paul, MN.

Meyer, M. and J.D. Johnson (1997), 'The effects of weak ties on perceived organizational innovativeness and innovation characteristics', paper presented to National Communication Association Annual

Convention, Chicago, IL.

Meyer, M. and J.D. Johnson (1998), 'Innovation roles: from souls of fire to devil's advocates', paper presented to the National Communication Association annual convention, New York.

Meyer, M., J.D. Johnson, D. Cox and J. B. Speyer (1997), 'Perceptions of innovation characteristics: a study of three contrasting preventive health innovations', paper presented to the Midwest Academy of Management, Ann Arbor, MI, Published in electronic proceedings.

Meyer, M., J.D. Johnson and C. Ethington (1995), 'Perceptions of innovation characteristics: a study of three contrasting preventive health innovations', paper presented to the Speech Communication Association Annual Convention, San Antonio, TX.

Meyer, M., J.D. Johnson and C. Ethington (1997), 'Contrasting attributes of preventive health innovations', *Journal of Communication*, **47**,112-31.

Miles, R.E. and C.C. Snow (1986), 'Organizations: new concepts for new forms', *California Management Review*, **28**, 62-73.

Miles, R.H. (1976), 'Role requirement as sources of organizational stress', *Journal of Applied Psychology*, **61**, 172-79.

Miller, D. and P.H. Friesen (1982), 'Innovation in conservative and entrepreneurial firms: two models of strategic momentum', *Strategic Management Journal*, **3**, 1-25.

Miller, K.I. (1995), *Organizational Communication: Approaches and Processes*, Belmont, CA: Wadsworth.

Minor, M.J. (1983), 'New directions in multiplexity analysis', in R.S. Burt and M.J. Minor (eds), *Applied Network Analysis: A Methodological Introduction*, Beverly Hills, CA: Sage, pp. 223-44.

Mintzberg, H. (1973), *The Nature of Managerial Work*, New York, NY: Harper & Row.

Mitchell, J.C. (1969), 'The concept and use of social networks', in J.C. Mitchell (ed.), *Social Networks in Urban Situations: Analyses of Personal Relationships in Central African Towns*, Manchester: Manchester University Press, pp. 1-50.

Mitchell, R.K., B.R. Agle and D.J. Wood (1997), 'Toward a theory of stakeholder identification and salience: defining the principle of who and what really counts', *Academy of Management Review*, **22**, 853-86.

Mizruchi, M.S. and J. Galaskiewicz (1993), 'Networks of interorganizational relations', *Sociological Methods and Research*, **22**, 46-70.

Moch, M.K. (1980), 'Job involvement, internal motivation, and employees' integration into networks of work relationships', *Organizational Behavior and Human Performance*, **25**, 15-31.

Moch, M., J.N. Feather and D. Fitzgibbons (1983), 'Conceptualizing and measuring the relational structure in organizations', in S.E. Seashore,

E.E. Lawler III, P.H. Mirvis and C. Cammann (eds), *Assessing Organizational Change: A Guide to Methods, Measures, and Practices*, New York: John-Wiley, pp. 203-28.

Moch, M.K. and E.V. Morse (1977), 'Size, centralization and organizational adoption of innovations', *American Sociological Review*, **42**, 716-25.

Mohr, L.B. (1969), 'Determinants of innovations in organizations', *American Political Science Review*, **63**, 111-26.

Mohrman, S.A., C.B. Gibson and A.M. Mohrman, Jr (2001), 'Doing research that is useful to practice: a model and empirical exploration', *Academy of Management Journal*, **44**, 357-75.

Monge, P.R. (1990), 'Theoretical and analytical issues in studying organizational processes', *Organization Science*, **1**, 406-40.

Monge, P.R. and N.S. Contractor (1987), 'Communication networks: measurement techniques', in C.H. Tardy (ed.), *A Handbook for the Study of Human Communication*, Norwood, NJ: Ablex, pp. 107-38.

Monge, P.R. and N.S. Contractor (2001), 'Emergence of communication networks', in F.M. Jablin and L.L. Putnam (eds), *The New Handbook of Organizational Communication: Advances in Theory, Research, and Methods*, Thousand Oaks, CA: Sage, pp. 440-502.

Monge, P.R. and N.S. Contractor (2003), *Theories of Communication Networks*, New York: Oxford University Press.

Monge, P., M. Cozzens and N. Contractor (1992), 'Communication and motivational predictors of the dynamics of organizational innovation', *Organizational Science*, **3**, 250-74.

Monge, P.R. and E.M. Eisenberg (1987), 'Emergent communication networks', in C.R. Berger and S.H. Chaffee (eds), *Handbook of Communication Science*, Newbury Park, CA: Sage, pp. 239-270.

Monge, P.R., R.V. Farace, E.M. Eisenberg, K.I. Miller and L.L. White (1984), 'The process of studying process in organizational communication', *Journal of Communication*, **34**, 22-43.

Monge, P.R. and K.I. Miller (1988), 'Participative processes in organizations', in G.M. Goldhaber and G.A. Barnett (eds), *Handbook of Organizational Communication*, Norwood, NJ: ABLEX, pp. 213-30.

Mooney, K.H., S.L. Beck, R.H. Friedman and R. Farzanfar (2002), 'Telephone-linked care for cancer symptom monitoring,' *Cancer Practice*, **10**, 147-54.

Moore, W.E. and M.M. Tumin (1949), 'Some social functions of ignorance', *American Sociological Review*, **14**, 787-95.

More, E. (1990), 'Information systems: people issues', *Journal of Information Science*, **16**, 311-20.

Morgan, G. (1986), *Images of Organization*, Beverly Hills, CA: Sage

Morra, M.E. (1998), 'Editorial', *Journal of Health Communication*, **3**, V-IX.

Morra, M., E.P. Bettinghaus and A.C. Marcus (1993), 'The first 15 years: what has been learned about the Cancer Information Service and the implications for the future', *Journal of the National Cancer Institute Monographs*, **14**, 177-85.

Morra, M., J.P. Van Nevel, E. Nealon, K.D. Mazan and C. Thomsen (1993), History of the Cancer Information Service', *Journal of the National Cancer Institute Monographs*, **14**, 7-34.

Morra, M., J.P. Van Nevel and W. Stengle (1993), 'Outreach programs and their effects within the Cancer Information Service', *Journal of the National Cancer Institute Monograph*, **14**, 45-59.

Morris, J.H., R.M. Steers and J.L. Koch (1979), 'Impacts of role perceptions on organizational commitment, job involvement, and psychosomatic illness among three vocational groupings', *Journal   of Vocational Behavior*, **14**, 88-101.

Moynihan, T. (1982), 'Information systems as aids to achieving organizational integration', *Information and Management*, **5**, 225-9.

Myers, P.S. (1996), 'Knowledge management and organizational design: an introduction', in P.S. Myers (ed.), *Knowledge Management and Organizational Design*, Boston, MA: Butterworth Heinemann, pp. 1-6.

Nadler, D.A. and M.L. Tushman (1987), *Strategic Linking: Designing Formal Coordination Mechanisms*, Glenview, IL: Scott, Foresman.

Nagpaul, P.S. and S. Pruthi (1979), 'Problem-solving and idea-generation in R&D: the role of informal communication', *R&D Management*, **9**, 147-49.

National Cancer Institute (NCI) (1993), *NCI Facts Book*, Rockville, MD: NCI.

National Cancer Institute (NCI) (1996), *Cancer Facts*, Rockville, MD: NCI.

National Cancer Institute (NCI) (1996), *CIS Policy and Procedures Manual*, Bethesda, MD: NCI.

National Cancer Institute (NCI) (2003), *The Nation's Investment in Cancer Research*, Rockville, MD: NIH.

National Library of Medicine (NLM) (1994), *Fact Sheet*, Rockville, MD: NIH.

New Economy Regional Plan for the Greater Lexington Area, (2001),   Focus Area 6, Area of Emphasis #2, Knowledge and Innovation Management Consortium, 6-11 to 6-16.

Newman, M.E.J. (2003), 'The structure and function of complex networks', available at http://arXiv:cond-mat/0303516.

Nicholson, P.J., Jr and S.C. Goh (1983), 'The relationship of organization structure and interpersonal attitudes to role conflict and ambiguity in different work environments', *Academy of Management Journal*, **26**, 148-55.

Noelle-Neumann, E. (1974), 'The spiral of silence', *Journal of*

Communication, **24**, 43-51.

Nohria, N. and R. Eccles (1992), 'Face-to-face: making network organizations work', in N. Nohria and R. Eccles (eds), *Networks and Organizations: Structure, Form, and Action*, Boston, MA: Harvard Business School Press, pp. 288-308.

Nohria, N. and R. Gulati (1996). 'Is slack good or bad for innovation', *Academy of Management Journal*, **39**, 1245-64.

Nonaka, I. (1991), 'The knowledge-creating company', *Harvard Business Review*, 21-45.

Nonaka, I. and H. Takeuchi (1995), *The Knowledge-Creating Company: How Japanese Companies Create the Dynamics of Innovation*, New York: Oxford University Press.

Nutt, P.C. (1986), 'Tactics of implementation', *Academy of Management Journal*, **29**, 230-61.

Nyblom, J., S. Borgatti, J. Roslakka and M.A. Salo (2003), 'Statistical analysis of network data - an application to the diffusion of innovation', *Social Networks*, **25**, 175-95.

Office of Rural Health Policy (1994), *Reaching Rural: Rural Health Travels the Telecommunications Highway*, Rockville, MD: Office of Rural Health Policy.

Oliver, C. (1990), 'Determinants of interorganizational relationships: integration and future directions', *Academy of Management Review*, **15**, 241-65.

Oliver, C. (1991), 'Network relations and loss of organizational autonomy', *Human Relations*, **44**, 943-61.

Organ, D. and C.N. Greene (1981), 'The effects of formalization on professional involvement: a compensatory process approach', *Administrative Science Quarterly*, **26**, 237-52.

Orleans, C.T., V.J. Schoenbach, E.H. Wagner, D. Quade, M.A. Salmon, D.C. Pearson, J. Fiedler, C.Q. Porter and B.H. Kaplan (1991), 'Self-help quit smoking interventions: effects of self-help materials, social support instructions, and telephone counseling', *Journal of Consulting and Clinical Psychology*, **59**, 439-48.

Osborne, D. and T. Gaebler (1993), *Reinventing Government: How the Entrepreneurial Spirit is Transforming the Public Sector*, New York: Penguin Books.

Ossip-Klein, D.J., G.A. Giovino, N. Megahed, P.M. Black, S.L. Emont, J. Stiggins, E. Shulman and L. Moore (1991), 'Effects of smokers' hotline: results of a 10-county self-help trial', *Journal of Consulting and Clinical Psychology*, **59**, 325-32.

Pacanowsky, M.E. (1989), 'Communication in the empowering organization', in J.A. Anderson (ed.), *Communication Yearbook 11*, Newbury Park, CA: Sage, pp. 356-79.

Pahl, J.M. and K. Roth (1993), 'Managing the headquarters-foreign subsidiary relationship: the roles of strategy, conflict, and integration', *International Journal of Conflict Management*, **4**, 139-65.

Paisley, W. (1980), 'Information and Work', in B. Dervin and M.J. Voight (eds), *Progress in Communication Sciences, Volume II*, Norwood, NJ: ABLEX, pp. 114-65.

Paisley, W. (1993), 'Knowledge utilization: the role of new communication technologies', *Journal of the American Society for Information Science*, **44**, 222-34.

Paisley, W. (1994), 'New media and methods of health communication', in L. Sechrest, T.E. Backer, E.M. Rogers, T.F. Campbell and M.L. Grady (eds), *Effective Dissemination of Clinical and Health Information*, Rockville, MD: Agency for Health Care Policy Research, AHCPR Publication No.95-0015, pp. 165-80.

Papa, M.J. (1989), 'Communication network patterns and employee performance with new technology', paper presented to the Annual Meeting of the International Communication Association, San Francisco.

Parrott, R. (2003), 'Media issues', in T.L. Thompson, A.M. Dorsey, K.I. Miller and R. Parrott (eds), *Handbook of Health Communication*, Mahwah, NJ: Lawrence Erlbaum, pp. 445-48.

Parsons, T. (1960), *Structure and Process in Modern Societies*, Glencoe, IL: Free Press.

Perry, J.L. and K.L. Kraemer (1978), 'Innovation attributes, policy intervention, and the diffusion of computer applications among local governments', *Policy Sciences*, **9**, 179-205.

Pescosolido, B.A. and B.A. Rubin (2000), 'The web of group affiliations revisited: social life, postmodernism, and sociology', *American Sociological Review*, **65**, 52-76.

Peters, T.J. and R.H. Waterman (1982), *In Search of Excellence: Lessons from America's Best-Run Companies*, New York: Harper & Row.

Pettigrew, A.M. (1990), 'Longitudinal field research on change: theory and practice', *Organizational Science*, **1**, 267-92.

Pettigrew, L.S. (1989), 'Theoretical plurality in health communication', in J.A. Anderson (ed.), *Communication Yearbook 11*, Newbury Park, CA: Sage, pp. 298-308.

Pfeffer, J. (1982), *Organizations and Organization Theory*, Boston, MA: Pitman.

Picot, A., H. Klingenberg and H.P. Kranzle (1982), 'Office technology: a report on attitudes and channels selection from field studies in Germany', in M. Burgoon (ed.), *Communication Yearbook 6*, Beverly Hills, CA: Sage, pp. 674-93.

Pierce, J.L. and A.L. Delbecq (1977), 'Organization structure, individual attitudes and innovation', *Academy of Management Review*, **2**, 27-

37.

Pinelli, T.E. (1991), 'The information seeking habits and practices of engineers', in C. Steinke (ed.), *Information Seeking and Communicating Behavior of Scientists and Engineers*, New York: Haworth Press, pp. 5-25.

Pobocik, S., J.D. Johnson, H.-J.Chang, S. Darrow and C. Thomsen (1996), 'The importance of planning for conference success: a case study involving the Cancer Information Service', paper presented at the meeting of the Speech Communication Association, San Diego, CA.

Pobocik, S., J.D. Johnson, S. Darrow, C. Muha, C. Thomsen, D. Steverson, W. Stengle and J.A. Ward (1997), 'Internal communication mechanisms within the Cancer Information Service', paper presented to the International Communication Association annual convention, Montreal.

Pollock, T.G., J.F. Porac and J.B. Wade (2004), 'Constructing deal networks: brokers as network 'architects' in the US IPO   market and other examples', *Academy of Management Review*, **29**, 50-72.

Pondy, L.R. and I.I. Mitroff (1979), 'Beyond open system models of organization', in S.M. Bacharach (ed.), *Research in   Organizational Behavior Vol. 1*, Greenwich, CT: JAI Press, pp. 3-39.

Poole, M.S. and R.D. McPhee (1983), 'A structurational analysis of organizational climate', in L.L. Putnam and M.E. Pacanowsky (eds), *Communication and Organizations: An Interpretive Approach*, Beverly Hills, CA: Sage, pp. 195-220.

Poole, M.S., A. Van de Ven, K. Dooley and M.E. Holmes (2000), *Organizational Change and Innovation Processes: Theory and Methods for Research*, New York: Oxford University Press.

Porter, M.E. and V.E.   Millar (1985), 'How information gives you competitive advantage', *Harvard Business Review*, **63**, 149-60.

Pouder, R. and C.H. St John (1996), 'Hot spots and blind spots: geographic clusters of firms and innovation', *Academy ofManagement Review*, **21**, 1192-25.

Powell, W.W. (1990), 'Neither Market nor hierarchy: network forms of organization', in S.B. Bacharach (ed.), *Research in Organizational Behavior*, Norwich, CT: JAI Press, pp. 295-336.

Prusak, L. and D. Cohen (2004), 'How to invest in social capital', in E. Lesser and L. Prusak (eds), *Creating Value with Knowledge:Insights from the IBM Institute for Business Value*, New York: Oxford University Press, pp. 13-23.

Putnam, R. (2000), *Bowling Alone - The Collapse and Revival of American Community*, New York: Simon & Schuster.

Rakowski, W., A.R. Assaf, R.C. Lefebvre, T.M. Lasater, M. Niknian and R.A. Carleton (1990), 'Information-seeking about health in a community sample of adults: correlates and associations with other health-related practices', *Health Education Quarterly*, **17**, 379-93.

Ray, E.B. (1987), 'Supportive relationships and occupational stress in the workplace', in T.L. Albrecht and M.B. Adelman (eds), *Communicating Social Support*, Newbury Park, CA: Sage, pp. 172-91.

Reder, S. and N.F. Conklin (1987), 'Selection and effects of channels in distributed communication and decision making tasks: a theoretical review and a proposed research paradigm', paper presented to the International Communication Association Annual Conference, Montreal, Canada.

Redding, W.C. (1979), 'Organizational communication theory and ideology: an overview', in D. Nimmo (ed.), *Communication Yearbook 3*, New Brunswick, NJ: Transaction Books, pp. 309-41.

Reichers, A.E., J.P. Wanous and J.T. Austin (1997), 'Understanding and managing cynicism about organizational change', *Academy of Management Executive*, **11**, 48-59.

Reinsch, N.L., Jr. and R.W. Beswick (1990), 'Voice mail versus conventional channels: a cost minimization analysis of individual's preferences', *Academy of Management Journal*, **33**, 801-16.

Renn, O. (1991), 'Risk communication and the social amplification of risk', in R.E. Kasperson and P.J. Stallen (eds), *Communicating Risks to the Public*, Boston, MA: Kluwer Academic Publishers, pp. 287-324.

Research!America (1995), *Press Release*, 23 June, Alexandria, VA: Research!America.

Reynolds, E.V. and J.D. Johnson (1982), 'Liaison emergence: relating theoretical perspectives', *Academy of Management Review*, **7**, 551-59.

Rice, R.E. (1993), 'Media appropriateness: using social presence theory to compare traditional and new organizational media', *Human Communication Research*, **19**, 451-84.

Rice, R.E. and Associates (1984), *The New Media: Communication, Research and Technology*, Beverly Hills, CA: Sage.

Rice, R.E. and C. Aydin (1991), 'Attitude toward new organizational technology: network proximity as a mechanism for social information processing', *Administrative Science Quarterly*, **36**, 219-44.

Rice, R.E. and W.D. Richards (1985), 'An overview of network analysis methods and programs', in B. Dervin and M.J. Voight (eds), *Progress in Communication Sciences*, Norwood, N.J.: Ablex, pp. 105-65.

Rice, R.E. and D.E. Shook (1990), 'Relationships of job categories and organizational levels to use of communication channels, including electronic model: a meta-analysis and extension', *Journal of Management Studies*, **27**, 196-229.

Richards, W.D., Jr (1985), 'Data, models, and assumptions in network analysis', in B. Dervin and M. Voigt (eds), *Progress in Communication Sciences, Volume VI*, Norwood, NJ: Ablex, pp. 105-66.

Riley, P. (1983), 'A structurationist account of political culture', *Administrative Science Quarterly*, **28**, 414-37.

Ring, P.S. and A.H. Van de Ven (1994), 'Developmental processes of cooperative interorganizational relationships', *Academy of Management Review*, **19**, 90-118.

Roberts, K.H. and C.A. O'Reilly, III (1979), 'Some correlations of communication roles in organizations', *Academy of Management Journal*, **4**, 283-93.

Robertson, T.S. and Y. Wind (1983), 'Organizational cosmopolitanism and innovativeness', *Academy of Management Journal*, **26**, 332-38.

Robinson, L.M. and F.B. Whittington (1979), 'Marketing as viewed by hospital administrators', in P.D. Cooper (ed.), *Health Care Marketing: Issues and Trends*, Germantown, MD: Aspen Systems Corporation, pp. 167-74.

Rogers, E.M. (1962), *Diffusion of Innovation*, New York: Free Press.

Rogers, E.M. (1983), *Diffusion of Innovations*, New York: Free Press.

Rogers, E.M. (1995), *Diffusion of Innovation, 4th edn*, New York: Free Press.

Rogers, E.M. (2003), *Diffusion of Innovations, 5th edn*, New York: Free Press.

Rogers, E.M. and R. Adhikayra (1979), 'Diffusion of innovations: an up-to-date review and commentary', in D.Nimmo (ed.) *Communication Yearbook 3*, New Brunswick, NJ: Transaction Books, pp. 67-81.

Rogers, E.M. and R. Agarwala-Rogers (1976), *Communication in Organizations*, New York: Free Press.

Rogers, E.M. and D.L. Kincaid (1981), *Communication Networks: Toward a New Paradigm for Research*, New York: Free Press.

Rogers, E.M. and F.F. Shoemaker (1971), *Communication of Innovations*, New York: Free Press.

Romanelli, E. (1991), 'The evolution of new organizational forms', *Annual Review of Sociology*, **17**, 79-103.

Rosenbaum, A. and J.F. Calhoun (1977), 'The use of the telephone hotline in crisis intervention: a review', *Journal of Community Psychology*, **5**, 325-39.

Rosovsky, H. (1990), *The University: An Owner's Manual*, New York: W.W. Norton.

Ross, P.F. (1974), 'Innovation adoption by organizations', *Personnel Psychology*, **27**, 21-47.

Rouse, W.B. and S.H. Rouse (1984), 'Human information seeking and design of information systems', *Information Processing and Management*,

20, 129-138.

Rousseau, D.M. (1985), 'Issues of level in organizational research: multi-level and cross-level perspectives', in S.M. Bacharach (ed.), *Research in Organizational Behavior, Volume 7*, Greenwich, CT: JAI Press, pp. 1-37.

Ruchinskas, J.E. (1983), 'Predictors of media utility: influence on manager's perceptions of business communications systems', paper presented to the Annual Meeting of the International Communication Association, Dallas.

Rynes, S.L., J.M. Bartunek and R.L. Daft (2001), 'Across the great divide: knowledge creation and transfer between practitioners and academics', *Academy of Management Journal*, **44**, 340-55.

Sabherwal, R. and D. Robey (1993), 'An empirical taxonomy of implementation processes based on sequences of events in information system development', *Organization Science*, **4**, 548-76.

Salancik, G.R. and J. Pfeffer (1977), 'An examination of need-satisfaction models of job attitudes', *Administrative Science Quarterly*, **22**, 427-53.

Salincik, G.R. and J. Pfeffer (1978), 'A social information processing approach to job attitudes and task design', *Administrative Science Quarterly*, **23**, 224-53.

Salmon, C.T. and C. Atkin (2003), 'Using media campaigns for health promotion', in T.L. Thompson, A.M. Dorsey, K.I. Miller and R. Parrott (eds), *Handbook of Health Communication*, Mahwah, NJ: Lawrence Erlbaum, pp. 449-72.

Sarbaugh, L.E. (1979), 'A systematic framework for analyzing intercultural communication', in N.C. Jain (ed.), *International and Intercultural Communication, Vol. V*, Falls Church, VA: Speech Communication Association, pp. 11-22.

Sarmento, A., J. Batista, L. Cardoso, M. Lousa, R. Babo and T. Rebelo (2003), 'The use of action research in the improvement of communication in a community of practice: the MOISIG case', in E. Coakes (ed.), *Knowledge Management: Current Issues and Challenges*, Hershey, PA: IRM Press, pp. 274-90.

Saunders, C.S., D. Robey and K.A. Vaverek (1994), 'The persistence of status differentials in computer conferencing', *Human Communication Research*, **20**, 443-72.

Scarbrough, H. and J. Swan (2002), 'Knowledge communities and innovation', *Trends in Communication*, **8**, 7-18.

Schendel, D. (1996), 'Editor's introduction to the 1996 winter special issue: knowledge and the firm', *Strategic Management Journal*, **17**, 1-4.

Schmitz, J. (1988), 'Electronic communication: a longitudinal view', paper presented to the Annual Meeting of the Academy of Management, Anaheim, CA.

Schmitz, J. and J. Fulk (1991), 'Organizational colleagues, media richness, and electronic mail', *Communication Research*, **18**, 487-523.

Schneider, L.A. (1962), 'The role of public relations in four organizational types', *Journalism Quarterly*, **62**, 567-76, 594.

Schon, D.A. (1967), *Technology and Change*, New York: Delacorte Press.

Schon, D.A. and M. Rein (1994), *Frame Reflection: Toward the Resolution of Intractable Policy Controversies*, New York: Basic Books.

Schopler, J.H. (1987), 'Interorganizational groups: origins, structure, and outcomes', *Academy of Management Review*, **12**, 702-13.

Schramm, W.S. (1973), *Men, Messages, and Media*, New York: Harper & Row.

Schulz, M. (2001), 'The uncertain relevance of newness: organizational learning and knowledge flows', *Academy of Management Journal*, **44**, 661-81.

Schuman, T.M. (1988), 'Hospital computerization and the politics of medical decision-making', *Research in the Sociology of Work*, **4**, 261-87.

Schwab, R.C., G.R. Ungson and W.B. Brown (1985), 'Redefining the boundary spanning-environment relationship', *Journal of Management*, **11**, 75-86.

Seabright, M.A., D.A. Levinthal and M. Fichman (1992), 'Role of individual attachments in the dissolution of interorganizational relationships', *Academy of Management Journal*, **35**, 122-60.

Sechrest, L., T.E. Backer and E.M. Rogers (1994), 'Effective dissemination of health and clinical information', in L. Sechrest, T.E. Backer, E.M. Rogers, T.F. Campbell and M.L. Grady (eds), *Effective Dissemination of Clinical and Health Information*, Rockville, MD: Agency for Health Care Policy Research, AHCPR Publication. No. 95-0015, pp. 1-7.

Seibert, S.E., M.L. Kraimer and R.C. Liden (2001), 'A social capital theory of career success', *Academy of Management Journal*, **44**, 219-37.

Seibold, D.R., R.A. Meyers and S.C. Willihnganz (1984), 'Communicating health information to the public: effectiveness of a newsletter', *Health Education Quarterly*, **10**, 263-86.

Senge, P.M. (1990), *The Fifth Discipline: The Art and Practice of the Learning Organization*, New York: Doubleday Currency.

Sennett, R. (1998), *The Corrosion of Character: The Personal Consequences of Work in the New Capitalis*, New York: W.W. Norton.

Shah, P.P. (1998), 'Who are employees' social referents? Using a network perspective to determine referent others', *Academy of Management Journal*, **41**, 249-68.

Shaw, M.E. (1971), *Group Dynamics: The Psychology of Small Group Behavior*, New York, NY: McGraw-Hill.

Sherer, C.W. and N.K. Juanillo Jr. (1992), 'Bridging theory and praxis: reexamining public health communication', in S.A. Deetz (ed.),

Communication Yearbook 15, Newbury Park, CA: Sage, pp. 312-45.

Short, J., E. Williams and B. Christie (1976), *The Social Psychology of Telecommunications*, New York: John Wiley.

Siefert, M., G. Gerbner and J. Fisher (1989), *The Information Gap: How Computers and Other New Communication Technologies Affect the Social Distribution of Power*, New York, NY: Oxford University Press.

Simonson, M.R., M. Maurer, M. Montag-Torardi and M. Whitaker (1987), 'Development of a standardized test for computer literacy and a computer anxiety index', *Journal of Educational Computing Research*, **3**, 231-47.

Singh, J., J.R. Goolsby and G.K. Rhoads (1994), 'Behavioral and psychological consequences of boundary spanning burnout for customer service representatives', *Journal of Marketing Research*, **31**, 558-69.

Sitkin, S.B., K.M. Sutcliffe and J.R. Barrios-Choplin (1992), 'A dual-capacity model of communication media choice in organizations', *Human Communication Research*, **18**, 563-98.

Smelser, N.J. (1963), *The Sociology of Economic Life*, Englewood Cliffs, NJ: Prentice-Hall.

Smith, H.A. and J.D. McKeen (2003), 'Creating and Facilitating Communities of Practice', in C.W. Holsapple (ed.), *Handbook of Knowledge Management 1: Knowledge Matters*, New York: Springer-Verlag, pp. 393-407.

Smith, K.G., S.J. Carroll and S.J. Ashford (1995), 'Intra-and interorganizational cooperation: Toward a research agenda', *Academy of Management Journal*, **38**, 7-23.

Smithson, M. (1989), *Ignorance and Uncertainty: Emerging Paradigms*, New York: Springer-Verlag.

Sneiderman, C.A., A.F. Hood and J.W. Patterson (1994), 'Evaluation of an interactive computer video tutorial on malignant melanoma', *Journal of Biomedical Communication*, **21**, 2-5.

Sparrowe, R.T., R.C. Liden, S.J. Wayne and M.L. Kraimer (2001), 'Social networks and the performance of individuals and groups', *Academy of Management Journal*, **44**, 316-25.

Spekman, R.E. (1979), 'Influence and information: an exploratory investigation of the boundary role person's basis of power', *Academy of Management Journal*, **22**, 104-17.

Starbuck, W.H. (1976), 'Organizations and their environments', In M.D. Dunnette (ed.), *Handbook of Industrial and Organizational Psychology*, Chicago, IL: Rand McNally, pp. 1069-1123.

Steen, R.G. (1993), *A Conspiracy of Cells: The Basic Science of Cancer*, New York: Plenum Press.

Steinfield, C.W., B. Jin and L.L. Ku (1987), 'A preliminary test of a social information processing model of media use in organizations', paper presented to the annual meeting of the International Communication Association, Montreal.

Steinke, C. (1991), 'Introduction', in C. Steinke (ed.), *Information Seeking and Communicating Behavior of Scientists and Engineers*, New York: Haworth Press, pp. 1-3.

Stevenson, W.B. (1990), 'Networks of interaction within organizations', *Social Science Research*, **19**, 113-31.

Stevenson, W. B., J. L. Pearce and L. W. Porter (1985), 'The concept of 'coalition' in organization theory and research', *Academy of Management Journal*, **10**, 256-68.

Steverson, D. (1995), Memo entitled 'FTS2000 Network Data', Rockville, MD: Cancer Information Service, 17 January.

Stewart, T.A. (2001), *The Wealth of Knowledge: Intellectual Capital and the Twenty-First Century Organization*, New York: Currency.

Street, R.L., Jr (1990), 'Communication in medical consultations: a review essay', *Quarterly Journal of Speech*, **76**, 315-32.

Sullivan, C.B. (1995), 'Preferences for electronic mail in organizational communication tasks', *Journal of Business Communication*, **32**, 49-65.

Susskind, A., V.D. Miller and J.D. Johnson (1998), 'Downsizing and structural holes: their impact on layoff survivor perceptions of organizational chaos and openness to change', *Communication Research*, **25**, 30-65.

Swan, J. (2003), 'Knowledge management in action?', in C.W. Holsapple (ed.), *Handbook on Knowledge Management 1: Knowledge Matters,* New York: Springer-Verlag, pp. 271-96,

Szulanski, G. (1996), 'Exploring internal stickiness: impediments to the transfer of best practice within the firm', *Strategic Management Journal*, **17**, 27-43.

Tagiuri, R. (1968), 'The concept of organizational climate', in R. Tagiuri and G.H. Litwin (eds), *Organizational Climate: Exploration of a Concept*, Boston, MA: Harvard Graduate School of Business Administration, pp. 11-32.

Taylor, M. and M.L. Doerfel (2003), 'Building interorganizational relationships that build nations', *Human Communication Research*, **29**, 153-81.

Thomas, J.B., S.M. Clark and D.A. Gioia (1993), 'Strategic sensemaking and organizational performance: linkages among scanning, interpretation, action, and outcomes', *Academy of Management Journal*, **36**, 239-70.

Thompson, B., S. Kinne, F.M. Lewis and J.A.Wooldridge (1993), 'Randomized telephone smoking –intervention trial initially directed at blue cross workers', *Journal of the National Cancer Institute*, **14**,

105-12.

Thompson, J.D. (1967), *Organizations in Action*, New York: McGraw-Hill.

Thompson, T.L. (2003), 'Provider-patient interaction issues', in T.L. Thompson, A.M. Dorsey, K.I. Miller and R. Parrott (eds), *Handbook of Health Communication*, Mahwah, NJ: Lawrence Erlbaum, pp. 91-3.

Thomsen, C.A. and J.T. Maat (1998), 'Evaluating the Cancer Information Service: a model for health communications, Part 1', *Journal of Health Communication*, **3**, 1-14.

Thorelli, H.B. and J.L. Engledow (1980), 'Information seekers and information systems: a policy perspective', *Journal of Marketing*, **44**, 9-27.

Tichenor, P.J., G.A. Donohue and C.N. Olien (1970), 'Mass media and differential growth in knowledge', *Public Opinion Quarterly*, **34**, 158-70.

Tichy, N.M., M.L. Tushman and C. Fombrun (1979), 'Social network analysis for organizations', *Academy of Management Review*, **4**, 507-19.

Tidd, J. (2000), 'The competence cycle: translating knowledge into new processes, products and services', in J. Tidd (ed.), *From Knowledge Management to Strategic Competence: Measuring Technological, Market, and Organizational Innovation*, London: Imperial College Press, pp. 5-25.

Tilley, C.B. (1990), 'Medical databases and health information systems', *Annual Review of Information Science and Technology*, **25**, 313-82.

Trevino, L.K., R.L. Daft and R.H. Lengel (1990), 'Understanding managers' media choices: a symbolic interactionist perspective', in J. Fulk and C. Steinfield (eds), *Organizations and Communication Technology*, Newbury Park, CA: Sage, pp. 71-94.

Trevino, L.K., R. Lengel, and R.L. Daft (1987), 'Reasons for media choice in management communication: a symbolic interactionist perspective', *Communication Research*, **14**, 553-74.

Tsai, W. (2001), 'Knowledge transfer in intraorganizational networks:effects of network position and absorptive capacity on business unit innovation and performance', *Academy of Management Journal*, **44**, 996-1004.

Tsui, A.S. and C.A.I. O'Reilly (1989), 'Beyond simple demographic effects: the importance of relational demography in superior-subordinate dyads', *Academy of Management Journal*, **32**, 402-23.

Turner, J.W. (2003), 'Telemedicine: expanding health care into virtual environments', in T.L. Thompson, A.M. Dorsey, K.I. Miller and R. Parrott (eds), *Handbook of Health Communication*, Mahwah, NJ: Lawrence Erlbaum, pp. 515-35.

Tushman, M. (1978), 'Technical communication in R & D laboratories: The impact of project work characteristics', *Academy of Management Journal*, **21**, 624-45.

Tushman, M.L. (1979), 'Work characteristics and subunit communication structure: a contingency analysis', *Administrative Science Quarterly*, **24**, 82-98.

Tushman, M.L. and R. Katz (1980), 'External communication and project performance: an investigation into the role of gatekeeping', *Management Science*, **26**, 1071-85.

Tushman, M.L. and T.J. Scanlan (1981a), 'Boundary spanning individuals: their role in information transfer and their antecedents', *Academy of Management Journal*, **24**, 289-305.

Tushman, M.L. and T.J. Scanlan (1981b), 'Characteristics and external orientations of boundary spanning individuals', *Academy of Management Journal*, **24**, 83-98.

Valente, T.W. (1995), *Network Models of the Diffusion of Innovations*, Cresskill, NJ: Hampton Press.

Valente, T.W. and R.L. Davis (1999), 'Accelerating the diffusion of innovations using opinion leaders', *Annals of American Academy of Political and Social Sciences*, **566**, 55-67.

Van de Ven, A.H. (1986), 'Central problems in the management of innovation', *Management Science*, **32**, 590-607.

Van de Ven, A.H. (2000), 'The president's message: the practice of management knowledge', *Academy of Management News*, **31**, 4-5.

Van de Ven, A.H. (2002), 'Strategic directions for the Academy of Management: this academy is for you!', *Academy of Management Review*, **27**, 171-84.

Van de Ven, A.H., A.L. Delbecq and R. Koenig (1976), 'Determinants of coordination modes within organizations', *Administrative Science Quarterly*, **41**, 322-38.

Van de Ven, A.H. and M.S. Poole (1990), 'Methods for studying innovation development in the Minnesota Innovation Research Program', *Organization Science*, **1**, 313-35.

Van Sell, M., A.D. Brief and R.S. Schuler (1981), 'Role conflict and role ambiguity: an integration of the literature and directions for future research', *Human Relations*, **34**, 43-72.

Varlejs, J. (1986), 'Information seeking: changing perspectives', in J. Varlejs (ed.), *Information Seeking: Basing Services on Users' Behaviors*, London: McFarland & Co., pp. 67-82.

Viswanath, K., J.R. Finnegan, Jr., P. Hannan and R.V. Luepker (1991), 'Health and knowledge gaps', *American Behavioral Scientist*, **34**, 712-26.

Viswanath, K., E. Kahn, J.R. Finnegan, Jr., J. Hertog and J.D. Potter (1993), 'Motivation and the knowledge gap: effects of a campaign to reduce diet-related cancer risk', *Communication Research*, **20**, 546-63.

Wager, L.W. (1962), 'Channels of interpersonal and mass communication in an organizational setting: studying the diffusion of information about a unique organizational change', *Sociological Inquiry*, **32**, 88-107.

Wallace, K. (2001), 'Knowledge management at NRC: a practical perspective to KM', in J. de la Mothe and D. Foray (eds), *Knowledge Management in the Innovation Process*, Boston, MA: Kluwer Academic Publishers, pp. 159-71.

Walsh, J.A. and T.W. Phelan (1974), 'People in crisis: an experimental group', *Community Mental Health Journal*, **10**, 3-8.

Walther, J.B. (1994), 'Anticipated ongoing interaction versus channel effects on relational communication in computer-mediated interaction', *Human Communication Research*, **20**, 473-501.

Walton, R.E. (1985), 'Strategies with dual relevance', in E.E. Lawler, III, A.M. Mohrman, Jr., S.A. Mohrman, G.E. Ledford, Jr. and T.G. Cummings (eds), *Doing Research That Is Useful For Theory and Practice*, San Francisco, CA: Jossey-Bass, pp. 176-204.

Wandersman, A., R.M. Goodman and F.D. Butterfoss (1997), 'Understanding Coalitions and How They Operate: An "Open Systems" Organizational Framework', in M. Minkler (ed.), *Community Organizing and Community Building for Health*, New Brunswick, NJ: Rutgers University Press, pp. 261-77.

Ward, J.A.D., K. Duffy, R. Sciandra and S. Karlins (1988), 'What the public wants to know about cancer: the Cancer Information Service', *Cancer Bulletin*, **40**, 384-9.

Waters, R. (2003), 'Can social networks give the net a new lease on life?', *Financial Times*, 30 December.

Waters, R. (2004), 'The enigma within the knowledge economy', *Financial Times*, 2 February.

Watt, J.H. and C.A. Van Lear (eds), (1996), *Dyanamic Patterns in Communication Processes*, Thousand Oaks, CA: Sage.

Watts, D.J. (2003), *Six Degrees: The Science of the Connected Age*, New York: W.W. Norton.

Webster, J. and L.K. Trevino (1995), 'Rational and social theories as complementary explanations of communication media choices: two policy-capturing studies', *Academy of Management Journal*, **38**, 1544-72.

Weedman, J. (1992), 'Informal and formal channels in boundary-spanning communication', *Journal of the American Society for Information Science*, **43**, 257-67.

Weenig, M. and C. Midden (1991), 'Communication network influences on diffusion and persuasion', *Journal of Personality and Social Psychology*, **61**, 734-42.

Weick, K.E. (1969), *The Social Psychology of Organizing*, Reading, MA:

　　　　Addison-Wesley.

Weick, K.E. (1976), 'Educational organizations as loosely coupled systems', *Administrative Science Quarterly*, **21**, 1-19.

Weick, K.E. (1996), 'Drop your tools: an allegory for organizational studies', *Administrative Science Quarterly*, **41**, 301-13.

Weimann, G. (1983), 'The strength of weak conversational ties in the flow of information and influence', *Social Networks*, **5**, 245-67.

Weiss, C.H. (1983), 'Towards the future of stakeholder approaches in evaluation', in A.S. Bryk (ed.) *Stakeholder-Based Evaluation,* San Francisco, CA: Jossey-Bass, pp. 83-96.

Wellman, B. (1988), 'Structural analysis: from method and metaphor to theory and substance', in B. Wellman and S.D. Berkowitz (eds), *Social Structure: A Network Approach*, Cambridge: Cambridge University Press, pp. 19-61.

Wellman, B. (1996), *An electronic group is virtually a social network*, unpublished paper, Toronto, Canada: University of Toronto.

Wennberg, J.E., B.A. Barnes and M. Zubkoff (1982), 'Professional uncertainty and the problem of supplier-induced demand', *Social Science and Medicine*, **16**, 811-24.

Wertz, D.C., J.R. Sorenson and T.C. Heeren (1988), 'Communication in health professional-lay encounters: how often does each party know what the other wants to discuss?', in B.D. Ruben (ed.), *Information and Behavior, Volume 2*, New Brunswick, NJ: Transaction Books, pp. 329-42.

White, M. (1985), 'Intelligence management', in B. Cronin (ed.), *Information Management: From Strategies to Action*, Oxon: ASLIB, pp. 21-35.

Wigand, R.T. (1977), 'Some recent developments in organizational communication: network analysis - a systematic representation of communication relationships', *Communications*, **3**, 181-200.

Womack, S.M. (1984), 'Toward a clarification of boundary spanning', paperpresented to the Speech Communication Association Annual Convention, Denver, CO.

Wood, E.H. (1994), 'MEDLINE: the options for health professionals', *Journal of the American Medical Informatics Association*, **1**, 372-80.

Wooldridge, J.A., J.A. Ward, M.A. Woodworth, K. Mashburn, D. Reusch and S.W. Davis (1993), 'Information-management technology in the Cancer Information Service', *Journal of the National Cancer Institute Monographs*, **14**, 61-6.

Wright, G. and A. Taylor (2003), 'Strategic knowledge sharing for improved public service delivery: managing an innovative culture for effective partnerships', in E. Coakes (ed.), *Knowledge Management: Current Issues and Challenges*, London: IRM Press, pp. 187-211.

Zaltman, G. and R. Duncan (1977), *Strategies for Planned Change*, New

York: Wiley.

Zaltman, G., R. Duncan and J. Holbek (1973), *Innovations and Organizations*, New York, NY: Wiley.

Zemore, R. and L.F. Shepel (1987), 'Information seeking and adjustment to cancer', *Psychological Reports*, **60**, 874.

Zenger, T.R. and B.S. Lawrence (1989), 'Organizational demography: the differential effects of age and tenure distributions on technical communication', *Academy of Management Journal*, **32**, 353-76.

Zook, E.G. (1994), 'Embodied health and constitutive communication: toward an authentic conceptualization of health communication', in B. Berelson (ed.), *Communication Yearbook 17*, Newbury Park, CA: Sage, pp. 344-77.

Zorn, T.E. and S.K. May (2002), 'Forum introduction', *Management Communication Quarterly*, **16**, 237-41.

Index

Acceptance 79, 81, 86, 88, 90,
   133-4, 149-50, 154, 157-8,
   168, 171-2, 176, 180, 183,
   186, 189, 193
Access 25, 33, 57, 70, 90, 106
Adaptability 147, 149, 152, 155,
   164-5, 169, 173, 177, 181,
   184, 187, 189-90, 193
Ad hoc meetings 52
Adoption 6, 14, 18, 73, 88, 97,
   100-101, 108-9, 112, 114,
   116, 119, 143, 145-6, 148,
   158, 164, 190, 192, 197,
   200-202, 215-16
American Cancer Society
   (ACS) 23, 48, 74-5, 219
Amplification 194
Appraisal 107
Atlanta *see* conferences
Attributes *see* innovation 20,
   82, 144-8, 172, 190-91,
   193, 197, 199, 212-13
Authority innovation decision
   14

Behavioral Research Program
   220
Boundary spanners 68-77
Broadband 38
Brokerage 16, 48, 51, 64, 122-6,
   127-8, 131, 205-9
Busy rates 19, 153, 157, 175

Call centers 40, 160
Call Record Form (CRF) 36,
   54, 161
Campaigns 73, 92, 147, 214
Cancer 3, 8, 24-6, 31-2, 70, 73,
   75, 143, 148, 160-61, 220
   centers 39, 47
   control 16, 97, 119, 201
   detection 5, 25
   prevention 5, 19, 25, 29, 35,
     201
   treatment 5, 8, 25-9, 31, 35,
     44
Cancer Information Service
   (CIS) 1, 3-5, 8, 10, 14-16,
   18-19, 23-4, 36, 41-69, 71-
   5, 77, 80, 82-5, 87, 89-91,
   93, 95-6, 98-9, 104, 116-17,
   128-9, 131-2, 135, 138,
   140, 143, 146-8, 151, 157-
   8, 160, 162-4, 169-72, 176,
   183, 186, 189, 197, 200-
   201, 204, 206, 210-14, 216,
   218-21
Cancer Information Service
   Research Consortium
   (CISRC) 1, 4, 6, 7, 9-11,
   13-4, 16-19, 51, 53, 66-8,
   77, 84-91, 96, 122, 126,
   128-32, 138, 140-41, 144,
   148, 158, 161, 191, 193,

197-8, 201-2, 206-7, 210-
11, 213, 218-19, 221
Cancer Information Service
Telephone Evaluation and
Reporting System
(CISTERS) 47, 83
Capital
intellectual 5
political 13
social 122
Centrality 101, 122-6, 128, 130,
204
Centralization 46, 65-7, 78-9,
82, 90-1, 100, 133-4, 147,
200, 205
Champions 128, 144, 218
Circular calls 18, 52, 65
Clients 5, 26-9, 69, 200
Climates 2, 14-5, 20, 49, 55-7,
59-60, 62, 77-89, 189, 191-
5, 197, 218
Coalition 8, 9, 68-78, 85, 89,
96, 99, 123, 197, 219
Codification 113-15
Cohesion 117-19, 122, 137
Collaboration 89, 92, 113, 209
Commitment 72, 82, 93
Communication 6, 82, 138-41,
162-3, 172-6, 199-200, 216
channels 37, 40, 47, 81, 102-
12, 132, 135, 137, 163, 198,
202-3
environment 78-81, 141
laboratory *see* laboratory
logs 76, 88
mechanisms, internal 49-55,
58-9, 64, 123, 162
quality 78-9, 93-4, 132-3
stars 76, 200
Community of practice (CoP) 1,
6, 9, 53, 65-6, 85, 117, 128-
31, 144, 160, 197, 203-4,
214, 218, 221
Compatibility 15, 84, 146, 149,
152, 155, 158, 164-5, 169,
173, 177, 181, 184, 187

Complexity 15, 145, 150, 153,
156-8, 167, 171-2, 175,
179, 182, 185, 189, 191,
193, 197, 205, 213
Computer knowledge 163, 167-
8, 171, 175, 179-80, 183,
186, 191
Computerization 143-4, 159-89,
201, 204, 213-14, 216, 219
Computerization Advisory
Group (CAG) 53-4, 144,
160, 163, 190, 204
Conferences 51, 54-66, 141,
143, 144, 203
Atlanta 55, 59, 61-3
Denver 18, 55, 60-63, 183,
204
Consumer/client 24-6, 28-30,
35, 37, 41, 201
Contractual network 3, 8, 54,
82, 84
Consortia 1-2, 4, 6-10, 12, 65,
86, 89-92, 132, 198, 205-
10, 218
Definition 8
Context 2, 97, 146, 217
Control 58-9, 63, 77, 98, 102,
123
Cooperation 19, 59, 77, 89, 92,
97, 112, 121, 210
Coopetition 220
Coordination 6, 8, 40, 49-50,
58-9, 63, 110, 123, 162
Cost minimization 105, 109-12
Costs 18, 20-21, 34, 66, 96,
106, 119, 163, 191, 205,
216
Creativity 2, 5, 12, 112, 114-15,
198, 210-11
Critical mass 101
Culture 6, 14, 58, 77-8, 84, 91,
146, 207
Cyclical explanation 76

Data 5, 36
bases 36, 38, 44, 46, 48, 70,
97
mining 36

storage 36, 38
transformation 36
transport 36-8
Density 127, 195
Decision–making 35-6, 40, 67,
    82, 93, 100, 105, 109-12,
    133-4, 158, 190, 200
Denver *see* conferences
Dialogue 210, 217
Differentiation 50-51, 55, 82,
    121-3, 125-6, 208, 211
Diffusion 2, 20, 49, 59, 69, 72,
    97, 100-101, 103-4, 108,
    116, 119-20, 123, 128, 136,
    138, 139, 163, 198, 202,
    204, 212, 215
Digital divide 30
Disseminating 4, 9, 18, 25, 44,
    88, 92, 136, 160, 164, 219
Division of Cancer Control and
    Population Services
    (DCCPS) 220-21
Dosage 126, 129, 139, 204

Effectiveness, efficiency 2, 13,
    18, 20, 51, 57, 60, 62, 68-9,
    97, 144-5, 160, 163-4, 190,
    193, 204, 212, 216, 219,
    221
E-mail 80, 104, 110-11, 128,
    135, 138-9, 162, 202-3,
    219-20
Environment 1, 7-8, 11, 14-16,
    19, 49, 67, 69-71, 78, 90,
    133-4, 208
    innovation *see* innovation
Explicit knowledge 13, 16, 54,
    58, 112-15, 200

Face-to-face *see* interpersonal
    channels 54, 64, 99, 103,
    141
Formal 48, 51, 57, 60, 64, 76,
    82, 84, 99, 102, 111-12,
    125, 130, 133-5, 140, 142
    indices 81-4, 127
    structure 51, 71, 82, 95, 98-
    9, 123, 197, 201, 204

Formalization 46-7, 65, 67, 78,
    80, 82-3, 90-91, 93-5, 100,
    133, 147, 161, 205
Framing 12-14, 19, 40, 197,
    211-12, 216-17
Functional roles 61-3, 71, 75,
    104, 130-31, 200, 217

Goals 12, 15-20, 50-51, 55-7,
    59-60, 62-3, 98, 122, 162,
    208, 211, 215-17
Government 1, 2, 5, 30, 66, 74-
    5, 186, 213, 216, 218

Health and Human Services
    (HHS) 14
Health Communication and
    Informatics Research
    Branch (HCIRB) 220
Health information 4, 14
Health literacy 23, 31-2, 73
Hierarchy *see* formal structure
Homophily 41, 55-7, 62, 97,
    114, 118-20
Horizontal communication *see*
    informal
Human side 68, 89, 92-3, 198

Idea generation 130-31, 205
Indices *see* formal
Influence 113-15, 119, 129
Informal 9, 60, 63, 67-8, 76, 81,
    97-8, 100, 132-5, 141, 193-
    4, 198, 214
Informatics 36
Information 3, 5, 24, 59
    carriers 24-5, 27
    environment 33, 50, 68, 212
    fields 31, 35-40, 119
    gaps 29-35
    health
    infrastructure 30-31, 35, 39,
    70
    needs 5
    processing technologies 36-9
    resources 161-2, 172, 180,
    184-6

Resources Task Force (IRTF) 54
seeking 6, 24-41, 85, 136-7
Specialists (IS) 18-19, 47-8, 86, 153, 156, 161, 172-89, 212
technology 4-7, 12, 24, 33, 35, 40, 50, 72, 88, 97, 99, 143-4, 147, 159-60, 164, 183, 198, 213-14, 217
innovation(s) 1-11,14-15, 17, 55, 67-8, 72, 77-8, 89-91, 95, 97-8, 100, 103, 143-4, 159, 197-205
   attributes 12, 15, 143-4,
   characteristics 172, 190, 194
   climates *see* climate
   cons 15, 193-5, 200, 213
   defined 5
   environment 12, 14-15, 20
   factory 86, 198, 202, 218
   implementation 6, 10-12, 21, 63, 67, 71, 81, 88-9, 91, 97, 100, 102-3, 109, 112, 114, 116-17, 121, 130-31, 135, 145-6, 148, 160, 163, 168, 190-92, 197, 200, 202, 204, 206, 213-14, 217
   meta- 2, 12, 198
   Profile 190-93
   pros 15, 194-5, 200, 213
   stage 113-14, 126, 137, 201-2
   themes 1, 2, and 3 16-18
Innovativeness, perceived 2, 77-80, 84, 93-4, 132-5, 144, 190, 192-3, 195
Integration 8, 49-51, 72, 98-9, 121-3, 125-6, 208
Interaction 58, 63
Interdependencies 14, 50
Interest 55-7
Internal communication mechanisms *see* communication, mechanisms, internal
Internet 30, 36, 38, 44, 220

Interpersonal channels 47, 104-5, 108-9, 111-12, 128, 136, 138-40, 142, 190-91, 202-4
Intervention strategies *see* knowledge delivery innovations
Involvement 57, 62, 81, 191

Knowledge 5, 24, 26, 34, 37, 49, 78, 92
   defined 4, 12
   delivery innovations 1, 3, 9, 52, 69, 74, 77, 87, 91, 126-7, 129-31, 143-4, 146-8, 163, 172, 198, 213-14, 219
   gap 31, 44
   generation 12, 16, 42, 67-96
   management (KM) 1-2, 4-11, 13, 23, 45-7, 52-3, 65-6, 68, 89, 100, 112, 114, 132, 135, 142-3, 145, 159, 197-200, 211, 217-20
   network 85, 95, 112-26
   sharing 54, 56, 69, 97, 112-13, 126
   transfer 69, 97, 114, 120, 124-5, 194, 205, 219
   utilization 24

Laboratory 3, 17, 210
   communication 3, 16, 66, 84, 201, 211, 218
   state-of the-science 3, 218
Learning, organizational 5, 61, 215, 218
Levels (of analysis) 6, 10-21, 140, 142, 186, 197, 205, 216
Liaisons 114, 122-3, 125
Linking roles *see* liaisons, brokerage
Links 97, 99, 103, 113, 115, 120-21, 127, 129-30, 141-2
Longitudinal research 4, 76, 126-8, 193, 198-200

Mailings 162, 172, 176, 180, 183, 187-9

Markets 98, 102-3, 113, 122, 125

Media Exposure and Appraisal (MEA) 107

Media richness 106-7, 137

MEDLINE 43-4

Mission 14-5, 68-9, 176, 213, 219

Multiplexity 101, 115, 120-21

National Cancer Institute (NCI) 3-4, 14-15, 17, 23, 41-3, 45, 48, 53, 66, 68, 73-4, 85, 89, 131, 158-9, 161-2, 201, 206, 211, 213, 219-21

National Institutes of Health (NIH) 14-15, 42, 219

National Library of Medicine (NLM) 43-4, 219

Network 7-8, 49, 67, 75, 91, 98, 103
analysis 10, 88, 100-101, 103, 108, 112-15, 122, 125-6, 132-3, 138, 142, 193, 205
radial 74-5
roles 123-4, 127

New organizational forms 3, 7-8, 46, 54, 66, 75, 82, 90, 93, 95, 102, 122, 189, 192-3, 197, 202

Norms 14, 51, 114, 117-18, 212

Observability 15, 147, 150, 153, 156, 167, 171, 175-6, 179, 182, 185, 188, 193

Office of Cancer Communications (OCC) 14, 18, 45, 47, 50, 53, 65, 73, 75, 83, 110, 127-8, 130, 147, 158, 160-62, 164, 200, 204, 213, 220

Office management 93, 160, 163-4, 172, 177-80

Orchestrators 13, 130-31, 215

Outreach 160, 162-4, 169-72, 201, 220

Managers 47, 49, 60, 69, 70, 73, 75, 84-5, 91-2, 110, 112, 117, 131, 200

Paradox 204, 208, 216

Participation 20, 56-7, 60, 62, 78, 81, 101-2, 121, 126, 133, 139, 191-2

Physician Data Query (PDQ) 43-4, 48, 161

Planning 57, 60-61, 63, 200

Policy 4, 13, 16, 30-31, 33, 145, 186, 198, 201

Power 14, 81, 119

Practitioners *see* researcher-practitioners

Prestige 13, 20, 212

Principle Investigator (PI) 16, 84, 129-31, 200, 221

Proactive counseling 86

Program project *see* CISRC 9, 18, 127-8, 130-31, 191, 200

Project Director (PD) 18, 47, 60, 65, 84-5, 109-10, 128, 131, 172, 189-9, 200-201, 207, 213, 218, 221

Projects 9, 96, 129, 148-58
1 9, 16, 86-7, 148-52, 157-8, 201
2 9, 16, 87, 148-9, 152-4, 157-8, 189, 193-5, 198, 200, 206, 215
3 9, 16, 87-8, 148-9, 155-8, 214

Prominence 193

Proximity 117-18

Publication subcommittee 16

Quality 47

Quality Control Monitoring System (QCMS) 88

Radial network *see* network, radial

Range 122, 133, 135, 193

Reciprocity 114

Record keeping 161, 172, 181-3

Redundancy 113, 115-16, 120

Regional Offices (RO) 3, 4, 8,
16-17, 46-7, 52, 54, 73, 75,
87-90, 93, 110, 117, 129,
158, 160-64, 169, 172, 206,
213, 218, 220-21
Reinvention 88, 160, 213, 216
Relative advantage 15, 145,
149-50, 153, 156, 158, 164-
5, 169, 173, 177, 182, 185,
188, 190, 193, 213
Reorganization 4, 62-3
Research 15, 50, 197
Research and development
(R&D) 7, 50, 69, 76, 91
Researcher-practitioner
relationship (RPR) 1, 2, 4, 7,
9, 16, 18, 19, 88, 192, 198,
200-201, 205-10, 219
Resistance 19, 81, 152, 160, 179,
212
Riskiness 109, 116, 145, 147,
149, 155, 158, 164, 166, 170,
172, 174, 178, 190-91, 193,
206, 217
Role(s) 118-19
ambiguity 93-6
conflict 76, 93-6
functional *see* functional roles
network *see* network, roles
Rules 121, 140

Satisfaction 2, 3, 72, 77, 93, 124
Sense making 11, 13, 23, 138
Slack resources 67, 78, 80, 82-3,
85, 90, 133, 205
Social
contagion 113-14, 116-19, 121,
136, 138
information processing 105,
109-11, 137
presence 106, 108-12
support 8
Sociometric 128-31, 192, 220
Spiral of silence 194
Sponsors 130
Stakeholders 5, 12-14, 20, 23,
68-9, 89, 144, 191-2, 200,
211, 213-14, 216

Strategy 4, 7, 20-21, 24, 39, 42,
54, 65, 68, 73, 96-7, 189-91,
211, 219
Strength of weak ties 59, 114-16,
121, 193-5, 200, 204
Strong ties *see* strength of weak
ties
Structural equivalence 97, 117-
19, 137, 139-40
Structural hole brokers (SHB)
see brokerage
Structure 15, 21, 67-9, 90, 98-
103, 118, 122, 132-3, 141,
143, 192, 198, 204, 220
Success 1, 6, 11-12, 14, 29, 56,
58, 61, 63, 117, 131, 135,
163, 180, 205, 209-19
Survey Methods Core (SMC) 16
Survival 4
Symbolic interactionism 210
System 14, 135, 138, 141, 144,
160, 204, 207-9, 211, 214,
218

Tacit knowledge 12, 16, 53-4, 56,
65, 91, 112-14, 116, 119-20,
200-201, 221
Task forces 51, 53-4, 64, 83
Team for Evaluation and Audit
Methods (TEAM) 18, 88,
130, 206, 219
Technology 1, 6, 30, 37, 49,
112, 164, 168
Telecommunications systems
37-8, 97, 159-60
Telemedicine 36, 38
Telephone (information and
referral) services 3, 4, 40-41,
47, 148, 160-62, 164-8, 172,
202, 219
Telephone Service Managers
(TSM) 60, 75, 84, 86-7,
109-10, 131, 158, 160-61,
163, 200, 221
Threshold 101

Trialability 12, 15, 146, 151, 154,
    157-8, 164, 166, 170, 172,
    175, 180
Trust 113-14, 207

Uncertainty 72, 99, 101, 146
    Management 90, 146
    Reduction 7, 25, 95, 102-4,
    106-12, 116, 120, 147, 168
Unified Medical Language
    System (UMLS) 45
Upward communication *see*
    formal
Utility *see* MEA

Weak ties *see* strength of weak
    ties
Website *see* Internet
Weekly packages 52, 112
Wisdom 5, 14, 24
Written channels 48, 104, 111-12